INSIDE IMMIGRATION LAW

Research in Migration and Ethnic Relations Series

Series Editor:
Maykel Verkuyten, ERCOMER
Utrecht University

The Research in Migration and Ethnic Relations series has been at the forefront of research in the field for ten years. The series has built an international reputation for cutting edge theoretical work, for comparative research especially on Europe and for nationally-based studies with broader relevance to international issues. Published in association with the European Research Centre on Migration and Ethnic Relations (ERCOMER), Utrecht University, it draws contributions from the best international scholars in the field, offering an interdisciplinary perspective on some of the key issues of the contemporary world.

Also in series

European Immigration
A Sourcebook
Edited by Anna Triandafyllidou and Ruby Gropas
ISBN 978 1 4094 5363 5

Ethnic Diversity and Social Cohesion
Immigration, Ethnic Fractionalization and Potentials for Civic Action
Merlin Schaeffer
ISBN 978 1 4094 6938 4

Full series list at back of book

ERCOMER

**EUROPEAN RESEARCH CENTRE
ON MIGRATION & ETHNIC RELATIONS**

Inside Immigration Law

Migration Management and Policy Application in Germany

TOBIAS G. EULE
University of Bern, Switzerland

Routledge
Taylor & Francis Group
LONDON AND NEW YORK

First published 2014 by Ashgate Publishing

2 Park Square, Milton Park, Abingdon, Oxon OX14 4RN
711 Third Avenue, New York, NY 10017, USA

Routledge is an imprint of the Taylor & Francis Group, an informa business

First issued in paperback 2016

British Library Cataloguing in Publication Data
A catalogue record for this book is available from the British Library.

The Library of Congress has cataloged the printed edition as follows:
Eule, Tobias G., author.
Inside immigration law : migration management and policy application in Germany / By Tobias G. Eule.
pages cm. -- (Research in migration and ethnic relations series)
Includes bibliographical references and index.
ISBN 978-1-4094-7013-7 (hardback)
1. Emigration and immigration law--Germany. 2. Emigration and immigration--Government policy--Germany. I. Title.
KK6044.E95 2014
342.4308'2--dc23

2013043988

ISBN 978-1-4094-7013-7 (hbk)
ISBN 978-1-138-24578-5 (pbk)

Contents

For Judy and Jörg, with love.

List of Tables

Preface

This book examines the implementation process of immigration law in Germany through an ethnographic lens. Based on participant observation, interviews and an analysis of public as well as confidential documents in four German *Ausländerbehörden*, municipal immigration offices, this study unveils the complex practices of decision-making and work organisation in a politically contested environment. While both law and migrant groups in Germany have been extensively studied, the *Ausländerbehörde*, site of the granting of permanent residence as well as efforts to expel and deport migrants, has been severely neglected. Yet, it assumes the central position in the interaction between the state and migrant population, as residence law is superior to all non-constitutional laws, directly affects and regulates all aspects of life from social welfare to employment and is of particular relevance in countries with low naturalisation rates such as Germany. The study will show how the implementation of immigration law to individual cases can be a chaotic, improvising and sometimes arbitrary practice, partially a result of the complex, politically laden and constantly changing nature of the German immigration law. As well as being heavily dependent on a bureaucrat's knowledge, skills and political position, the implementation process is greatly influenced by interventions from several sub-state levels of both executive and judicial power, and local representatives of civil society.

This study assesses the variation of the implementation of immigration law in federalist Germany and examines the different political and organisational forces that influence the process. Through its set-up, the study can compare and critically evaluate the work of four different immigration offices regarding the discretion and client interactions of individual bureaucrats, the management of legal knowledge and symbolism as well as the relations to external political forces from media to courts, from NGOs to higher echelons of state bureaucracy. This research project on which this book is the first extensive, comparative and in-depth analysis of the management of migration in Germany ever conducted and thus of exploratory value as well as contributing to discussions on the sociology of law, migration and bureaucracies.

The present work has been greatly improved by the trust and guidance of Göran Therborn, who supervised my doctoral research at the University of Cambridge. Christian Joppke encouraged me to write this book and provided me with the necessary intellectual freedom. Himself a veteran of immigration office research, Thomas Scheffer offered insights and suggestions from afar. Carrie Heitmeyer, Jörg Hüttermann, Ruth Mandel, Julie Smith, Tobias Trappe and Harald Wydra all provided valuable support along the way. Amongst others, Anna Bachmann,

Martin Fuller, Patricia Lenz and Jonathan Ong were forced to play intellectual ping pong with me so many times that we would certainly win gold if this were ever to be an Olympic discipline.

My friends and family supported me greatly and were always there to provide me with the reality check when needed. Apologies for prolonged phases of restraint and ignorance; and for all those emails I never replied to. I am well, really.

Chapter 1
Can I Stay? Migration Policies in Germany

Amira's family came to Germany escaping the chaos of a civil war. Their plea for asylum was denied in the late 1990s but due to the father's bad health and the family's three underage children the local immigration office decided not to deport them to their state of origin. Amira has never possessed a residence permit; instead, for over a decade she has resided in Germany on the sufferance of the immigration office. She cannot remember living anywhere other than in Germany, has only attended school in Germany. In a few weeks, Amira will turn 18 and, as an adult, her case will be judged independently from that of the rest of her family. Without a right to remain in the country, and on her own, she could be deported to a country she barely remembers having lived in – she has lived in Germany for most of her life, has her entire social network here. Today, Amira has gone to the immigration office to extend her certificate of sufferance, and to ask her caseworker about her future. Can she stay?

Yu studies Chemistry at the local university and is about to finish his Master's degree with a good result. His studies were funded by a German foundation, and through them, he has been offered an internship at a pharmaceutical company that, if successful, could turn into a full-time job. His residence permit does not allow him to work and expires with the end of his degree. Can he stay?

Hassan has worked for a construction company for the past three years. He has enjoyed the work, and his supervisor has suggested that he could have his contract renewed. His residence permit and work permission expire with his contract, and his boss wants him to have them renewed first. Also, his wife and daughter have been living without him in his home country. Today, Hassan is visiting the immigration office to enquire about his residence permit, and the possibilities of bringing his family to Germany. Can they come? Can he stay?

Ursula has been visiting her daughter for the last three months, celebrating her seventy-fifth birthday with her grandchildren. Since the death of her husband, it has been difficult for her to cope on her own. During the past few months, she has enjoyed being around her grandchildren very much, and made life considerably easier for her daughter, who struggles with balancing work and being a single parent. Since Ursula's visa expires next week, she is at the immigration office today to see if it could be extended for a few weeks, perhaps even for longer. Can she stay?

Saadi is Amira's older brother and found it harder to adapt to living in Germany. He dropped out of school early and has struggled to keep a job for more than a few weeks. As a teenager, Saadi got into all kinds of trouble and has been charged with drug possession, theft, and assault. He has a son with a woman he no longer sees, but a residence permit because of the child, who is German. Last month, he had a huge argument with his ex-girlfriend because he cannot provide for his son. Also, he has been caught twice evading bus fares in the last couple of weeks and is now afraid that due to this, he will be considered a repeat offender and will not have his residence permit renewed. Today, Saadi has an appointment with the immigration office. Can he stay?

The lives of the five people waiting at the immigration offices could not be more different, and yet they share a crucial commonality: all five are at a decisive moment of their lives, at which it is not up to them to determine what will happen. All five individuals, their lives, hopes and imagined futures have to be assessed and decided on by the staff of the immigration office. Here, they become cases, organised not by name but by a code of letters and numbers, categorised by nationality and legal status. Here, they wait to be called into a conversation from which they hope to gain the answer to the one important question: Can I stay?

Who Can Stay – And Why

This book is based on a simple but often forgotten premise: that what actually happens in practice is significantly different from what is theoretically supposed to happen. Through an analysis of migration policy application, it reminds us that we need to take the frictions and discretionary practices of immigration bureaucrats seriously in order to fully understand the management of migration. In this, the book contributes to the field of migration studies and the public debate on immigration in Europe, but through on a detour from the more traditional approaches to the field. Over the course of the last decades, scholars have amassed crucial information about the nature, size and consequences of migration. Thanks to their work, we know a lot about specific migrant groups, distinguished by age, religion, gender, ethnicity or trade. There are also great treatises on hybrid, changing and unsettled (national) identities shaped by, and numerous comparative analyses of policies and legislation that respond to recent waves of immigration. However, we know only very little about how these policies are applied to individual cases, and have almost no insights into the institutions in which the legal status of migrants, and thus their fate as acknowledged members of public life, is decided. In focussing on processes of decision-making in immigration offices in Germany, this book offers to fill this gap, through an account of policy application and implementation on the 'street-level', where state officials and migrants interact face to face.

This book is not about individual stories, but the system that assesses and processes their requests. It is based on four four-month periods of participant observation in different immigration offices, gaining repeated in-depth and longitudinal insights into the implementation of immigration law in Germany. However, the study is neither a technical assessment of the efficiency of German immigration bureaucracy nor does it measure the application of individual paragraphs and passages of the law. Instead, this book adopts a broader approach and examines the law as well as those who apply it, the conditions under which it is applied as well as the forces that shape these conditions. In looking at the 'human face' of migration policy and immigration policing, this study sheds light on the practice of decision-making, and illuminates the dilemmas, troubles and hazards faced by immigration caseworkers in exercising their power: to decide who can stay – and why.

Migration is a topic that continues to occupy the mind of almost all European nations, from the cheap populism of right-wing parties to highbrow newspaper editorials, from pub brawls to the echelons of the university lecture hall. Indeed, the face of Europe and its member states seems to be changing dramatically, from the diversity of fast food joints to the possibly challenged relationship between religion, politics and private life. Germany, the focus of this study, has been late to acknowledge its role as 'country of immigration' and still, many political discussions are instigated much later than in other European states. In the 20 years since the fall of the Soviet Union and its allied states, however, Germany has 'caught up' with many developments faced by its neighbours: the rise and fall of populist anti-immigrant parties, a swell of immigrants with ethnic or national ties to Germany as well as high levels of asylum seekers, heated public debates, movements to move towards 'multiculturalism' followed by pronouncements of its death, and finally, federal legislation to deter, integrate, remove, naturalise and select migrants on their way into Germany. More recently, migration developments have become somewhat synchronised in Europe, to a great extent as a product of European Union legislation on migration issues, but also of the impact of global events. Thus debates over the nature of Islam in Western societies, counterterrorism legislation that focussed on migrants and targeted specific ethno-religious groups seen as potential enemies in the 'clash of civilisations' and increased levels of asylum seekers from countries of war have impacted all European countries, albeit not always to the same extent.

The immigration office – site and subject of this study – is more often than not about as far removed as possible from these debates about the political direction of migration politics and citizenship. Indeed, apart from occasional reporting on the gross mistreatment of individual migrants and their families, immigration offices usually do not appear to bear great relevance to the experts in politics, media and academia – and understandably so: The implementation of law to individual cases is complicated, technical and decidedly unglamorous. Furthermore, individual offices lack both legislative and political power to exert influence or be a part of the immigration debate. Yet decisions made by bureaucrats in the immigration offices have an immense impact on the lives of individuals and families, as residence law is superior to all other laws save the constitution, directly affects and regulates all aspects of life from social welfare to employment and is of particular relevance in countries with low naturalisation rates such as Germany. After all, it is these officials who decide on the conditions of residence as well as the eligibility to stay at all and often, these officials are the first and main points of contacts newly arrived migrants have with the German state. In a way, the bureaucrats of the Ausländerbehörde (Foreigner's Office) thus represent the whole state apparatus and legal system; in short, they are 'the State' to migrants. Their behaviour, their treatment of individuals and their 'cases' might thus have a significant impact on the migrants' perception of the state overall, and consequently hold a great potential for both integrating and alienating foreign nationals. As this study will show, there is value in analysing the procedures and practices of immigration offices. After all, understanding the decision-making processes and the social interactions in the practice of immigration law can not only further our understanding of migration management, but also of the ways in which migrants adapt to and are socialised into society.

This book is based on participant observation, interviews and an analysis of public as well as confidential documents in German Ausländerbehörden, municipal immigration offices. The primary research was conducted in four different phases of four months each between February and May 2009 and between December 2009 and November 2010, with each phase covering a different office in a different city. This led to several follow-up interviews and group discussions with local councillors and state officials, and consulting work on institutional change in 2012 and 2013. Through its research design, the study can thus compare and critically evaluate the work of four different immigration offices regarding the discretion and interactions of officials and their clients, the management and application of legal knowledge as well as the relations to external political forces from media to courts, from NGOs to the higher echelons of state bureaucracy. The study shows how the implementation of immigration law to individual cases can be a chaotic, improvising and sometimes arbitrary practice, partially a result of the complex, politically charged and constantly changing nature of the German immigration law. As well as being heavily dependent on an individual's knowledge, skills and political position, the implementation process is greatly influenced by interventions from several sub-state levels of both executive and judicial power, and local representatives of civil society.

The individual stories presented at the outset of this chapter are thus more like trappings to the analysis of what happens 'inside' immigration law. They serve to remind the reader why this study is relevant, namely that in immigration offices decisions are made about real people, concerning real fates. Immigration offices might be situated at the lowest point in the hierarchy of migration politics, but they matter most to the individuals who move to a new country. This work is not primarily about those individuals, but in a way, it is for them.

The aim of this book is thus to examine the process of applying immigration law to individual cases through an investigation into the practice of decision-making and migration management in German immigration offices. Over the course of the next eight chapters, four significant variations found in the work of the four case studies are explored, and contextualised and explained through a presentation of four different dimensions that impacted the practice of Ausländerbehörden. The notion of law as clearly defined black letter text is challenged and its application shown to be based on techniques of collective memorisation rather than a rational process. The organisational structures and routines in the offices are portrayed as quite inefficient and constantly changing, resulting in unpredictability and uncertainty likely to have a lasting impact on the making of migrants through the interactions of 'state' and applicants. Political debate and interventions, especially on the local level, are revealed to greatly affect the work practice in Ausländerbehörden. Finally, strategies of coping and the question of individual responsibility of officials are discussed in order to explain the distance and disassociation between caseworkers and migrants.

The book can thus be read in at least two ways: As a study on migration management in Germany, since the data collection was completed there; or as a study on migration management, based on a case study, Germany. As largest economy and most populous country in the EU, Germany is an interesting case in itself, as national interests strongly influence the European Union and EU-level migration policies. However, the points raised over the course of the work are also valid for other cases. While of course both policy framework and institutional setting vary from country to country (even among the 'harmonised' European Union member states), the process of implementation and face-to-face interactions between state officials and migrants will in any case deviate from 'black letter law' and always be influenced by the variables presented here: divergent legal practices, bureaucratic friction, local political interests and individual officials. In every national setting, street-level bureaucracy will impact the socialisation of individuals into their role and category as immigrants. There is, perhaps, then, knowledge to be gained here that might further our understanding of the management of non-national residents in Western states and to the sociological discussion of law and public administration.

The Political and Legal Framework of Migration Management in Germany

This section will provide an introduction into the development of migration policy in Germany, describe its current legislation and consider the impact of EU-level harmonisation patterns. However, as the intricacies of migration policies are rather complex and the pace of legislation change is quite hastened, this section is not intended to provide an extensive overview, but only to offer necessary information to follow the argument covered in the remainder of the book. In the immigration offices, it is estimated that it takes between nine and 12 months to acquire expert knowledge on immigration law; to attempt this in a mere chapter would be futile. Chapter 3 explicitly deals with the use of law as basis of decision-making, provides several in-depth examples and argues that 'black letter law' is in fact less central to its implementation than collective recollections and rules of thumb. Readers interested in more detailed descriptions of migration policies are thus advised to further consult the excellent contributions of my colleagues that are mentioned in the text.

Trends in European Migration Management

Over the past decade or so, policies and the 'management' of migration control have become central foci of the academic debate on immigration. Specifically, academic approaches seem to have shifted from normative arguments about ideal forms of policy to a more dispassionate analysis of the concrete nature of migration control regimes (Geiger and Pécoud 2010: 1). Key aspects of such studies have been the international harmonisation of migration policies (e.g. Boswell and Geddes 2011; Duncan 2012; Fischer 2012; Geddes 2003; Thym and Snyder 2011) and increased cooperation in the management of migration, particularly within Europe (e.g. Geiger and Pécoud 2010, 2012; Ghosh 2000; Koslowski 2011). Within Europe, a general trend towards convergence of migration policies can be identified, partially as a 'spill over effect' of the harmonisation of European policies in general (Triandafyllidou and Illies 2010: 23).

This trend towards convergence is visible particularly regarding four aspects, the first and most sweeping being internal mobility through the 1985 Schengen Agreement or the Treaty of Maastricht from 1992. Both the abolition of border controls and the freedom of movement for EU citizens and their spouses increase the difficulty for states to control its migrant population considerably. Especially the gradual EU enlargements of 2004, 2007 and 2013 and the elimination of visa requirements for citizens of EU member candidates have drastically altered the nature of migration management in the old EU-15, with hundreds of thousands of former deportees and irregular migrants enjoying freedom of movement.

The second trend towards convergence is related to specific modes of migration control and return policies like the Dublin I and II regulations and shared information on visa granting and biodata of asylum applicants (Feldman 2012; Fischer 2012; Geddes 2003; Menz 2011; Triandafyllidou and Illies 2010). The Dublin regulation intends to ensure efficient asylum procedures and to prevent asylum seekers from making various asylum claims in different European countries. They should instead get access to one asylum process, namely in the state where the person has entered the Schengen Area. If asylum seekers try to apply for asylum in another country, the latter can transfer them back to the country of their first arrival (for information on Dublin II see Hruschka 2011) – a common practice, since many still try to claim asylum in a country different from the one of first arrival (Schuster 2011). Hence, the Dublin II regulation seeks to limit the movements of asylum seekers made possible through the Schengen Agreement.

Collaborative European border regimes, the third trend of convergence, are a direct outcome of the previous two trends and have received wide-spread academic attention in recent years (e.g. Andersen et al. 2012; Carling 2007; Carr 2012; Hess and Kasparek 2010; TRANSIT MIGRATION Forschungsgruppe 2007;

Zaiotti 2011). While the Schengen Agreement has significantly eased mobility within Europe, external border control has been improving quickly, making it ever harder for irregular migrants to enter Europe (Carr 2012: 3; Klepp 2011: 33). Mau and colleagues (2012) show that alongside increased deterrence, entry into Europe is eased for members of selected nationalities or with specific skillsets, making the border regime not so much a 'fortress' than a site of selective permeability. One of its key characteristics has been the strategy of externalising border control and maintaining surveillance of migrants before they reach the border (cf. Boswell and Geddes 2011: 133; Gruszczak 2012; Klepp 2011; Lahav and Guiraudon 2006; Ryan and Mitsilegas 2010; Seiffarth 2011). This includes attempts to prevent migration flows to Europe through a triple approach of development, deterrence and information-spreading in countries of origin (Niederberger and Wichmann 2004; Pécoud 2010). As a result, legal migration opportunities have been limited and illegal entry been rendered more difficult (Andrijasevic 2006; Bloch et al. 2011; Collyer 2010; de Haas 2008). Hence, migrants are pushed to take ever riskier routes and means of transportation (Carling 2007: 340; Lemberg-Pedersen 2012: 38).

The final trend of convergence relates to the increasing importance of supranational court decisions by the European Courts of Justice and Human Rights. These bodies have increasing capacities to oversee the due implementation of European-level decisions into national practice (Boswell and Geddes 2011; Guiraudon 2000). One key aspect has been the application of supranational treaties, especially constitutional and human rights norms to migration law cases (see Council of Europe 2013). Chapter 3 discusses this example of multi-level migration policy in more detail.

Despite these developments, the process of harmonisation should neither be seen as linear progression towards a coherent European migration framework, nor as anywhere nearing completion. Studies on national and European policy making thus see migration policies formed on the basis of particularistic interest and bureaucratic simplification rather than scientific knowledge or rational means-ends analyses (Boswell 2009; Feldman 2012). Efforts to coordinate harmonisation set out by the 1999 Tampere Agreement evaporated, and the EU's recent Stockholm Programme of coordinating legislation stresses national autonomy, ensuring that significant differences between national policies continue to exist (Boswell and Geddes 2011; Fischer 2012; Guiraudon 2003; Zincone 2011).

Significant national differences can be found even within the field of irregular migration control, where harmonisation is probably most advanced. This is especially true regarding internal responses to irregular migration, which are especially relevant as irregular migrants increasingly consist of visa overstayers who legally entered Europe (Triandafyllidou and Vogel 2010: 294). The few compilations that exist (e.g. Brochmann and Hammar 1999; Doomernik and Jandl 2008; Guiraudon and Joppke 2001; Martin 2003) highlight significant variations of national approaches. One of the few harmonised actions is employer sanctions, as decreed in a 2009 EU Directive (Triandafyllidou and Illies 2010).

However, since existing studies mainly focus on policies rather than practice, there is relatively little knowledge on the actual workings and implications of migration control. We thus cannot clearly judge how evenly even the harmonised migration policy areas are applied.

Limits of Migration Management

This leads to a key point of this work: it is impossible for states to fully manage immigration. This is by no means a novel observation (see Benz and Schwenken 2005: 365; Castles 2004; Hess and Tsianos 2007: 23f; also Massey 1998 on the United States), and various explanations for this are on offer. First and as mentioned above, the common external efforts are not matched by an internal harmonisation of migration policy and control practice, especially in the field of irregular migration and asylum-seeking (Boswell and Geddes 2011; Feldman 2012; Fischer 2012). A 'bricolage' of laws, agencies and interests causes significant friction between actors (Sciortino 2004), despite an overall (long-term) tendency towards greater European integration of the 'migration apparatus' (Feldman 2012: 13ff). Second, several authors argue that, in fact, restrictive migration policies are never meant to fully work. Instead, irregular migrants are seen as necessary and highly flexible underbelly of the workforce, deliberately held vulnerable to exploitation under questionable labour conditions (Calavita 1998; Castles and Miller 2009; de Genova and Peutz 2010). It is further argued that, third, restrictive migration policies never need to be fully implemented as they evoke a disciplinary effect exactly through their uneven implementation (Wicker 2012). In this respect, the existing threat of deportation is more important than its actual use.

While the intentionality of creating partly failing policies is difficult to prove (and not part of this project), the practical difficulties of applying un-implementable policies are more discernible – and highly relevant. Thus migration agencies have to permanently react to new – and often creative – strategies of irregular migrants to circumvent controls that lack a coherent legal framework (e.g. Bojadžijev and Karakayalı 2007: 204; Engbersen and Broeders 2011; Hess and Tsianos 2007: 23f; Martin 2003). Although some studies show the interconnections between migration policies and migrants' strategies, they often fall short of depicting the practices of migration control authorities (but see Guiraudon and Joppke 2001). The exploratory studies brought together by Düvell (2006b) suggest a tacit toleration by some state authorities in some countries. Engberson and Broeders (2011) too mention a certain tolerance amongst Dutch control agencies, but stress that increased control efforts matter just as much. Studies of migrants in particular cities stress the importance of the 'local' as a field of policy investigation is supported by (see Alexander 2007; Anderson 2003; Fauser 2012; Penninx and Martiniello 2004; Wilmes 2011; Wilmes and Bommes 2007), since specific local constellations regarding welfare policies, but also police practices and migrant agencies frame the field of autonomy for irregular migrants. Engbersen and Broeders (2011) also point to the importance of local 'informal institutions' in shaping migrants' opportunities and objects of intervention for control agencies.

Many of these observations relate to the results of the fieldwork in the immigration offices. Indeed, it is the contention of this book that no policy can be expected to be ever fully implemented, and that considerations of the actual management of migration needs to consider this. Rather than choosing one of the above suggestions, this work provides a framework of four interrelated factors that impede the implementation of immigration law. Each of them will be explained in an individual chapter, I thus mention them only briefly here. The first impediment to full implementation is the law itself, which, due to its multi-level origins based on compromise and piecemeal tactics leaves much room for interpretation and in fact forces agents to materialise the law on the lowest level of the executive. The second factor is the nature of organisation in public administration, the spatial and organisational distance between policy promulgators and implementers as well as the limits of ideal-typical Weberian rational bureaucracy. The third factor relates to political interventions to the implementation process, both from state and non-state actors. The continued debates over immigration in Europe prove that neither means nor goals of migration policy are based on a societal consensus. These conflicts are inherent in the formulation and execution of the law, and are fought on the street level of bureaucracy. The fourth factor is the immigration officials themselves. Struggling to fulfil their politically charged duties, they utilise methods of organisational survival, take short cuts and duck away from responsibility.

It should be clear from this overview that the aim of this book is not to overhaul our theoretical understanding of society. Instead, it utilises well-established knowledge from other sub-disciplines of the social sciences (mainly legal anthropology and organisation studies) to further our level of understanding within the field of migration studies. None of the claims made in this book should be especially controversial – we have just never had the opportunity to delve into the practices of migration management to make the connections. Many scholars have noted that if we want to understand how states manage their non-citizen population, it is not sufficient to merely analyse policies (see, for example, Boswell and Geddes 2011; Morris 2002). After 16 months of working in immigration offices, over 60 interviews and more than one year of advisory work for city councils, it has become quite apparent that practice is not only a question of law-to-case translation, but a more complex affair that impacts migrants beyond their residence status. As representatives of the state (Dubois 2010), street level bureaucrats are significant in establishing the expectations and self-image of migrants in relation to the state. As will be argued in the concluding chapter, we should thus take implementation practices seriously not only in order to calculate the deviation from the black letter law, but also to critically assess the process of socialisation that migrants undergo.

A Very Short Introduction to Migration in Germany

Although Germany infamously has been extremely reluctant to acknowledge its status as a country of immigration, migration from, to and within Germany has always happened (Fahrmeir 2000; Scheffer 2001). Immediately after the Second World War, the majority of migrants to the FRG were ethnic Germans (Aussiedler) who had left the formerly German territories in Eastern Europe (Geddes 2003: 80), as well as internal refugees from the socialist German Democratic Republic. This drastically changed from the mid 1950s, when imminent labour shortages spurred the West German government to recruit temporary 'guest' workers. As a result, bilateral agreements were made with Italy (1955), Spain (1960), Greece (1960), Turkey (1961), Portugal (1964), and Yugoslavia (1968) through which some 2.6 million mainly male low- and un-skilled workers arrived in the FRG (Oezcan 2004; Schmahl 1995). This immediately came to a halt in 1973, when the first serious post-war recession and the 'oil shock' hit Germany and the demand for labour plummeted, which caused the FRG government to proclaim an 'Anwerbestop', a ban on further recruitment (Schmahl 1995).

Given the prevalence of German citizens migrating to the FRG in its first decade, there had not been much of a need for an immigration law focussing on non-German nationals.[1] Furthermore, §119 of the Basic Law decreed that matters concerning refugees and expellees could be decided via edicts by the Bundestag. As a result, while the Federal Expellee Law (Bundesvertriebenengesetz, BVFG) was enacted in 1953, for foreign immigrants the 1938 Ausländerpolizeiverordnung (Police Regulations on Foreigners) remained the legal basis until 1965 (Dollinger and Speckmeier 2007; Töpfer 2002).[2] Rising guest worker numbers in the late 1950s and early 1960s resulted in the enactment of the 1965 Ausländergesetz (Foreigners' Law). The 1965 Ausländergesetz transferred substantial levels of decision-making to the individual states of the Federal Republic of Germany (FRG), while simultaneously setting most decisions onto a discretionary basis, to be decided by the responsible Ausländerbehörde – the foreigners' office of every city or county (Geddes 2003: 81). The 1965 Ausländergesetz has been severely criticised for being mostly devoid of any substantive content as well as based on ill- or non-defined terms (Dollinger and Speckmeier 2007; Schuback 2002: 65–7). Furthermore, it did not include any passages on family reunifications, which increasingly became the major reason for migration in the 1970s (Geddes 2003: 81–2).

1 The German Basic Law of 1949 includes under §116 a general granting of citizenship to all those who had been granted citizenship or asylum in Germany until 1937, and explicitly permitted the re-entry into nationality of those who had been expelled from citizenship during the Third Reich.

2 In practice, the Ausländerpolizeiverordnung was 'de-nazified' through §123 of the German Basic Law.

In addition to family reunions, the FRG increasingly became a main goal for asylum seekers from across the world.[3] The Basic Law had promulgated in §16 (2) that 'Persons persecuted on political grounds shall have the right of asylum' – as a result, asylum was granted on a considerably generous level, leading to continuously rising numbers of applications and the asylum procedure law (Asylverfahrensgesetz, AsylVfG) of 1981 (Scheffer 2001). A new Ausländergesetz was instigated in 1990, and now regulated the granting of residence in considerably higher detail, although retaining some general clauses and ill-defined terms (Dollinger and Speckmeier 2003, Schuback 2002: 68). With the rise of immigration in the late 1980s, political pressure to reduce and control migration culminated in the so-called Asylkompromiss (asylum compromise) of 1993, in which the generous clause of the Basic Law was severely curtailed by a 'judicial monstrosity' (Die Zeit, 30 April 2009), which complicated the entry for asylum seekers, and eased the immediate rejection and deportation of 'obviously unjustified' applicants (Marshall 2000; Schmahl 1995). As a result, the numbers of asylum applications drastically decreased from 440,000 at the peak of the Yugoslav civil war in 1992 to a staggering low of 19,164 in 2007 (Bundesamt für Migration und Flüchtlinge 2009; Guiraudon and Joppke 2001).

However, the debates around immigration of the mid 1990s brought with them the realisation that despite continuous contrary claims, Germany had now become a country of immigration. By 1993, 7 million foreigners – immigrants without German citizenship – inhabited Germany (BAMF 2009). Of these, 70 per cent had been living in Germany for 10 years or more, and 1.5 million had been born in the FRG, with naturalisation rates at less than 0.5 per cent of the immigrant population (Geddes 2003: 94–5). The centre-left government elected into power in 1998 included in its coalition agreement the reform of both citizenship and immigration law, resulting in the reformed Staatsangehörigkeitsgesetz (nationality law, StAG), enacted in 2000, and the new Aufenthaltsgesetz (residence law), enacted in 2005, although the first draft had to undergo several changes to appease the states governed by the Christian Democrats (Geddes 2003; Groß 2004). The new nationality law marks a radical departure from the previous *jus sanguinis* basis of citizenship in Germany and significantly eased the naturalisation process for immigrants and granted automatic German nationality to children born in Germany to parents with secure legal residence. However, the law has also been severely criticised for not going far enough and not allowing for dual citizenship (Mandel 2008; Schiffauer 2006) – although §12 of the Citizenship Act does tolerate dual citizenship in several circumstances and leaves room for further agreements of public international law (H. Hofmann and R. Hofmann 2008). While naturalisation rates initially increased, they have rather steadily declined since 2000 and actually fell below the 1998 level in 2008 (Reichel 2012).

3 This was a striking development, considering the gruelling history of fascist Germany in the 1930s and 1940s (Marshall 2000).

The Aufenthaltsgesetz

While most studies focus on the granting and withholding of citizenship (Brubaker 1992; Davy 2008; Fahrmeir 2000; Joppke 1999; Kivisto and Faist 2007; Kymlicka 1996; Wunderlich 2005), in reality the scope of laws attempting to coordinate immigrants and immigration is much wider. Immigration law in Germany can be divided into three main categories; nationality law, asylum law, and residence law. While nationality law regulates the attainment of citizenship and asylum law dictates the process of granting or denying asylum, residence law includes all rules concerning the entry, stay and exit of non-German nationals in Germany (Morris 2002). It is the application of this last set of regulations on which this study focusses, although of course the former two directly impact on the latter by defining the categories with which it is dealing. Given the decline of naturalisations compared to relatively stable continued immigration to Germany, and the relative neglect of residence law compared to citizenship policies, this seems appropriate.

Literature on immigration law in Germany as well as elsewhere is almost exclusively published by legal scholars, usually lawyers and judges who work in the field. As a result, most works published are general commentaries on the legal text (H. Hofmann and R. Hofmann 2008; Hailbronner 2008; Dienelt 2010), geared at other practitioners, as well as law students (Armbruster 2003) or police forces (Westphal and Stoppa 2001; Schuback 2002). These texts have been extremely useful in understanding the law itself; however, they are of limited sociological value, since they only rarely focus on the implementation practice within the German Ausländerbehörden. Notable examples are the commentary by Hofmann and Hoffmann (eds, 2008), which offers some strategies of dealing with 'common' (mal)practices of Ausländerbehörden and the journal Anwaltsnachrichten Ausländer- und Asylrecht ('lawyers' news [on] foreigners' and asylum law'), which publishes summaries and critiques of state decrees on immigration law as well as having a regular section on the 'funny/sad' episodes of dealing with institutions that apply immigration law, as well as their 'derailments', thus especially severe instances of malpractice or xenophobia. However, since these spectacular – and indeed often shocking – anecdotes serve a polemical rather than analytical purpose, they are not representative of everyday life in any Ausländerbehörde and therefore of limited comparative value to this study, although they do suggest that some of the problems in the implementation process I encountered were not unique to my four case studies and thus encourage a comparative look at the implementation.

The most current residence law is the 'Gesetz über den Aufenthalt, die Erwerbstätigkeit und die Integration von Ausländern im Bundesgebiet' (law on the residence, employment and integration of foreigners in the federal territory [of Germany]), or Aufenthaltsgesetz (residence law), which has been operative since 1 January, 2005. The Aufenthaltsgesetz includes all rules concerning the entry, stay and exit of non-German nationals in Germany and distinguishes between five general types of permission to stay in Germany:

- A tourist visa (Visum) is granted by a federal embassy and usually valid for up to three months within the Schengen Area, although it can be extended in Germany;
- A residence permit (Aufenthaltserlaubnis) is the non-permanent regular permission to stay in Germany. Contrary to previous law, it is the 'same' type of permit regardless of the reason of residence, although the residence permit indicates the paragraph on which the residence permit is based, thus rendering transparent the legal basis of the immigrant's sojourn. The Aufenthaltserlaubnis also regulates the access to the labour market;
- A settlement permit (Niederlassungserlaubnis) allows permanent residence in Germany and usually also includes unlimited access to employment and independent work;
- An EU permanent residence (Daueraufenthalt EU) is a settlement permit for the whole European Union (except the UK, Denmark and Ireland);
- A temporary suspension of deportation (Aussetzung der Abschiebung) or sufferance (Duldung) is, as the title implies, not actually a permission to stay in Germany, but denotes a status in which the migrant is legally bound to leave the country but cannot be forced to, for reasons that are delaying the deportation. Usually, this is either due to a pending application to asylum status or a residence permit, or personal or structural reasons that hinder the departure of the migrant, such as severe personal ailment or not having a passport. Despite this not actually being a secure legal status, historically many migrants have stayed in Germany on the status of sufferance for a number of years, sometimes decades (Morris 2006; Trier 2010).

Citizens of European Union member states and their immediate relatives enjoy freedom of movement, but until 2013 needed to acquire a certification of free movement (Freizügigkeitsbescheinigung) to fulfil their obligation to register with local authorities if they decided to stay in Germany and wanted access to the German welfare system.

Due to the sometimes lengthy process of determining the granting or withholding of residence, migrants who apply for a new residence permit from a secured legal status have their old residence status extended until the decision is made. To certify this, applicants receive a certification of application (Fiktionsbescheinigung).

The Institutional Hierarchy of Immigration Law Application

The promulgation of immigration legislation in Germany is a federal affair; a new residence act can thus only be passed by the Bundestag. The federal ministry of the interior has an immigration law department that provides legal expertise and interacts with similar departments of other European states. However, the legal oversight of the application of immigration legislation has been passed down to the individual Länder, the 16 states of Germany. In each of the states, a department, usually situated within the ministry of the interior, is responsible for interpreting and clarifying the law. While not able to pass laws, the state immigration law departments can issue decrees that are binding to all immigration offices within that state, but not to the administrative courts that decide on cases in which the applicant has appealed against the immigration office's decision. The Ausländerbehörden themselves are sub-departments of the 418 counties (Kreise and kreisfreie Städte). As a consequence, the organisational oversight is in the hands of the local council, but based on federal legislation amended by decrees of the state departments. Decisions made by officials of the Ausländerbehörden are thus technically those of the local councils, which apply migration policies on the lowest possible administrative level.

The hierarchy of immigration administration in Germany therefore includes all three levels of government – the federal, the state and the local – with the local councils being legally accountable for decisions made by the immigration offices. Given that the (federal) executive branch that provides expertise on legal change is not the branch that interprets it for implementation, and that the legal oversight (by the states) is disassociated from the (local) organisational oversight and accountability, there is thus ample organisational distance between offices that could allow different practices of implementation and interpretation – which is what this study aims to unveil. This system differs significantly from that of other European states: While almost all states have local subdivisions that micromanage migration, in many cases these subdivisions are directly accountable to the federal department on immigration and do not involve state and local authorities in the process (Boswell and Geddes 2011; Guild and Peers 2001; Morris 2000, 2002).

Outline

The remainder of this chapter will briefly map out the remainder of the book. Chapters 2–6 present the fieldwork data and explanatory dimensions for the variations in practice encountered. Together, they explore the workings of migration administration in German immigration offices. Chapters 7 and 8 concludes the book by summarising the findings and analysing the possible impact on immigrants.

Chapter 2 introduces the reader to the four offices and cities in which the research took place. Given the agreement to keep the identities of the participating offices anonymous, only the information most relevant to an appreciation of the comparative value of the study will be given. Having thus set the scene, central elements of the work routines of immigration officials are introduced. Based on suspicions of marriages of convenience, some of the significant differences in which these work routines were carried out are examined, which call to question the view of a stable and reliable decision-making process. The chapter then outlines the most relevant findings in terms of the variation of implementation and decision-making processes found both between and within immigration offices. Since the aim of the research was to go beyond a mere technical comparison of legal decisions and beyond a simple presentation of individual office routines, the data will be presented on four different levels of variation: decisions, decision-making, handling, and political alignment. My results show that for the majority of cases, the final decisions on residence and deportation are more similar than the processes that lead to them. Furthermore, where variations in decisions taken do exist, they are most commonly due to different structural and political factors that shape the nature of decision-making, and often an incoherent network of accountability and control.

The subsequent four main chapters of analysis cover different explanatory domains that roughly coincide with the levels of variation in work practice; law, organisation, politics and actors. However, each explanatory dimension impacts on more than its primary level of variation, with Chapter 3, on law, being the most far-reaching, since it examines the ways in which law is learned, understood and applied by caseworkers. 'Street-level' law (borrowing the phrase from Michael Lipsky's seminal work on caseworkers, 'Street-Level Bureaucracy' (Lipsky 1980)) in German immigration offices is found to be a flexible and opaque set of rules, and furthermore undergoing constant change. The very practical and almost a-legal approach to law found in immigration offices will be presented as the dominant modus operandi in how the complex and constantly changing nature of immigration law is handled in Germany. Officials charged with deciding the fate of migrant cases struggle with, on one hand, the inherent ambiguity within the law itself as well as, on the other, the immense difficulty in matching legal requirements with the social reality. Ultimately, the research suggests that officials overcome this by basing decisions on an orally transmitted tradition of learning the legal text and calculations of risks of selective and improper implementation. Similarly, distinguishing between different types of discretion – one of which is legal and outcome-oriented and one influencing the decision-making process – it is argued that applying discretionary powers is not part of a rational and rule-bound process, but a question of the creative use of autonomy. While Chapter 3 presents most of the findings regarding the implementation of law and decisions on the future stay of migrants, the following chapters will each examine a fundamental dimension that shapes the decision-making process and thus accounts for the differences and variations encountered in the four different immigration offices.

Since no decision on the stay of migrants is made in a vacuum, Chapter 4 considers the organisational structures and differences encountered in the four Ausländerbehörden, as well as the interactions between officials and clients, which are shaped by these structures. The first part of the chapter examines how the management of migration is framed within an institutional context at the local level. All four case studies are shown to struggle with finding a suitable structure for case working; in all four offices, reform was common. Both general organisational responses as well as strategies to increase the cohesion of practices are discussed, as a result of which it is argued that rather than a stable organisation in which operations are embedded in transparent and fixed structures, the Ausländerbehörden are engaged in a constant effort to establish and maintain order.

Chapter 5 considers these outside interventions and aims to illustrate the political nature of the local level management of migration. It will be shown how immigration offices can be the site of intense attempts at political interventions from different sides, with impacts both on the structure and working conditions within immigration offices as well as the decisions made inside them. Three main types of potential political interventions are distinguished and discussed. Firstly, influence of local politics and administrations is considered. Since immigration offices are situated within city councils, they are susceptible to interventions on both structural and substantial levels, for example through the allocation of workforce, the provision of legal advice and funds for specific programmes targeting illegal migrants or highly skilled workers. Since decisions on immigration can be highly contested, city councils and higher city administration often have an interest in presenting their immigration office in a specific way (as tough guys on failed asylum seekers or a friendly community service to the hard-working migrant population) and will thus try to steer decisions – and their publicity – in a certain direction. Secondly, the chapter will analyse the influence exerted by higher administrative bodies such as state ministries of the interior, that can amend the law and steer implementation through the issuing of decrees and memorandums that are binding to immigration offices, although not relevant in court settings. State ministries, especially in states governed by coalitions different to the federal coalition, often use this power to reinterpret recent legislative changes, especially during election campaigns. Finally, pressures from individuals and organisations of the 'public sphere', often aligned with local and regional media outlets are examined. Most commonly, these initiatives roam around either individual cases (usually families that face imminent deportation) or specific groups, often illegal immigrants, asylum seekers or ethnic grouping such as Roma or Turks. While of little importance in the debates around legislative change, these groups can be powerful forces in local debates over the interpretation and ethics of immigration law. For immigration offices and their supervising city councils, dealing with publicity is thus one of the most important tasks if they are to retain their institutional 'independence'. Some of the strategies to deal with these political interventions will be discussed in the chapter.

The final chapter in the analytical part of this study deals with the individual caseworkers who have to make decisions over the fate of other people's lives. Invisible in most public discussions and academic considerations unless defamed as racist and right-wing, these individuals are faced with complex decisions under immensely difficult conditions, as the previous chapters will have shown. This chapter will consider some individual responses and reflections on the decision-making process and work in immigration offices. After a quick survey of the main issues considered problematic by caseworkers, the chapter will give an overview of different coping strategies which they routinely draw on and discuss how individuals deal (and fail to deal) with their professional struggles. All four immigration offices studied suffered from high levels of long-term sickness leaves, many of which were caused by stress and other work-related problems. Yet none of the agencies had developed institutionalised approaches to help their employees in dealing with their difficulties, other than a training course in intercultural competence that was supposed to ease communication with applicants, but clearly failed in this goal. Indeed, a lack of trust and paranoia for betrayal and deceit pervaded most immigrant-official interactions, often caused by individual experiences combined with work on particularly difficult cases. Low levels of trust among both officials and applicants reinforce each other, with rather negative effects on the accuracy and empathy of case working and decision-making. Finally, the chapter will examine the professional work ethic and issues of individual responsibility prevalent for the immigration office employees. Due to the sometimes chaotic organisation and highly hierarchical but thinly controlled structure, responsibility for the accuracy, speed and transparency of individual decisions are often rejected by employees on all hierarchical levels, leaving many errors unaccounted for and, much more often, causing applications to disappear into a flux of nothingness, increasing the length of the decision-making process to years, sometimes decades. The chapter will conclude with a typology of case working which takes into account varying levels of power, trust, motivation and responsibility as a means of understanding the different ways in which bureaucracy could work more efficiently.

Chapter 7 considers the effects of this chaotic, uneven and varying implementation practices. It is argued that the lack of transparency further increases the already existing stark power asymmetry between officials and their clients. In addition to the power of determining the fates of their applicants' lives by enforcing residence law, bureaucrats appear even more fearful and potent if their legal powers are applied in a context that is incomprehensible to those who are subjected to them. Not being able to distinguish between the rejection of applications for which there was no legal basis and the dismissal of cases by the whim of an individual employee is thus likely to have a lasting impact on immigrants, particularly given the important role the Ausländerbehörde plays in their lives. The chapter will conclude with an analysis of the mechanisms by which 'untamed' immigrants with no previous experience of German administration are socialised into docile subjects who know what is expected of them, and base this discussion on the work of Erving Goffman and Michel Foucault. Within the field of migration studies, then, the study gives ample evidence for the critical re-evaluation of assumptions hitherto taken for granted. Residence law rather than citizenship doctrines are of primary importance for immigrants in countries with low naturalisation rates; furthermore, looking at the socialising effects the micro-management of migration has on its 'cases' helps to understand the often problematic relationship between immigrants and state, that is perhaps not predominantly due to a democratic deficit of the host countries

Chapter 8 links variations and explanatory domains back to the original research question and its theoretical foundation. By summarising what could be learned by studying four different immigration offices, the implications of the work within the wider field of migration studies, but also the sociology of law and organisations will be shown. Understanding how immigration law works as applied rather than taking the 'scripture' of law for granted has important implications for the conceptualisation of law as a fluid, contextual set of norms. Similarly, the in-depth look at how German bureaucracy operates on its lowest hierarchical level suggests that the Weberian approach to bureaucracy is less useful when used to analyse organisations and should perhaps rather be limited to more historic arguments.

Since this is an ethnographic work as well as the first systematic and comparative study of immigration offices, this study entails some very descriptive parts which are necessary to familiarise the reader with the setting. In this rather strange sense, the German administrative system is no less exotic than the 'pre-modern' tribes of classic anthropology. As is customary with such approaches, the data will be presented through ethnographic anecdotes that originate from the author's field notes. In the case of this book, they represent specific case constellations and implementation strategies that were routinely observed. Excerpts from the field notes and longer anecdotes are indented.

Chapter 2
Inside Immigration Law

> My first day at the Ausländerbehörde: After meeting with the head of office and being shown around the different departments, I begin my fieldwork of decision-making practice in a random office with two kind strangers (I am introduced but did immediately forget their names) who allow me to take a seat next to them and observe their work routine, which is already at full throttle. After her number is called out by an automated system, a middle-aged woman enters the room, presents her passport and, when asked, sits down opposite the official on my left and heaves a big yellow plastic bag onto the desk, full with documents that "might be relevant, because you never know", as the applicant explains with a nervous laugh. When the woman starts explaining her case (something with disability pay and child benefits), the official merely nods and sends the woman out to wait "a little while". Then, the caseworker rummages through the papers in the plastic bag, searches and finds a file amongst a huge stack of – unordered – other files, transfers a few sheets from the plastic bag to the file, spends a couple of minutes entering data from the passport into the office database, prints out a green sheet of paper, glues it onto a page in the woman's passport, signs and seals it, prints out, signs and files another page, then gets up, calls the woman in, hands her passport and plastic bag and tells her that "that will be all for now". The woman, confused, asks about her cases and the decision that has – apparently – just been made, the official merely replies that "everything is in the passport" and that the woman need not worry. As the woman, her plastic bag and the passport leave the room, the official turns to me and tells me that the applicant "would not have understood, anyways". Then, without further ado, she calls for the next person to enter the room. Less than 10 minutes into my first observation, I am as confused as the clients, and seriously start doubting the possibility of succeeding in this venture.

For the immigrant in the above example, the decision on her residence was made behind closed doors, based on mysterious criteria and an unclear set of data, and she will probably have to compare the permit in her passport with that of her peers to understand its implications. The gap identified in the literature thus has a real life parallel: for many migrants, the immigration office is a 'black box' where you enter a yellow plastic bag full of paperwork and receive a residence permit that allows you to stay, work, study or claim benefits. With this chapter, we truly move *inside immigration law* and investigate how and under what conditions immigration law is applied to individual cases. For this, a twofold purpose has to be achieved: first, to present key aspects of the case studies as an entry point to the 'inside' of immigration law and secondly, to assess the different levels of variation between the four different offices studied. This chapter is thus dominated by a presentation of the results of comparing the work practices of four Ausländerbehörden. The following four chapters examine specific aspects of the decision-making process and work routines more closely. All four case studies will be briefly introduced first, followed by a discussion of the tasks Ausländerbehörden are supposed to fulfil. Through discussing instances of suspicions of marriages of conveniences, the complexity of these tasks will be illustrated, and shown that not only the outcomes, but also the decision-making process itself differ greatly and merit an in-depth analysis. From this, four different areas of variation will be presented that reflect the ways in which case working differed in the four offices. Several examples based on my participant observations serve to explain and exemplify each variation.

Four Ausländerbehörden

> It is Wednesday morning, a cold, rainy April morning, a few minutes to eight a.m. While I gather a chair from the common room, caseworker 22 has turned on the radio, and takes the kettle to the bathroom to gather water for his fruity tea, which he always offers me, and I always decline. Carrying my chair across the corridor, I pass caseworkers 17 and 32, who stand by the window. Outside, a group of probably 25–30 people has clustered in front of the entrance. Through the rain, we can see people from all kinds of ethnic and social backgrounds huddled together in much closer proximity than appropriate for usual societal conventions. What unites this diverse crowd is their aim to be among the first to enter the Ausländerbehörde, and for this they endure rain, cold, and standing shoulder to shoulder with complete strangers. 17 draws my attention to a group of people under a shelter in front of the neighbouring building. "Also ours", he mutters. 32 follows me into his office, and while watching me heaving my chair over the monitors and piles of files, asks me to follow him downstairs for the opening of the Ausländerbehörde. 17, still observing the crowd in front of the building, consults his watch and assures 32 that there is "still a minute or so" until eight, and the start of opening hours. We pause, 32 checks his watch, and slowly makes his way down the stairs. I follow, and stand beside him as he unlocks the door, which opens to the outside. 32 has to ask the crowd to move back to enable him to open the door, and tells a young man off for trying to barge in before the door is completely open. Once 32 has stepped back, people start to flow in, pushing their way, running up the stairs towards the offices. Most know their way. The end of the long carpet runner flips over. An older man with a walking stick carefully bypasses this obstacle, causing people behind him to complain. A young woman trips, but it is impossible to flip the carpet back into position: too many feet are in the way. As we walk up the stairs, 32 tells me that during the civil war in Yugoslavia, the entrance to the Ausländerbehörde was overseen by two policemen to prevent accidents. As we reach the first floor,

> there are already a dozen people waiting outside 32's office. 22, who shares the office with 32, is still shuffling through some papers, but as we enter, he bellows "who's first?" The fight against the clock has begun.

Four ethnographic case studies in four different German immigration offices form the basis of this analysis in order to achieve both in-depth insights into the individual offices and a comparative perspective. Several factors influenced this choice, which is a compromise between different theoretical and practical concerns. A pilot study was conducted, which showed that three main external factors were of immense influence: the size of the city and especially overall municipal budget, the number of immigrants residing within the municipal borders and the governing political coalitions and traditions of the federal state. Applying a strategy approximating maximum variation sampling (Patton 2002; A. Rubin and Babbie 2009), I decided to choose three further samples that were as diverse as possible and yet still somewhat typical of Germany. Since the majority of non-citizens in Germany live in urban areas (Statistisches Bundesamt 2007), I further decided to concentrate on cities with more than 100,000 inhabitants. Given the access difficulties described above, I relied on the help of officials in the Middlestadt Ausländerbehörde to arrange contacts with other immigration offices. While not all could be persuaded to grant access, the three cases do fit my outset criteria rather well. In addition to Middlestadt with its 300,000 inhabitants (17.8 per cent of whom are immigrants without German citizenship), I gained access to East Middlestadt, a city in the former GDR with 250,000 inhabitants (3 per cent immigrants), Steelstadt with 600,000 inhabitants (11 per cent immigrants) and Metrostadt with well over a million inhabitants (17 per cent immigrants). While Middlestadt is in a state which is governed by a conservative coalition with a notoriously hard-line approach to immigration, both Steelstadt and Metrostadt are in a state with a strong Social Democratic tradition. Since reunification, East Middlestadt's state has seen both Social Democratic and Christian Democratic governments and is currently governed by a 'grand coalition' between the two parties.

Middlestadt

Middlestadt is a relatively affluent city in an urban conglomeration of settlements dominated by classical German industries – chemical processing, production of machinery and finance. The city accommodates the whole variety of migrants: guest workers, family resettlers, asylum seekers, highly skilled migrants, military personnel, but has a comparably small international student population. The Ausländerbehörde is located in significantly refurbished military barracks well outside the city centre. Its head of office, a veteran of over 30 years' experience in working in immigration law, likes to think back to the 'older and simpler days' of migration management but has come to accept that the 2005 legislation has meant a sea change for the work and organisation of his office. However, taking on responsibility, enlarging his staff and attempting to professionalise the office towards becoming a provider of services came at the cost of losing the sense of a tight-knit community amongst caseworkers. This leaves the head of office in a dilemma between defending unpopular measures against a disgruntled staff and linking back to the spirit of times past. Opening hours are in the mornings of three days a week and on one afternoon, with service at a first-come, first-served basis. Given the generally high caseload of officials and lack of coordination of service provision, the demand for case working can be very high and differ drastically between quiet Monday mornings and frantic Wednesday afternoons.

Steelstadt

Unlike Middlestadt, Steelstadt is situated within an area that was hit hard by de-industrialisation and has undergone significant economic decline since the 1970s. Unemployment in August 2011 was almost double that of Middlestadt, which stands just above the average national rate of 6 per cent (Bundesagentur für Arbeit 2011). Consequently, a lot more migrants struggle to stay above welfare level. Nevertheless, immigration remains high, mostly due to the pull factor of already established migrant populations (cf. Castells and Miller 2009) and, to some extent, the local university. In response to a relatively low staffing level, the Ausländerbehörde has seen a rather drastic increase in caseworkers in the past few years, mostly young administrative staff were posted to the office immediately after their apprenticeship. While caseworkers would have preferred to work in other divisions of the city council, most have accommodated themselves within the Ausländerbehörde, although at the time of my research quite a few were considering or starting part-time further vocational training as a way out. The head of office works in close cooperation with his deputy and the other staff in higher positions, focusing on an equal distribution of tasks that include responsibilities for publicity and court cases. Opening hours are in the mornings and early afternoons on four days of the week, with Thursday openings extended until 6pm.

The Ausländerbehörde in Steelstadt shares a nondescript office block with another subdivision of the city council, which however does not provide face-to-face services to the public. While the building is in good shape from the outside, the inside is in a rather shabby state. After passing intense security checks by unwelcoming private security personnel (an incident occurred at the immigration office of a neighbouring city), applicants can choose to wait for the one, desperately slow elevator, or take the narrow stairs to the upper floors of the building. Along the staircase, frustrated migrants have tagged their anger onto the walls, which has been more or less well covered up by housekeeping. On the four floors of the Ausländerbehörde, there are big waiting areas, including vending machines for snacks and drinks but lacking furniture, and narrow corridors with ample seating, causing regular blockages during peak hours. A plethora of signs and corrections of signs, trying to explain the confusing – and constantly changing – organisational layout of the floors only add to the difficulty of finding one's way to the correct reference person within the Ausländerbehörde. Most office doors are securely locked even during office hours. Inside, some officials have taken great care to personalise their work space, flocking the walls with posters of punk bands and brand logos, while others prefer to use all available space to stack incomplete or not yet returned files.

East Middlestadt

East Middlestadt differs quite drastically from the other three cases by virtue of having been part of the GDR until reunification. While the other three cities have had rather sizeable and established migrant populations since the 1970s, there are very few visible indicators within East Middlestadt's public sphere that a migrant population actually exists. Immigration levels are extremely low and currently at only 3 per cent, but have nevertheless quadrupled in the past 25 years. Two factors have been dominant in this dramatic increase: asylum seekers who are distributed within Germany according to the overall population size and migrant quota of counties and cities, and the university, which successfully advertises itself to potential international students. However, since employment opportunities are few, most students leave East Middlestadt after their studies, and many asylum seekers pooled to East Middlestadt by quota try to have their restriction of free movement transferred to another city in which they hope to find better opportunities and more peers who share a similar fate and history. The immigration office is located at one of the city's main council offices in the city centre, immediately opposite the town's famous cathedral. Opening hours are on four mornings and one afternoon, extending until 6 pm.

As a consequence of the low migration rate, the immigration office is tiny, with only 15 staff members, and a very familiar, friendly atmosphere predominates amongst the caseworkers. Colleagues greet each other and say goodbye with a firm handshake, some of the caseworkers attend evening classes to learn English and exchange their homework during quiet periods. Problems are confronted and attempted to be resolved collectively; it sometimes appears as if resoluteness was one of the key expectations to potential job candidates. All caseworkers on consultation duty share one office and since many clients are remembered from previous meetings, take over from another to speed up the handling process of cases. The friendly climate within the Ausländerbehörde is somewhat dampened by the thick security glass panels that separate the officials' work space from their clients, who have to stand during consultations. All office doors are heavy and locked on all occasions. These precautions are welcomed by most employees, mostly women, who refer to past instances of aggressiveness of previous clients. While students are welcomed with enormous kindness, other migrants are eyed with more suspicion. After a client leaves the office, the officials often share their suspicions and worries about the individual case, causing them to enter comments to the file to forewarn and remind the next colleague dealing with the case.

Metrostadt

As a centre of commerce, trade, media and manufacturing with an international airport and one of the largest cities in Germany, inhabitants of Metrostadt traditionally see it to shine well beyond its immediate region – and indeed, nation state. While unemployment is above the national average, so are the opportunities for people of all trades. Migration rates have traditionally been high, and Metrostadt has been both a city of immigration settlement and transit since the Middle Ages. The Ausländerbehörde, by far the largest of my sample, reflects this attitude of representing a vibrant, cosmopolitan city, and the head of office frequently liaises with high state officials to express what is, after all, the opinion of one of the county's major migration management institutions. Control over internal matters is thus far more delegated to the division heads, who lead sections that are each the size of the immigration offices of Middlestadt or East Middlestadt. The majority of – standard – cases are handled in individual district offices within the city districts, while the most difficult and the most important clients are dealt with at the headquarters, which is located in a huge city council building well outside of the city centre. Opening hours vary and in the case of the headquarters, consultations are usually arranged through appointments fixed well in advance.

> My start in Metrostadt is rather chaotic and overshadowed by a minor surgery that I have to undergo. As a result, I am not formally shown around or introduced and thus employees who do not know me initially eye me with suspicion. Two months into the research, I introduce myself to a subsection of the Ausländerbehörde that I have not yet been to. However, since neither the director of the subsection nor the section head, both of whom I have spoken to in advance, are in, I am left at the mercy of the subsection's deputy, a resolute woman who claims to have never heard of me or my research, and stresses that she could not imagine the head of the immigration office agreeing to what in her view clearly sounded like a lot of nonsense, letting an outsider "sniff around" without a leash! When I suggest contacting the office head and resolving the issue, however, my persistent caseworker hesitates. "I am not sure that THAT will be necessary", she ponders, clearly intimidated to go out of her way and contact the "big boss" for so trivial a matter. I offer a list of other people in the Ausländerbehörde that she might know and find trustworthy enough to establish my credentials, or to come back another time. The former finally is agreeable, and I am told to wait outside while the caseworker researches me. After a short while, I am called in, sat down, offered a coffee and spend the most pleasant and informative morning with one of my key caseworkers-to-be. All that is left of the incident earlier on is to remark that "in this office, one hand never knows what the other is up to".

What Do Ausländerbehörden Do?

Given that the central aim of the research is to examine how immigration offices fulfil their role as institutions of migration management and analyse the differences of practice and legal application, it appears wise to shortly reflect on the official role of the 'foreigners authorities', as Ausländerbehörden are referred to in the official translation of the Residence Act. Section 71 of the *Aufenthaltsgesetz* (AufG) states:

> The foreigners' authorities shall be competent for residence- and passport-related measures and rulings in accordance with this Act and in accordance with provisions relating to foreigners which are contained in other acts.

Simply put, immigration offices apply immigration law. In practice, this means deciding on the stay of immigrants in Germany through different technical steps. However, immigration law is not a mere set of technical guidelines, but a political instrument. The *Aufenthaltsgesetz* states that it:

> serves to control and restrict the influx of foreigners into the Federal Republic of Germany. It enables and organises immigration with due regard to the capacities for admission and integration and the interests of the Federal Republic of Germany in terms of its economy and labour market. At the same time, the Act also serves to fulfil the Federal Republic of Germany's humanitarian obligations. To this end, it regulates the entry, stay and economic activity of foreigners and promotion of the integration of foreigners. (Ibid.)

In a wider context, then, the role of immigration offices in Germany is to execute the migration policy of the Federal Republic of Germany.

In practice, not much of this abstract role is immediately intelligible. The day-to-day work of Ausländerbehörden is not dominated by political debates around or even references to the migration policy of Germany. Instead, there is a predominance of rather menial and routine activities, exchanges and interactions that seem to follow constant patterns and informal codes of conduct.

Three Ideal–Typical Official–Client Interactions

> The next applicant is called in, greeted, asked to sit down, and presents his passport unasked. Caseworker 133 enters the migrant's date of birth into the administrative software, finds the client and his case number, and opens the corresponding entry in the database: a "28–1–1", a migrant holding a residence permit based on section 28, first paragraph, first sentence of the Residence Act; the spouse of a German. Caseworker 133 gets up and asks us to wait for a moment while he searches for the file. Two minutes later, he returns with a slim brown file containing all relevant information on the case, sits down, and

enquires whether the migrant's spouse is accompanying him today. He affirms this, and is asked to bring her in, as a result of which the migrant gets up, opens the door and calls for his wife. After she enters, he closes the door and they sit down. Caseworker 133 asks them if the couple is still married – they are – and if they still live together – they do. He then prints out a declaration of co-habitation that both have to sign, and hands over an application form for the migrant. The client declines the form, takes out an already completed one from his bag, and hands it over to the caseworker, who quickly examines it and then files it into the folder along with the now-signed declaration. While the applicant's wife enquires about the possibility of her spouse attaining permanent residence and the caseworker explains that that will only be possible in a year's time, 133 enters a new residence permit valid for two years into the database. He then prints out a residence label for the passport and a paper copy for the file, attaches the label to an empty passport page, stamps and signs it, enters the number of the residence label along with the migrant's name and case number into a second database, updates the client's entry in the online central registry of foreigners and hands the passport over. The couple get up, exchange short greetings with the caseworker and leave, while 133 signs and files the copy of the residence label, gets up, stows away the file and opens the door to call in the next applicant.

The next client too is greeted, asked to sit down, and too presents his passport unasked. Again, Caseworker 133 enters the migrant's date of birth into the administrative software, finds the client and his case number, and opens the corresponding entry in the database. This time, we have a "16–1", holding a residence permit based on section 16, first paragraph of the Residence Act; a student. Caseworker 133 gets up and asks us to wait for a moment while he searches for the file. Two minutes later, he returns with a slim brown file containing all relevant information on the case, sits down, and enquires if the client has brought the application form along with all necessary documents. The applicant provides a half-filled out form and five pages of documentation, including his matriculation certificate, his tenancy agreement with a duplicate, and a bank statement indicating that 8,000 Euro have been paid into the migrant's account, of which the client is only allowed to withdraw 650 Euro per month. Caseworker 133 quickly reviews these documents, files the matriculation certificate, the copy of the tenancy agreement and the bank statement and at the same time explains to the student what he is supposed to fill into the remaining gaps of his application form. The client then hands over the form, which too is filed. 133 then asks for a proof of having health insurance and a current, biometrical photograph. The migrant replies that he has forgotten both, to which 133 retorts that without these documents, the application cannot be processed and a new residence permit not granted. The client promises to provide these as soon as possible, but since it is already shortly before closing time and the old permit expires today, caseworker 133 decides to issue a certificate of application, valid for six weeks. He thus enters the certificate into the database,

> prints out an official document, a corresponding label and a paper copy for the file, attaches the label to the document, stamps and signs it, enters the number of document and label along with the migrant's name and case number into a second database, updates the client's entry in the online central registry of foreigners and finally prints out an invoice, that the client has to pay at the cashier located on the ground floor of the Ausländerbehörde. The student gets up, leaves the room, and returns five minutes later with a receipt, in exchange for which he receives his passport and his certificate of application, after which he leaves. While waiting for the client to return, 133 has already signed and filed the copy of the certificate and label, and stowed away the file, so that he can now open the door and call in the next applicant.
>
> Again, the next client is greeted, asked to sit down, and presents her passport unasked; again, the migrant's date of birth is entered into the administrative software, client and case number found, the corresponding entry opened. This client already has a permanent residence title according to section 9 of the Residence Act, but has a new passport and thus requires a new residence label. The new passport is photocopied and its identity number typed into the client's database, after which 133 enters a new permanent residence permit into the database, prints out a label and a paper copy, attaches the label to an empty passport page, stamps and signs it, enters the number of the residence label along with the migrant's name and case number into a second database, updates the client's entry in the online central registry of foreigners, prints out an invoice and hands it over. The client gets up, and leaves the room while signs and files the copy of the residence label, gets up, picks up the file, puts the copies of passport and residence label into the folder and stows it away again. Five minutes later the migrant returns with a receipt, in exchange for which she receives her passport, after which she leaves. Again, Caseworker 133 can now get up to open the door and call in the next applicant.

On the street-level, the process of implementing migration policies is thus unquestionably unglamorous. The majority of migrants living in Germany either hold permanent or secure residence permits, the transfer or renewal of which is a standardised, routine task. Deciding on applications like the ones presented above closely resemble very technical and mechanical ways of case working that were described as 'people processing' by various organisational theorists in the 1970s (McKinlay 1975; Prottas 1979), referring to the making and handling of cases according to clear regulations within a stable administrative system. However, because these cases are so straightforward, they do not have to come to the Ausländerbehörde very often and if they do, they do not take a lot of time to deal with. While the overall caseload consists of relatively simple matters to process and decide, the main workload for immigration offices is comprised of rather more difficult cases. As the next example shows, the difficulty lies not only in the decision to be made, but also in getting to the decision, the processing and handling of cases.

Marriages of Convenience

In 1990, ‘Green Card’ a light-hearted romantic comedy starring Gerard Depardieu and Andie MacDowell was released. In this film, a Frenchman (Depardieu) persuades an American woman (MacDowell) to marry him in order to allow him to stay in the United States. In the ensuing troubles of two relative strangers pretending to be a harmonious couple, the two fall in love so that at the end of the film, the two renew their marriage vows no longer ‘out of convenience’, but because they actually mean it. In reality, cases like these are decidedly less romantic, and often much less comical. A marriage of convenience, thus a marriage entered ‘solely for the purpose of allowing one of the participating parties to attain a residence permit’, as one state decree stated, is not only a reason to deny or revoke residence, but also a criminal offence. All four Ausländerbehörden studied in this research took the issue very serious, but all struggled to find ways to prove the existence of such a bogus marriage.

Since there is no federal regulation on dealing with abuses of the Residence Act by way of a marriage of convenience and only few state decrees actually exist on the matter, immigration offices were left more or less to their own devices in addressing the issue. In East Middlestadt, the caseworkers regularly exchanged their experiences in investigating suspected bogus marriages, and in Middlestadt, an unofficial collection of court decisions and internal memorandums was circulated among some caseworkers. The heads of both Metrostadt and Steelstadt had issued communiqués with examples of how to deal with suspicious cases, but not included indicators of when a case actually was suspicious. Given the fact that caseworkers would usually deal with clients on a one-to-one basis, often sharing their office with a colleague who worked on his or her own cases, the initial detection of grounds for suspicion was almost entirely up to the individual official. Since this was a rather common problem, I talked to most caseworkers about how they went about both detecting relationships that only existed to attain residence and gathering evidence to support their suspicions. The results were striking: the threshold that raised a suspicion of a marriage of convenience varied greatly both between the four offices and between their employees. Thus despite being responsible for only a fifth of the migrant population of Middlestadt, I observed more than twice as many instances of suspicions in East Middlestadt as in Middlestadt. In both cases, the semi-official discussion of the issue had led to a very lenient (Middlestadt) or very distrustful (East Middlestadt) attitude among caseworkers. In both Steelstadt and Metrostadt, the variation among caseworkers was considerable.

Comparing all four offices, there were thus significant differences in the expectations of the behaviour of immigrants. Similarly, the individual factors that contributed to raising suspicion varied greatly in all four case studies, although both Middlestadt and East Middlestadt showed a higher internal coherence. These indicators ranged from a large age difference between the spouses (e.g. more than five, 10, or 20 years, with greater distrust if the wife was older than the husband), an otherwise precarious status of the applicant (e.g. a failed asylum seeker facing deportation, an unskilled worker seeking to enter Germany), to significant differences in appearance (a scruffy, squat man and a neat and elegant woman) and 'unusual' ethnic mixes (e.g. a Eastern European and Caribbean couple, a Latin American and African couple). Thus not only how often officials would become suspicious of applications to such residence permits, but also on what basis they formed their suspicion diverged significantly. Some caseworkers especially struggled to distinguish between arranged marriages (which, if consensual, would be legal) and marriages of convenience (which are not legal, even if consensual), something that further complicated the seeking of proof.

> Caseworker 78 has suspected a bogus marriage in a case of hers. A young woman who has just come of age has recently arrived in Germany and now seeks a right to abode based on her marriage to a permanent resident from the same ethnicity who is in his thirties. In order to settle the issue, 78 has prepared a questionnaire that both spouses will have to answer simultaneously, and asked her colleague next door to interrogate the husband while "we will take on the girl", as she puts it. The questionnaire consists of just over 20 questions concerning the history and current state of the relationship, and includes items such as "where did you first meet your spouse", "on which side of the bed do you sleep", or "what does your partner drink for breakfast". After the questioning, 78 compares the results and comments each item loudly, for me to understand. For the majority of questions, both interviewees have responded alike or given corresponding answers. Both claim that they were introduced by their families when the husband visited his country of origin, and while the husband claims to sleep on the right side of the bed, the wife claims to sleep on the left. Some questions were phrased incorrectly and thus do not lend themselves for comparison; both have answered what their respective partner drinks for breakfast without indicating what they themselves drink for breakfast. On the question of what present the wife gave the husband for his last birthday, the responses actually differ (the husband: "nothing", the wife "perfume and a shirt"), but 78 rejects this as irrelevant because "that's just how men are". More serious to her are the failures to correctly identify the vocational training of the wife and the highest degree of education of the husband, two things that for 78 "a couple just knows". In the end, 78 decides to grant a residence permit for a year and includes an entry into both the file and the database to remind the next caseworker of her suspicion.

Questionnaires like these were common in all four immigration offices, although in all cases, employees would phrase their own questions, since many officials explained that immigrants would prepare for specific questions and it would thus be wise to use new questions each time. As a result, the quality and depth of the questions varied greatly. When I raised the issue of marriages of convenience with judges and lawyers during my expert interviews, many provided anecdotes of 'impossible questions' asked by the Ausländerbehörde, and one judge told me that he had tried to answer all the questions asked in one particular case. In evaluating his answers, he found that he could remember neither the maiden name of his mother-in-law, nor the colour of his current bed linen, and certainly had no clue if they had blinds or curtains in their guest bedroom, and thus wondered if he had to question the soundness of his own marriage.

Acknowledging the problematic nature of questionnaires, many caseworkers preferred sending a colleague to the applicant's home to check on the way the suspects lived together. Many employees who adopted this method regularly did not see this as problematic at all and had no concern to intrude into the privacy of the applicant's home and marriage. I never actually observed such a home visit since all three instances when I accompanied an official failed: two because no one was home and one because we were denied entry, which in itself was considered highly suspicious. Many lawyers I interviewed complained about the insensitive nature of these visitations, with caseworkers rummaging through the personal belongings of the applicant and his or her spouse. However, all lawyers also told me that they advised their clients to let the employees of the Ausländerbehörde into their homes without warrants or any other legal basis, since not allowing for this intrusion of privacy would be seen as indicator for a marriage of convenience, which concurs with my observations. The officials that were responsible for these checks told me that they were looking for clear indicators that two people were living together as a couple, such as both male and female clothes and shoes, a double bed instead of two single beds in different rooms, and two toothbrushes. Interestingly, almost all of the judges I interviewed mentioned very different indicators of proof of marriages of convenience. These indicators all focused on the economic aspect of a marriage and included shared property or cars, access to each other's bank accounts, or a common insurance and retirement fund plan. However, in none of the four Ausländerbehörden I studied did economic indicators matter, or were seen as good alternatives when I suggested them in the presentation of my results.

The example of the marriages of conveniences is indicative for many of the issues and variations of practice I observed during my fieldwork. Since actually comparably few residences were denied on the basis of an alleged marriage of convenience and many immigrants won the appeals to such denials of residence in court, the outcomes to these suspicions were not that different in the four Ausländerbehörden. Markedly different however were the attitude with which the issue was approached in the office or by the individual official, the level of vigilance caseworkers adopted despite their or their office's official attitude, and the process of investigating the suspicion. The exploration of the process of implementing immigration law thus yields very different results to what an analysis of the implementation outcomes would deliver. These differences in practicing immigration law as well as the outcomes of these practices will be presented in the next section, through a framework of four different levels of variation.

How Differently do Ausländerbehörden Fulfil their Role?

The previous chapter has shown that the management of migration in Germany involves all three levels of executive authority, federal, state, and local. In addition to being a decentralised process as in most European states, the German immigration administration is characterised by a disassociation of legal innovation, interpretation and accountability for application (Boswell and Geddes 2011; Guild and Peters 2001). That immigration offices work differently, as shown in the previous section, is thus hardly surprising; it is the aim of this book to assess how and in what ways variations can be found between the four case studies, and to explain these variations. As starting point it is worth briefly discussing the few studies that go beyond a discussion of policies and legislative intent. Boswell and Geddes (2011) try to give an estimation of practice mostly based on court decisions, and admit to not having a solid basis of evidence. Similarly, Morris finds evidence for a differential application of residence law according to Land and city in Germany (2002: 31), but she did not gather sufficient evidence to pursue the issue further. More in-depth approaches include Scheffer's (2001) ethnography on asylum seeking in Germany and Juss's (1997) study of visa granting in British embassies (see also the short pieces by Cyrus and Vogel 2003; Bouchard and Carrol 2002; Marchetti 2010; Rousseau et al. 2002; Triandafyllidou 2003). All of these works provide an in-depth analysis of specific aspects of attempts to regulate migration and indicate that individual bureaucrats can exercise varying levels of discretion in applying policy to practice.

Triandafyllidou's study of the Florence foreigners' office (2003) and Cyrus and Vogel's study of work permit granting in German labour offices (2003) both have comparable research goals in analysing the levels of discretion available to officials, but come to extremely differing conclusions. While Triandafyllidou's study reveals moderately high levels of formal and informal discretion (2003: 276–84), Cyrus and Vogel conclude that the scope for discretion is relatively low (2003:253). Bouchard and Carroll (2002) interviewed border bureaucrats who oversee Canadian border crossings, and like Triandafyllidou found relatively high levels of discretion, which appears to be exercised rather arbitrarily. Ellermann (2006, 2009) analyses responses of German and US American bureaucrats to the divergence between a 'general' public opinion that appears to support restrictive policies towards migrants, and fierce public opposition upon the realisation of deportations. According to her findings, bureaucrats manage to pre-empt or contain such conflicts through avoiding publicity and using their autonomy to resist interventions by local politicians. Juss's study of discretion in the visa permission process in the UK as well as UK embassies in South Asia (Juss 1997) reveals severe shortcomings in the implementation process due to weak internal controls and quality assurance mechanisms. According to Juss, visas are stalled by unfair and culturally insensitive behaviour, inaccuracy in the handling of cases and unnecessary delays (1997).

Varying levels of discretion, differing procedures and internal controls, as well as individual variations were all discernible in my findings and will be further discussed and explained below. However, it is difficult to compare the results of the above-mentioned studies, as they all focus on different aspects of the implementation, and provide little to no explanation to their observations. Thus Scheffer and Cyrus and Vogel both focus on migration management in Germany, but in different institutions and with different foci (face-to-face interactions and discretion). While the basis of work is the same legal text, none of them refer as to how there might be different interpretations or practices relating to it. Similarly, Triandafyllidou shares a similar framework with Cyrus and Vogel, but since neither legal, political, nor organisational factors influencing the work are considered, it is impossible to say why they come to different conclusions.

In order to broaden the analysis, I will now discuss the breadth of variations of practices found, each with a set of examples based on relatively regular observations to illustrate the implication of this variation. While it is difficult to compute actual numbers of observed cases since many interactions were observed in passing or only partially, with only the initial application or only the final decision observed and the rest reconstructed from the file and the recollection of the caseworker, all examples are based on at least 25–30 observed cases, often more.

It is worth noting at this stage that even though the primary framework of the research was to assess the variance between the four cases, in effect, the variance within them was almost as big, especially with variation levels A and B (see below). The four levels of variation all refer to different aspects of the implementation process; together, they represent the dominant ways in which the Ausländerbehörden were found to work differently during my fieldwork. In that, they are thus results of the inductive process of participant observation and interviewing and not *a priori* categories according to which the data was collected.

Variance A: Decisions

Immigration offices differ in their application of residence law in the decisions they make. This is perhaps the most straightforward variation among the four cases, although by far not the most prevalent of the four types of variance considered in this chapter. While it can be very difficult to compare individual cases, in general, there was a wide congruence in the decisions made by the immigration offices. This is not surprising given the prevalence of standardised, straightforward cases in immigration offices: In all offices apart from East Middlestadt, the majority of migrants hold a permanent residence; furthermore, all offices had relatively high levels of immigrants from European Union countries that in most circumstances are free to move and settle in Germany – provided that they have collected their certification of free movement from the immigration office. In fact, while the majority of cases are extremely unproblematic, cause little workload and are handled with great congruence, they are often only peripheral to the everyday work within the immigration office, which predominantly deals with the relatively few problematic cases that require frequent consultations and in which the process of decision-making can extend into several months, sometimes years and decades. Table 2.1 provides an indication of this: in general, the more precarious the residence status of an immigrant is, the greater are both the workload the immigrant's case and the variance in decision-making. As a consequence, the impression of the share of difficult cases prevalent in the immigration office held by most caseworkers widely exceed the actual caseload of these types, simply because the workload of any single insecure or rejected case greatly exceeds that of a permanent case by far.

Table 2.1 Typology of observed cases

	Permanent	**Secure**	**Insecure**	**Rejected**
Examples of Status	Settlement Permit, Citizen of EU	Family of German citizens, students, migrant workers with steady employment, accepted asylum seekers	First time applicants, holders of probationary residence permit, temporarily accepted humanitarian immigrants	Failed asylum seekers, rejected residence applicants, irregular immigrants, migrants on suspension of deportation
Caseload	Majority of cases in all immigration offices	Most cases with a residence permit, vast majority of non-permanent migrants	Sizeable populations in all four offices	Less than 10 per cent of all cases in all immigration offices
Workload	Very low	Low-medium	High	High
Outcome Variance	Extremely low	Low	Medium	Medium-High
Examples	Migrants with settlement permit living abroad, EU Citizens on welfare	Changes in the situation of the migrant, Possibility to attain permanent residence, Granting of permanent work permit	Estimations and assessments of securing ones livelihood	Decisions to grant (probationary) residence permit, Decisions to deport, Possibility to work

Within the categories of migrants with an insecure or virtually nonexistent legal status, the variation in decisions made is significant, but not to a level suggesting utter arbitrariness. Bearing in mind the difficulty of properly calculating data from the Ausländerbehörden, especially when gathered through ethnographic means, and the impossibility of estimating decision of third parties, it is safe to assume that around 30 per cent of cases with either insecure or rejected legal status would have been decided differently if presented to a different official or within a different immigration office.

Typical Examples of Variations in Decisions made:

> Never having worked before in Germany and without qualifications, a woman struggles to find employment that allows her to secure the livelihood for herself after divorcing from her husband. According to section 31 AufG, the residence permit can be renewed despite the woman relying on welfare.

Here, the different immigration offices had internal regulations or established practices that expressed that in regular cases, the residence permit should (Steelstadt, East Middlestadt) or should not (Middlestadt, Metrostadt) be renewed. These regulations and practices were adhered to in all cases that I observed, so that in this example, two women with the same above mentioned legal predicament would get the same outcome within any office, but different ones if one applied in Steelstadt and the other in Metrostadt.

> After a long phase of application, trial, and retrial, a humanitarian migrant was denied asylum but granted probationary residence due to the ongoing civil war in his home country that prevented the immigration office from deporting him. He has spent the past decade in Germany, the past five years of which he has obtained a renewed probationary yearly residence permit. Has he fulfilled the seven year requirement to obtain a settlement permit as humanitarian migrant?

Here, negative decisions are often made during initial consultations without a proper evaluation of the case. Officials in all four immigrations offices advise that a settlement permit is unobtainable prior to having seven years' worth of residence permits, which is incorrect, as according to section 26 AufG, the period of the asylum trial can be counted towards the seven years of residence. This, however, is often forgotten in informal discussions, thus pre-empting positive decisions. Since most evaluations are done during an informal consulting process and thus the migrant is discouraged from applying in the first place, these practices never undergo juridical review, as no decision is ever made that could be appealed.

For some residence permits, especially in the case of migrants that have been living on a suspension of deportation or on and off residence for many years, not securing ones livelihood – and thus relying on social benefits – can be disregarded if a positive prognosis of secure employment without receiving welfare is possible.

Some immigration offices, notably Middlestadt, have been rather lenient in deciding to make a positive prognosis, for example in the case of probationary residence permits according to section 104 AufG, while in Metrostadt, full employment can be of much more central importance.

> A family of four (parents, two children) have been rejected in their claim for asylum, have been unsuccessful in applying for residence and rely on welfare. Both parents have been charged for multiple offenses. However, the family has been in Germany for more than 10 years, both children were born on German soil.

While cases like these are almost nonexistent in East Middlestadt in the period studied, in Steelstadt, officials would try very hard to deport in such instances. In Metrostadt, it is much more likely that the situation of the family would be tolerated despite the precarious legal situation and perspective.

> A student is currently completing her Master's degree at the local university and has been offered to continue working with her supervisor towards a PhD, which will be funded through the university's excellence stipend fund. Seeing herself in a new phase of life and supported by her department, she applies for a research residence (§20 AufG) rather than a student residence (§16 AufG), which would probably allow her to apply for a settlement permit towards the end of her doctorate, and allow her spouse residence and work permits.

This case was hotly debated in the East Middlestadt office, which tended to regard PhD students as students and only allow for research residence permits in exceptional circumstances, while in Metrostadt this was handled much more leniently.

Other examples include the issuance of passports for immigrants and of work permits for migrants with suspended deportation orders. As to the variance within offices, East Middlestadt was the only case study in which decisions were highly predictable and with minimal internal variation in decisions made could be found. Middlestadt had moderate levels of internal variation and predictability depending on the case, while Steelstadt had the greatest internal variation of all four cases. In Metrostadt, patterns existed similar to those in Middlestadt, with the striking exception that whereas negative decisions – once under review in the central headquarters – had a relatively low variance, positive decisions like the second, third and fifth example that were handled in the district offices had a rather significant intra-variance. These results will be considered more closely in chapters 3 and 4, on law and office organisation.

Variance B: Decision-making

This second level of variation in the work of immigration offices focuses on the process that leads to a decision, on the decision-making rather than their respective outcomes. As the example of the marriages of convenience has shown, the path to the same residence permit can lead over very different demands and obstacles. The diverse requirements, especially the demand for and interpretation of documents to support an application, but also the varying levels of proof expected by employees differed significantly both within and between the four case studies.

Typical examples of variations in the decision-making process include the following:

> Upon renewing his residence permit to work as a laboratory technician for a pharmaceuticals company, a migrant is unsure what documents to bring to prove that he is able to provide for his family without relying on social welfare.

During my research in Middlestadt, the issue of what 'securing one's livelihood' actually meant was still debated and resolved through a court decision of the Federal Administrative Court of Germany (BVerwG 1 C 32.07), which stated that, basically, it meant not being able to attain social welfare if one applied for it. The Federal Government has since introduced a clarification of the matter in section 9c AufG. However, these measures left practice in immigration offices widely dispersed, centring around the question of how exactly one proves that one actually earns enough to not be able to claim benefits. None of the immigration offices actually managed to settle the issue in a way that persuaded caseworkers from deviating from their own preferred interpretation. Documents requested vary from only the work contract to the work contract and the three most recent payslips (the most prevalent version) to every payslip from at least the past nine months, a recently written statement from the employer guaranteeing employment beyond the granting of residence and evidence that one doesn't actually, through blunt betrayal, claim benefits after all. Variations of this theme relate to the inclusion of probationary periods and short-term contracts to the calculation of secured likelihood.

Linked to the previous examples, some immigrants are suspected to only work when an upcoming renewal of their residence permit requires them to be in paid employment; and in a few cases work contracts and payslips have been found to be bogus. With this threat of being cheated into granting residence in mind, caseworkers are unsure how to deal with situations in which they suspect potential misinformation.

The main variation here is in the awareness of caseworkers in the potential document fraud and their mistrust of being cheated. Some of the more extensive documentation requirements are linked to this issue, but other measures are taken in some instances, notably in East Middlestadt and, to a less extent, in Middlestadt and Steelstadt. A further variation lies in the criteria that have to be fulfilled to successfully defuse a suspicion. Sometimes, the in-house executive department or other employees of the city council are sent to the immigrant's work place to investigate and question employers and colleagues of the applicants. In Metrostadt, cases like these often disappear under the radar of other issues.

As relatively short-term migrants, students often have a cheap contract with private health insurers. Immigration officials are at odds whether to accept this as a sufficient cover or not. Section 9c AufG requires an insurance that is 'equivalent in substance' of the statutory German health insurance. While decrees are actually rather clear on how to interpret this matter, many officials struggle with evaluating the appropriateness of an insurance cover.

Another very common example of this will be discussed in Chapter 3 (on the suspicion of, and investigation into, potential terrorists). Variance in decision-making was prevalent in all four immigration offices; with the exception of East Middlestadt on most documentary issues, none of the Ausländerbehörden actually managed to introduce a coherent system of case working that made requirements posed to applicants in any way transparent. Chapter 4 will deal with these failed attempts to bring order into the at times bizarre and chaotic instances found in immigration offices, and the concluding chapter will consider the finding that in this study none of the offices have been able to introduce a good level of effectiveness and its implications for the wider study of bureaucracy and public administration. Especially striking was that even the most disinterested and noncommittal caseworkers could be engaged in a heated debate with their colleagues over the question of charging applicants for photocopies.

The Photocopy War

In order to prove that she fulfils the criteria of residence, an applicant does not only have to provide proof through documentary evidence, but also copies of that evidence for the files in the immigration office. A standard first time application for work related residence will include the provision of the passport, biometric passport photos, the preliminary work contract, a rental agreement, bills of water and electricity, evidence of health insurance, possibly family-related documents such as marriage licences, children's birth certificates or family registers, child benefit documentation, most likely also evidence of having completed necessary language course requirements, all, of course, photocopied. Perhaps unsurprisingly, most applicants fail to deliver all documents and copies in one go – an instant classic and author's favourite amongst forgotten documentation is a photocopy of every page in the tenancy agreement that 'either refers to costs, size of the rented property or entails a signature of either of the contractual parties'. Consequently, several visits to the immigration office are necessary to get the documents in order, while applicants who copy the whole tenancy agreement are regularly told off for wasting precious natural resources.

Often, the renewal of the residence (or, in dire cases, start of the decision-making process) depends on only a few forgotten photocopies. While some caseworkers just do the task of photocopying themselves and spare the client the hassle, most officials point out that with caseloads well into the thousands, providing free photocopies is actually a very expensive service and in times of severe municipal budget constraints one that is highly unethical to provide (the ethical constraints to using photocopiers for private purposes, however, are considerably less). Also, some caseworkers stress that since it is the applicant, not them, who wants to remain in Germany, it is alone the migrant's responsibility to obey his duty to cooperate. Again other officials suggest that since providing photocopies to the applicant is an extra service not covered by the administration's duty to serve the public good, they should charge immigrants for it, and indeed many immigration offices have a semi-official policy of charging clients for the burden of unwarranted photocopying, some as much as 50 pence per page. However, even these drastic policies do not hinder individual officials from absolutely refusing to photocopy in any case, while others continue to provide the service free of charge.

Since all offices have at least two officials assigned to a set of cases and the variety of opinions on photocopying approximates the total number of caseworkers, the chances are quite high for a migrant to having to adapt to and face the explanation of quite a number of different attitudes to photocopying. Even the installation of publicly accessible, coin-operated photocopiers where clients can do the work themselves does not solve the problem – the photocopiers are on different floors and thus difficult to find in each immigration office except in Middlestadt, where no photocopier is provided at all; in fact, getting from the immigration office to the next public photocopier requires a 10 minute bus ride to the city centre. Where photocopiers do exist, the machines (usually no longer needed staff equipment) are prone to being out-of-service, especially when used by hundreds of different people without a proper background in photocopying on a daily basis. Thus the copy problem remains, and with every attempt to come to an office-wide compromise, the different positions grow further apart, provoking individual caseworkers to make a point in being especially lenient/restrictive/ethical in the provision of the service of digital reproduction. During 16 months of fieldwork, I bore witness to hundreds of photocopy discussions and two heated internal meetings on the matter. This is significant because in a few cases, applicants with proper documentation but without proper copies actually could not start their studies or work, and a few flights booked to reunify families had to be rescheduled not because of missing paperwork, but due to missing reproductions of paperwork.

While these casualties of the photocopy war are extreme examples, a plethora of similar cases happens every day at the immigration offices. After waiting times of up to three hours, applicants are routinely sent away for not having photocopies of the documentary evidence, or for missing minor parts. In some instances, this has consequences for the applicant's life plans. In all cases, it is extremely annoying and of course drastically increases the number of necessary appointments and thus, workload for the immigration office. A true microsociologist could spend a full book on issues such as this, but given the wealth of other data to present, the Photocopy War will only appear again in Chapter 4.

Variance C: Case-handling

The Photocopy War, while nominally based around the question of necessary or superfluous documents needed for decision-making, of course really embarks on a completely different issue: how should case working be done? The third variance reflects this, in that many practices within the observed offices varied greatly and are relevant to the study despite not being relevant to the immediate decision-making process. Instead, the issues summarised in this section affect the nature and quality of immigrant–bureaucrat interactions (chapters 4 and 6) and are in turn greatly influenced by discussions of the orientation and overall goal of Ausländerbehörden (Chapter 5).

Typical cases are as follows:

> A migrant who has been living on the sufferance of the immigration office for years presents his application for residence to the responsible caseworker. After listening for a few minutes, the official gets up, looks for the file, flicks through it briefly and explains that unfortunately, the client will not be able to obtain a residence permit. When enquiring about reasons – after all, a cousin had received a residence permit in a similar situation from a different city – the official quietly, but firmly repeats that unfortunately, in this case there was nothing the immigration office could do. A loud discussion follows, as a result of which the client is asked to leave, and indeed finally leaves when threatened with removal by security personnel. Swearing and calling the immigration office racist and arbitrary (in the general sense of "That man just holds a grudge against me and my people, he does not want to give me what I rightfully deserve"), the applicant finally exits the office, leaving a fuming caseworker behind.

While this rather common example of the degeneration of a consultation into a cockfight actually is significant in many ways, the crux of the misdirected interaction clearly lies in the applicant not understanding – or not accepting – the situation and the official not giving an explanation that is deemed sufficient. The immense sense of frustration and anger is clearly inappropriate, but understandable considering what is at stake for the migrant. Linked to the example of the confused woman (and ethnographer) in Chapter 2, one of the central issues in all four Ausländerbehörden was the lack of transparency during most of the implementation process. In most cases, neither the legal basis of decision-making nor the necessary criteria to be met are clearly explained, rather, the applicants are asked to provide a mass of seemingly random documents without understanding what they are good for.

> Within the total migrant population of each immigration office, the situation of one particular cultural or ethnic group was particularly difficult: as a young woman, followed by an older woman and three little children, enter the office, the (also young) caseworker next to me rolls his eyes and, rather loudly, tells me to watch carefully, as "this is what makes this job so unpleasant". In the

> following 10 minutes, the otherwise friendly and service-oriented official rants about unreliable applicants and snarls at the young woman, who is obviously used to the treatment. Perhaps unsurprisingly, it turns out that she has not brought any of the documentary evidence (again) and waits patiently until her temporary suspension of deportation is renewed for another two weeks, then turns and leaves the office, her entourage behind her.

In cases like the above, a stalemate between applicant and bureaucrat has been reached: The applicant has grown accustomed to (in some cases, was born into) the precarious, permanent temporariness of living in Germany without residence, while the office cannot deport the migrant due to logistical reasons, most commonly caused by the applicant himself. For some caseworkers, especially when they are assigned to these specific groups, dealing with these cases is almost like a crusade, an almost desperate attempt to do anything to attain what he sees as due process. Since these situations usually last for years, often decades, both applicants and officials tend to lose their grip on reality, lacking a certain realism to resolve the situation. Similar situations will be discussed in Chapter 6.

Other examples include the length and intensity of a consultation, the preferential treatment of specific groups, assessments of the credibility of documents, and, again related to the photocopying incidents, the factors that cause repeat appointments on the same or very similar issues.

Variance D: Alignment and Self-representation

Similar to differing greatly in the way individual interactions take place, Ausländerbehörden also present themselves in extremely different fashions. Both the internal organisation and external publicity are often tailored to a specific 'style' of immigration office, varying from the provider of services to valued members of society to a restrictive law enforcement agency. This orientation is defined by the city councils in interaction with the local public, and also in reaction to political tendencies on the state level. This aspect of variation will be part of Chapter 5, in order to avoid unnecessary repetition and because there are only four relevant examples – the immigration offices themselves – a further analysis is relegated to that later chapter.

Conclusion: What Ausländerbehörden Do, and How Differently They Do It

Through presenting a cross section of the data of 16 months of fieldwork, this chapter has provided insights in to the way immigration law is applied in German Ausländerbehörden and considered four key variations in the process of the application of law to individual cases. The first lesson of looking 'inside immigration law' is that what happens inside immigration offices amounts to an immensely complex and at times chaotic process that cannot be captured by an analysis of law or decisions made alone. Looking at the variance in decisions made shows that in the majority of cases – comprising those who already have a secure residence status – complexity, workload, and variance in decisions all are actually rather low. It is the comparably few cases of immigrants with precarious, insecure, changing or not yet established legal status where substantial variations can be found. Looking beyond decisions, it is evident that the processes of reaching a decision, but also ways of case-handling and institutional self-presentation, differ even more greatly both between and within immigration offices. As a consequence, even if migrants with comparable cases in Steelstadt and Middlestadt attain the same residence permit at the end, the process of attainment can diverge very much: in terms of how the applicant is welcomed and treated, what documentation he has to provide to match what levels of suspicion and expectations of credibility, how many times he has to turn up at the Ausländerbehörde, how long he has to wait, how much empathy he receives for his decision, and in how far the decision is actually made transparent to him.

Of course, to find that processes matter greatly when doing research on processes comes as no surprise. What is remarkable, though, is the extent of variations in the practice of the four offices, which, after all, have the same political mission: To apply federal German migration policy to individual cases. Now that it has been established what immigration offices do and estimated how differently they go about their mission, we can analyse how they are able to work so differently. The following chapters will examine the structural reasons for these variations, starting with an analysis of the law and how it is applied in immigration offices, then looking at the organisation of the individual offices and the political interventions that shape immigration law application. Finally, the caseworkers as actors in their own right will be portrayed, enquiring how they cope with doing what they do.

Chapter 3
Making Immigration Law

After the presentation of some of the findings on the variations of legal implementation, this chapter focuses on the basis of decision-making: immigration law, examining how it is constituted and worked with. The two factors, constitution and implementation of law, are intrinsically intertwined. The implementation practice in immigration offices contains aspects of interpretation and selection of legal documents, making 'the law' not simply a basis of decision-making but part of it. Chapter 2 has demonstrated that while the application of law is a routine procedure in the majority of cases, both the majority of time spent by caseworkers on cases and the majority of caseworker-immigrant interactions are spent on cases that are rather complex. Here, the legal text is not straightforward, but at times unclear and based on a multitude of different documents. Employees of immigration offices, hardly any of whom are trained in law, are thus faced with considerable challenges in their daily work, which are amplified by the ways in which knowledge of law, and legal interpretation, is gathered and transferred. Both legal complexity and at times highly unorthodox, unsystematic approaches to law create areas of ambiguity, which can result in a high variation in both the decision-making process and the decisions themselves. While the first part of the chapter will present the immigration law as constantly changing, inherently difficult and rather enormous set of legal documents, the second part will consider the ways in which immigration officers deal with the complexity at hand both on individual and organisational levels. Both factors go a long way to explaining the variations in decision-making found in the four Ausländerbehörden studied presented in the previous chapter.

The Complexity of Law

The development of the 2005 *Aufenthaltsgesetz* as successor of the *Ausländergesetze* of 1990 and 1965 was outlined briefly in Chapter 1. This forms the basis of the daily work of the bureaucrats in the Ausländerbehörde. However, this is by far not the only body of law that the officials need to be acquainted with. The *Aufenthaltsverordnung* (residence decree, AufenthVO) regulates exceptions and specificities of the implementation of the *Aufenthaltsgesetz*. The *Ausländerzentralregistergesetz* (law on the central registry of foreigners) organises the rules regarding the entry of immigrants' data into a central federal registry. Officials furthermore have to deal with work permits, welfare claims and the now obligatory integration courses for immigrants

(*Integrationskursverordnung*). The relevant legal texts alone comprise a 500-page strong book, while additional EU regulations, bilateral agreements, state-level decrees, local directives and major court decisions are further to be considered. Since immigration law directly impacts and depends upon other fields of law, many officials are expected to have knowledge of the basic welfare laws, criminal law and, of course, executive laws for the administration. The superiors, who oversee case working, write injunctions and represent the Ausländerbehörde in court cases as part of their job, further need to be well-acquainted with state court acts, civil law, state registration law, passport and identity card acts, federal border security acts and foreign nationality acts, among other things.

Employees of immigration offices usually have completed a three-year vocational training in the city administration or a three- to four-year general administration course at a college of applied science. In East Middlestadt and Middlestadt, none of the employees of the Ausländerbehörde were trained lawyers, while both in Steelstadt and Metrostadt, one official had a formal background in law. All employees have had to familiarise themselves with the immigration law on the job, as a specialisation in immigration law is not part of the curriculum of either the vocational training or the college course in public administration. As a result, the scope of knowledge and competence in dealing with the law relies almost entirely on the individual employee's effort and the in-house training at the Ausländerbehörde. Lacking a background in law myself, I could greatly empathise with the struggle of new employees to come to terms with the wealth of legal literature.

Further than a wealth of legal texts existing that are disseminated from a variety of sources – with the German Bundestag being the most important, but by far the most prolific promulgator of law – residence law in Germany is undergoing constant changes. Since its introduction in 2005, the Aufenthaltsgesetz has been altered 28 times, in 13 cases with major amendments (BGBl. I 2005: 721; 2007: 748, 1566, 1970; 2008: 162, 213, 2846; 2009: 1970; 2011: 610, 1266, 2258; 2012: 1224). Being chiefly responsible for overseeing the implementation of immigration law, the state officials from the four different German states that I interviewed all agreed that on state level, roughly three decrees per two months were issued, thus totalling to well above 100 additions, clarifications and extensions since 2005. In addition, several relevant court decisions on European, federal, state and county level, federal decrees, application guidelines and internal regulations as well as a wealth of legal interpretation is issued on a monthly basis. As a result, even after a filtering process for relevance at the top level of the immigration offices, where one official usually oversees the influx of new legal documents, caseworkers are expected to accommodate three to five changes, additions and clarifications to the legal basis of their decision-making per week. Thus at least with regard to immigration law, the main sources of law and innovation in law are not the Bundestag, but a variety of mainly executive and judicial branches – perhaps striking, given the overall strong civil law tradition in Germany (Fisher 2009).

The European Court of Justice and the Ankara Agreement

These very different sources from very different disseminating bodies are not only constantly changing, but also enormously complex and possibly conflicting. One of the most prominent – and striking – examples of this is the relationship between German residence law, decisions made by the European Court of Justice, and the consequences of the 1963 *Agreement Creating an Association between the Republic of Turkey and the European Economic Community*, or Ankara Agreement.

In 1963, the member states of the European Economic Council and the Republic of Turkey signed the Ankara Agreement, an association agreement to create a customs union between Turkey and the EEC and eventually lead Turkey to full EEC membership in a three-step process. In 1970, an additional protocol was signed, which went into force in 1973 (Schuback 2002: 246). Furthermore, an association council met on irregular occasions and passed association council decisions to continuously reduce the trade barriers between the EEC and Turkey. One of these decisions, Association Council Decision no. 1 from 1980 (ACD 1/80), states in §6 that Turkish employees had the right to access the EEC member labour markets without barriers once they had been in continuous legal employment in the EEC for four years. These decisions, although legally binding for the EEC members, were only partially included into federal law of many member states (Sieveking 2001, Guild and Peers 2001). In particular, the German government had decided that there was no basis for any right of residence for Turkish workers in the ACD 1/80, which was confirmed by several German court decisions (Schuback 2002: 247). However, in the landmark 1990 'Sevince' decision, the European Court of Justice (ECJ) decided against the Dutch government who had decreed similar rules that this right to freedom of employment was useless without the right to reside. Furthermore, the ECJ decided that the ACD 1/80 was immediately applicable to national law (ECJ C-192/89). However, contrary practices remained, and were confirmed by German administration courts who denied the responsibility of the ECJ (see Guild and Peers 2001, Schuback 2002). Only another court decision by the ECJ in 1992, this time against a German Ausländerbehörde, made explicitly clear that a residence permit followed from the right to employment in ACD 1/80 ('Kus', ECJ C-237/91). Thus 12 years after the initial signing of the protocol, the German authorities were forced to put the ADC 1/80 into practice – against prevailing national law.

The implementation of the Ankara agreement and in particular ACD 1/80 continues to be a source of contestation between national government, Turkish immigrants and the European Court of Justice. In February 2009, the ECJ decided in the 'Soysal'-case (ECJ C228/06) that the 'standstill clause' of §41–1 of the 1970 additional protocol prohibited new barriers for Turkish citizens to enter the EEC. This standstill clause states that given that the aim of the Ankara Agreement was to eventually lead Turkey to full EEC membership, legislation could not discriminate against Turkish citizens by imposing restrictions on the access to the labour market that had not been in place by 1973. In the Soysal case, two truck drivers had sued against having to apply for visas to enter Germany and exercise their trade. As the German visa regulations were from a federal regulation from 1980 and thus introduced after the additional protocol came into force in 1973, the ECJ declared the visa regulations invalid, and declared that Turkish citizens could enter the EU to provide or use services without a visa. This decision has consequently come to question all visa regulations for Turkish citizens wishing to enter Germany (Dienelt 2009). A number of legal commentators view tourism as a service industry, and argue that as a result of the Soysal ruling, Turkish citizens should be able to enter the EU without any visa requirements (Geyer 2009; Westphal 2009) – thus effectively abolishing all entry barriers for short-term stays. This, however, has been disputed by the federal interior ministry (Dienelt 2009), and the federal police went as far as barring internal access to the website of two immigration law lecturers of the federal police academy, which had publicised the opinion that the ECJ decision meant the end of visa requirements for Turkish Nationals (Westphal 2009). However, this was not the end of the matter: more recently, an administrative court in Lower Saxony ruled that entering Germany without a visa is not an illegal entrance for Turkish citizens (Amtsgericht Hannover, 286 Os 7911 Js 100048/10 (123/10)), while a state administration court in Berlin has referred a similar matter to the ECJ for clarification (OVG Berlin-Brandenburg OVG 12 B 46.09). In practice, both the interpretation and application of the ECJ decision was delegated to the lowest possible branch of the executive: the Ausländerbehörde.

In another recent decision, the ECJ decided that the standstill clause of ACD 1 80 was dynamic and thus not only prohibited the introduction of new restrictions but also the abolition of liberties granted in the meantime. Thus in the Toprak case (ECJ C-300/09), the federal government of the Netherlands was disallowed to introduce fees for working visa for Turkish immigrants. In relation to the Toprak decision, the German federal government has stated that it saw only little direct implication of the decisions and that it refrained from translating ECJ decisions regarding ACB 1/80 into federal law in general as the ECJ decisions were immediately applicable and superseded national law 'when relevant' (Bundestag Drucksache 2011 17/5539). Rather, the 2005 Residence Act states under section 4 that, in some cases, a 'right of residence exists as a result of the agreement to establish an association between the European Economic Community and Turkey of 12 September 1963'. In its recent statement, the government further states that it did not plan to enter a dispute in legal scholarship about the interpretation of the ruling, since the application was a matter of the states and individual immigration offices. Possible differences in interpretation and implementation were thus seen to be 'systemic' by the German government (Bundestag Drucksache 2011 17/5539: 5).

Regarding the Soysal ruling, the senior officials of the Ausländerbehörden who were aware of the decision generally agreed that this was likely to result in the abolition of many visa regulations for Turkish citizens. However, since no federal or state-wide decree had been issued concerning this, they agreed simply to ignore the decision until further notice – notwithstanding the fact that they were quite aware that the ECJ decision was immediately binding and required no federal reaction. In a seminar to police officers, a senior official in Middlestadt used the example of the Soysal case to illustrate the complexity of the immigration law and the influence of EU law over national law. He also admitted quite openly that in his opinion, this would very likely mean the end of all tourist visas for Turkish citizens. However, he continued to explain that the Ausländerbehörde would not act accordingly since the federal ministry had a different opinion on this. As a consequence, often migrants can only claim their rights according to the ECJ ruling by appealing against the immigration offices' decisions and hoping to find the support of courts, as in the examples in Lower Saxony and Berlin given above. An official of the immigration law section in one of the state interior ministries explained that the ECJ decisions on the standstill clause could very likely have substantive implications, but that immigrants would have to sue to get their rights acknowledged. Rather than being steered from federal or state levels, the implementation practice would simply 'adapt' to the decision over time, leaving room to 'see' what would happen.

The example of the issues surrounding the Ankara Agreement neatly shows two central problems in the analysis of the implementation of immigration law I encountered: firstly, 'immigration law' is not merely the Aufenthaltsgesetz, or even the legal codes published by the federal government. The entire legal basis of both the Soysal and Toprak decisions are *outside* German federal legislation, and a 'limited' view of the implementation of a certain section of a certain law would not be able to cover this. This development, with European Agreements and the European Court of Justice being the driving forces of innovation in law and the implementation practice playing a catch up game through various court cases, has been predominantly limited to Turkish immigrants and citizens of the former Yugoslav republics that have signed association agreements. However, this group includes over 2.5 million out of the 6.8 million non-naturalised migrants in Germany and is thus relevant for over a third of the immigrant population (Statistisches Bundesamt 2011). Furthermore, after the passing of the Lisbon treaty, the European Court of Justice has been granted much wider influence in migration and asylum issues (Boswell and Geddes 2011: 56–7). Similarly, the move towards a common European asylum policy will enhance the influence of supranational legal change (cf. Boswell and Geddes 2011).

One of the central problems in the implementation of law is the immensely complex, constantly changing law itself (Marshall 2000: 103, Moore 1978). An important part of the organisation of the Ausländerbehörde is thus the organisation of knowledge acquisition and transfer. Secondly, the implementation of immigration law can be intertwined with political interventions on several levels, and sometimes – as in the Soysal case – the illegitimate continuation of practices is legitimised by the federal and state administrations. Choosing to ignore the ECJ decision does not halt the legal conflict altogether, but merely relegates it to lower levels. Since the Ausländerbehörde is both responsible for the consultations on visa applications from abroad and the organisation of deportations of illegal entrants, it is in these offices that hopeful applicants and entrants are likely to clash with the official ignorance of the federal government, and in which the actual implication of supranational rulings has to be established.

Fighting Terror with Bureaucracy

A very similar relegation of conflict happened in the case of security checks that were introduced after the terrorist attacks of 11 September 2001. In response to the internal and external security discussions following the attacks, the federal government issued an anti-terror act (*Terrorismusbekämpfungsgesetz*) in January 2002. This law decreed that an Ausländerbehörde could undertake 'security checks' to enquire about extra-legal activities of an immigrant. These are enquires to federal and state police, the district attorney's office, the national intelligence service, the military intelligence service, the office for the protection of the constitution (*Verfassungsschutz*) and the customs police. The federal interior ministry provided list of the most 'suspicious' nationalities consisting of all countries with a Muslim majority except Bosnia and Herzegovina and Malaysia, in accordance with the rising political discussion about Islam as a danger in Europe (cf. Schiffauer 2006; Buruma 2007). The more specific implementation was – in accordance with the federalist principle of the FRG – left to the individual states. As a consequence, the different governments of the individual states issued greatly varying orders of how to implement the requirement for security checks (cf. Hessischer Landtag 2004, Drucksache 16/1931: 7). Variations included the group of people to issue checks on (varying from everyone to people aged 16–75), the numbers of checks (at the initial application stage, prior to every renewal, every few years, only upon suspicion), and the intensity of checks (enquiries to all services, only to state police, only to state police and *Verfassungsschutz*). Perhaps the most crucial variations were found in the response time of the different intelligence departments (3–9 months in Middlestadt, 2–5 working days in Metrostadt) and the additional material that the Ausländerbehörden were required to gather from the immigrant.

In East Middlestadt, Steelstadt and Metrostadt migrants had to complete a questionnaire with questions similar to those frequently found on arrival cards, for example 'Have you ever held membership of a banned political organisation' or 'Have you previously been convicted of terrorist activities'. While in East Middlestadt these questionnaires were handed out as part of the general application process and applicants filled them in while waiting for their residence permits to be printed, in both Steelstadt and Metrostadt the questionnaire had a much more crucial role. A separate appointment had to be made with a specific subdivision within the immigration offices that did nothing but these security interviews. Due to low staffing levels in both these subdivisions, this meant that applicants had to wait for months until an appointment could be made. According to state regulations, no residence permit was to be granted without the completion of the security interview, and Steelstadt followed this order carefully. In Metrostadt, however, it was decided that in many cases, an interview could happen after the granting of residence, since, after all, a residence could be revoked if there were risks to public security. This was decided 'in the interest of service', since it was seen to be ridiculous to expect immigrants with a right to reside in Germany to wait for a security interview with questions few officials expected to yield relevant results anyway. After the evaluation of the 'interview', which consisted of applicants completing the questionnaire under supervision of a caseworker, the immigration office was supposed to inform the state police and office for the protection of the constitution whenever a suspicious answer (usually a 'yes') was given and when there were substantial differences between the questionnaire and the immigrant's file. In East Middlestadt and to an extent also in Metrostadt, these two issues were evaluated together, and the intelligence services only informed if a suspicious answer could not be explained easily by examining the case. In Steelstadt, however, in most cases either a suspicious answer or a difference between claims made in the questionnaire and the file were sufficient for the intelligence services to be involved.

> Thus while in Metrostadt information on an Iraqi who had served in the army under the Saddam Hussein regime would not be forwarded to police and intelligence because, due to conscription, every adult man had to do military service (accounting for one suspicious answer), was trained to use a hand fire weapon (another suspicious answer of this type) and had been affiliated with a prohibited organisation (a third), in Steelstadt, these three suspicious answers were often enough to lead the caseworkers to the conclusion that in order to "better be safe than sorry", the personal information should be sent off. Usually, the short feedback from the state police and Verfassungsschutz stated that no further information could be found, however, in some cases applicants had to be called in for further questioning, which was typically rather intense and lasted for several hours.

> An elderly man is called in for further questioning because of a disparity between his security questionnaire and immigration file. While the man had denied any involvement with banned political organisations in the questionnaire during the initial questioning, he had claimed to have been involved with guerrilla forces in his home country in his claim for asylum over 20 years ago. This claim was denied on the basis of implausibility, with the responsible court deciding that it had been a bogus claim in order to attain residence in Germany. In Germany, he had worked as a journalist and consequently gained asylum for his regime-critical publications. The interview lasts for four hours in which the three caseworkers present take turns in questioning and go through every last detail of this case. In the end, they conclude that the man poses no security threat because

> in fact he never worked for the guerrilla forces, but warn him that in the next time, he should be more careful about his statements.
>
> I accompany a senior official of the immigration office to a court hearing, in which a migrant has appealed against the office's decision to withhold residence on the basis of suspected support of terrorism. The main reason for the decision was that the man had shared membership of a club with a known financier of terrorist groupings in the Middle East. Intelligence reports suggested that the club might be a front organisation for the gathering of funds for terrorism, but no conclusive evidence could be found. During the hearing, it transpired that this club provided after-school lessons for children and was founded by a friend of the applicant, who could prove that when the dubious financier joined the club, he had already stopped being involved because his children had left school by then. After the hearing, the judge goes out of his way to explain the distinction between evidence and wild guesses and that if he were to decide, the ruling would hardly be in favour of the immigration office. On our way back, the Ausländerbehörde official is quite apologetic of bringing me to this case, but explains that while she personally agreed with the judge and thought that there was no basis for denying residence, this trial was not about evidence, but about defending the Ausländerbehörde. After all, if the office had not attempted to withhold residence and the man had been found out to be involved in terrorism, the immigration office would be blamed.
>
> In Middlestadt, a state decree ordered caseworkers not to tell their applicants about the security checks; it was thus completely unclear to the clients why their application had not been decided, and of course they saw the Ausländerbehörde as being responsible for this delay. As a result, the caseworkers had to deal with many insults, and some clients threatened to sue the Ausländerbehörde for inactivity. To ease the pressure, it was internally agreed to explain the situation to the angry applicants, however, during my fieldwork, many clients still expressed their anger towards the officials. In late February 2009, a new electronic enquiry procedure was introduced, which drastically reduced the delay from a couple of months to a couple of days – for a while. By the end of May, backlogs of five to six weeks were rather common, while a few of the old backlog cases still had not been processed.

The introduction of security enquiries thus created an administrative problem that had not been foreseen, and after several years of practice not been successfully tackled. The resulting delays were – quite understandably – a great nuisance to the clients, some of whom had had to wait for their residence permit for longer than the residence permit was actually valid. Simultaneously, the introduction of security checks created a considerable dilemma for the street-level bureaucrats, who are still daily facing complaints for delays they did not cause, but for which they had to vindicate themselves. Almost all officials thought this situation to be highly annoying, but many shared the sentiment of the senior official who went to trial even in cases they themselves considered rather ridiculous. The case of introduced security measures again shows the diversity and complexity of the law, and the difficult position the immigration offices and their employees find themselves in by being at the lower end of a migration management hierarchy that hands down immensely difficult issues to be resolved without much support or help.

The 'flood of decrees' and the management of legal knowledge

Given the enormous amounts of regulations and important information relevant to the work of the Ausländerbehörde, the management of knowledge and strategies to keep abreast of legal change was a central concern in the immigration offices. There was a general sense of being overwhelmed amongst the employees, all of whom admitted that they struggled or had struggled with the difficulty of the legal basis of their job. Many caseworkers in particular expressed their feeling of being 'flooded' by legal changes and new developments. Indeed, one of the first new expressions I learned was that of the 'flood of decrees' (*Erlassflut*) that swept over the Ausländerbehörden. This was especially true for new employees, for whom learning the 'basic' residence law, managing their individual cases and keeping up with recent developments was often a frustrating experience. But seasoned caseworkers with many years of experience also expressed difficulties in continually staying on top of legal developments. Many also enjoyed this challenge, which meant that rather than merely 'pushing paper', they had to 'use their head'. 'Things never get boring around here' was an expression I often heard, both with positive and negative connotations. The assessment that immigration law was particularly complex was shared by legal professionals, lawyers and judges alike, who, despite all their criticisms, almost unanimously also recognised the immense accomplishment staying on top of the law means for administrative staff untrained in law. Given the universal acknowledgement of the difficulty of the task at hand, it is perhaps understandable that the vast majority of bureaucrats admitted to not reading and certainly not remembering every new court ruling, legal interpretation or decree that they received, usually via email. In all offices, knowledge gaps were accepted as given, the task for both individual officials and overall office system was consequently not to eradicate all gaps in knowledge, but to minimise them to the greatest possible extent and to provide a means of finding the relevant information when necessary.

Managing Knowledge

Three main factors can be identified as means of attaining and maintaining high standards of knowledge in public institutions (Flynn 1997): the initial schooling of employees for the job, the continuous evaluation of knowledge levels and responses through internal or external training sessions, and the provision of an information database. Since the vocational training of employees usually did not cover immigration law, the schooling of new officials was crucial for the successful integration of the colleague and the attainment of a good basis to execute the given task. However, despite this importance, the initial schooling in the immigration offices I studied varied greatly and was usually dependent on a few motivated colleagues rather than a system of schooling. The introduction to the new job was more or less through learning by observing and after a couple of weeks, doing, with an experienced colleague supervising and giving advice to the new recruit. In Middlestadt, new employees usually spent three months observing before taking on their own cases, and after another three months were usually expected to have gained sufficient experience to no longer rely on extensive supervision.

In East Middlestadt, training was much more informal, with new employees starting on their own cases as early as two weeks into the job. Similarly, in both Steelstadt and Metrostadt new officials were simply paired with more experienced colleagues and more or less left to themselves, resulting in an enormous variety of how the pairs worked, some of which worked on cases collectively for about six months, some of which solely relied on a consultative process. Some subdivision heads made a point of meeting with their new colleagues rather frequently in the first couple of weeks of their employment. However, no formal process was instigated to evaluate how far new employees had actually gathered the required levels of expertise and experience to competently make decisions on their own. Furthermore, all officials agreed that in order to be fully competent, at least nine to 12 months of experience were necessary, in many cases, much longer. The attainment of the necessary qualification was thus ultimately heavily dependent on the proficiency of the initial supervisor and, ultimately, the new employees own initiative. Many officials told me that in times of a high turnover of employees, which all immigration offices except East Middlestadt had experienced or were experiencing, some newer employees had been trained by officials who themselves struggled with many aspects of the law. As a result, and with rising complexity of the law, the level of competence had declined considerably. As a consequence, the individual levels of competency varied greatly, and many superior officials often expressed shock at the immense gaps in even the most basic requirements of legal knowledge.

Evaluation and Training

The varying levels of competency and substantial gaps in knowledge that some officials showed were usually only realised by their immediate peers who either helped them out or dealt with some of their cases and found flaws in the case-working and decision-making. Indeed, one of the main reasons for variations in decisions and decision-making was not a differing interpretation, but a different level of knowledge of the law. None of the Ausländerbehörden had developed a system according to which employees could evaluate their own competence, or could be evaluated by others, the only way knowledge gaps and misinformation became evident was when employees actively sought help and when cases went to trial after an immigrant had appealed against the office's decision. The direct superiors of the caseworkers usually argued that they could not be too strict in exercising control over the caseworkers in order not to endanger the working climate within the office. They acknowledge immense demands on individual caseworkers and rather accepted substantive knowledge gaps and answered queries to legal issues as they arose. In Middlestadt and Metrostadt, there was even a lack of departmental or group meetings in which issues in implementation could have been shared and discussed other than informally or on a case-to-case basis. Furthermore, neither internal nor external training sessions occurred very frequently. Usually the deputy head or another high ranking official was responsible for arranging training sessions, but due to time constraints was unable to provide training as often as he wished or might have been necessary. In Middlestadt, Steelstadt and Metrostadt employees usually did not receive more than three or four training sessions per year, one of which – and usually the longest – was the compulsory fire and safety training. Topics on these training courses were usually either dictated by major legal changes, with revisions of existing legislation only given when a substantial and systemic gap in knowledge was detected – often through a court case. Thus when asked how topics for training sesions were chosen, I was referred to 'Commissioner Chance', who apparently worked in all immigration offices in his mysterious ways. In East Middlestadt, due to the small size of the office, employees took turns in attending external training sessions organised by legal associations or state ministries and then presented what they had learned to their colleagues over a weekly communal breakfast. This was of great help to the caseworkers, who due to a lack of varied caseload missed vital cross-case comparisons to which other offices had access and often benefited from feedback from bigger offices and experts. However, this also meant that training could not be tailored to the individual needs of the employees of the office, because both the opportunities for immigration law seminars and the funds for attending were rather limited.

Knowledge Databases

Given the flood of decrees that continuously arrived at the immigration offices and the tendency of individual employees to read and forget – or simply not bother to read – many of the more minor additions and changes to legislation, keeping track of the body of documents that were relevant to decision-making in Ausländerbehörden was quite an important task for the officials. As a true metropolitan city, Metrostadt had one official whose main task was to keep a knowledge database up-to-date. The other cities, however, did not have the resources. In Steelstadt, there was a database, but apart from the minutes from the meeting of departmental heads and information on the passports of the nations of the world, it was hardly ever updated and thus only of limited use, unless one needed to find out about, say, Tongan Protected Person Passports. In Middlestadt and East Middlestadt, no such central database existed, and some division heads kept their own, mostly paper-based databases that usually were far from complete. In three of the four Ausländerbehörden, employees had access to an online commentary to the Residence Act that was provided by a small publishing house. This online commentary made reference to some of the main court rulings, but did not include federal and state decrees or, of course any internal regulations and guidelines. Thus some kind of database was usually available to caseworkers, although only in the case of Metrostadt close to being complete. Since both initial and later on-the-job training were not particularly systematic and intense, using the databases provided appeared to me to be the most reasonable method of learning and keeping up to date with the legal basis of decision-making. As it transpired, however, this was not the case.

The Oral Tradition of Legal Self-Education, and Group Intelligence

One of the assumptions that I had not even considered to be naive was that in order to apply immigration law, the officials of the Ausländerbehörde would require one particular instrument – the legal text itself. In my perception of work in immigration offices, the bureaucrats would be surrounded by paperwork including files, legal interpretations and decrees, crafting their decisions similarly to how I craft my academic work: based on a creative chaos of text. As it turns out, many immigration officials are surrounded by paperwork – but these are usually unsorted files and the menus of pizza delivery services. In fact during my fieldwork, the time officials spent studying the pizza menus vastly exceeded the time officials spent studying the law. Many officials, especially those who write rulings on denials of residence applications, actually have a much-used text version of the residence act. However, these texts are usually rather outdated, as is the time in which they were used most, namely either the introduction of the new Residence Act or the official's entry into the immigration law system, whichever is more recent. Many law textbooks I encountered withered away in drawers or served as saucers to protect more important documents (such as the pizza menu) from mug stains. Almost without exception, officials referred to a textual version of the law in only the most desperate situation. Law is omnipresent in the immigration offices, and most decisions made are in accordance with the residence act and related documents – but these documents, to my utter astonishment, do not appear to matter.

Always a little pert, one head of office usually introduced me as 'searching for the soul of the Ausländerbehörde', implying that as sociologist without proper legal or administrative background, all that mattered to me were the wishy-washy 'cultural' elements of the implementation of immigration law.[1] While the

1 Indeed, most people I encountered immediately assumed that I was a studying law, and when I explained to them that I was in fact a sociologist, usually mistook me for a management consultant.

work in immigration offices appeared decidedly soulless to me, I did encounter something of a *Conscience Collective* (Durkheim 1915), a collective tradition of sharing knowledge and experiences of law that unified the caseworkers in their behaviour and conceptualisation of their work. Janis (1972) has famously discussed the negative impact of such *groupthink*, and others have built up on that work and challenged communal strategies of decision-making (cf. Lee and Lawrence 1985: 94–6). Given the lack of other means of improving knowledge, sharing knowledge was the most successful strategy to reduce variations in decision-making in the Ausländerbehörde. When in doubt, caseworkers would usually ask their colleague in the same room first, and then phone or go to their direct superior. Since the relationship between caseworkers and superiors was usually very good, these instances of admitting ignorance did not mean losing face. Rather, all accepted that 'no one can know all of this [immigration law]', and thus the only way of dealing with being overwhelmed with new regulations and complex laws was to support each other, both on the same and across levels of hierarchies. Uncertainties caused by gaps in knowledge or difficult and new case constellations were resolved by making use of the greatest available resource to the immigration officials: their peers.

> One Wednesday afternoon, an older man accompanied by his son consults caseworker 19 about his application for a settlement permit. 19 inspects the applicant's file and find that the client has yet to bring proofs of having paid into the pension fund for 60 months. The client dissents, and argues that he is ill. After browsing the file for a while, 19 finds that the client has medical certificates that attest his ailments. Now turning to his previous residence permits, she finds that they have been granted exceptionally based on a decree from the early 2000s concerning citizens of a certain war-torn state. 19 turns to 18, who shares the office with her, and asks about the decree. Both agree that they have never heard of it, and 19 tries to contact her superior, 9, who has just gone for a cigarette. Thus, 19 asks caseworker 8 in the office next door. 8 has heard about a decree on this state, but thought that this was much older than from the early 2000s. Together, they inspect the applicants file and find a number of notes by both 18 and 8 that refer to the decree, all without explicitly stating what the decree entails. In the meantime, their superior, 9, is back, and 8, 19, 9 and I gather in 9's office to consult on the case. 9 has no recollection of such a decree, and consults her collection of relevant decrees. However, she fails to find a decree for the relevant date, and for a while, there is an air of confusion about what to do. Eventually, 9 suggests granting the same permit as last time – which is a residence for two years. All agree on this procedure, and 9 adds that probably in two years' time, the old man can finally get his permanent residence permit.

This example shows a classic case of collaborative and – to an extent – inventive decision-making prevalent in difficult and unusual cases like these. Not knowing what to do was not criticised or stigmatised in these situations, rather, all shared in being confused and unsure about what to do, and all share in finding a possible solution. The decision – to simply repeat the decision made last time and defer the settlement permit to later – is pragmatic, but really not more than an act of good faith in better knowledge two years ago. These 'acts of good faith', the trust in group knowledge and tradition, was prevalent in all four immigration offices. Not the law as text, but colleagues are the main sources of information. In complex cases, decisions were made less on the basis of studying commentaries, decrees and court decisions but through gaining a feeling of what action would be correct through a process of consultation with colleagues.

With increasing experience in the field, officials sometimes turned to me during phases of uncertainty. However, they were usually not interested in my assessment of a certain case or a specific legal issue, but in my knowledge of the practice of the other immigration offices. 'What do you think' usually meant 'how do the other offices solve this matter', not 'what is your opinion of that matter'. My experience with other systems of shared practice was more important than my individual expertise (no matter how significant or nonexistent) or common sense.

After my fieldwork, I gave a number of presentations on my findings, including all immigration offices and one of the state interior ministries, who invited me to give a talk after a number of interviews. One of the central findings I presented to both groups was about the oral tradition of law and the collective memory that predominates over a text-based problem solving approach. While these findings were merely acknowledged in the immigration offices – after all, this was standard procedure and hardly noteworthy – they caused quite a debate and exclamations of horror amongst the state officials, all of whom are trained lawyers. Similarly, when discussing my suggestions for improving organisation and service in the immigration offices, one of the things that were constantly ignored were ideas to improve transparency to clients by referring to the residence act text.

Thus the implementation of immigration law is from the outset an extremely difficult task, which is exercised by employees without any special legal training, who solely rely on the education they receive in their respective Ausländerbehörden. Further compassing a huge range of legal literature and being a relatively difficult set of rules and regulations, the immigration law is constantly changing. While structural remedies to ease dealing with the complexity of the job were almost nonexistent, the informal practice of sharing complexity and knowledge was prevalent in all four cases. *Law in action*, as applied rather than as written, is thus a distinctly different affair than a logical, highly structured image of people processing organisations might suggest. This is of course not a new insight, since studies by anthropologists like Sally Falk Moore have examined *law as practice* many decades ago (Moore 1978). Studies of court procedures have shown that the practice of law differs according to specific cultures of jurisprudence (Scheffer, Hannken-Illjes, and Kozin 2010). Outside the courtroom, Bittner's classic study on police officers (1967) found that on the street, the implementation and enforcement of law was not executed by the book, but rather based on routine ways of doing the job (Hobbs 1988;

Behr 2006). In his study of street-level bureaucracy in France, Dubois (2010) too finds that policies are not simply applied in the day-to-day work of officials, but 'materialises' through practice. In that sense, the application of law to cases is a craft, a practical skill that is refined through practice and mastery of which requires experience in usage rather than a broad theoretical foundation.

Discretion

In examining the implementation of immigration law in Germany, one of the key aspects to consider is the levels of discretion available to individual officials when making their decision. Four of the five model studies identified in Chapter 2 have found medium to high levels of individual judgement, which seems to confirm Lipsky's findings on street-level bureaucrats. Similar to Blau and Meyer (1971), Peters (2001), or Bardach (1977); Lipsky stresses the high levels of autonomy officials handling cases have. Due to the specialisation and diffusion of power in modern states, street-level bureaucrats are seldom directly accountable to the persons who promulgate the rules the bureaucrats have to implement (Lipsky 1980: 17). In combination with secure job positions and a relatively small catalogue of sanctions or benefits, officials have a substantial scope to withhold cooperation from both legislators and managerial elites (Lipsky 1980: 23–5). Furthermore, since law is seldom precise enough to fit an individual case, there are bound to be certain grey areas in which the official is not bound by a rule, but has to interpret it and exercise her discretion (Lipsky 1980: 14–15).

However, the term discretion itself has been applied rather discretionally and the differentiation of types of discretion is not always persuasive. Davies's definition that any 'public officer has discretion wherever the effective limits on his power leave him free to make a choice among possible courses of action and inaction' (1969: 4) is as helpful as it is all-pervasive. Lipsky's (1980) distinction between discretion and autonomy is a rather arbitrary distinction of the same phenomenon. In practice, autonomy from the legislation allows for discretion, while the necessary exercise of discretion and division of labour within modern states require substantive amounts of autonomy. Two of the studies that are most comparable to mine, Cyrus and Vogel (2003) and Triandafyllidou (2003), use the concept of formal and informal discretion to analyse the implementation process of immigration law. Both see the formal variant as explicitly stated in the law – basically whenever the verb 'can' is used in legislation – and informal discretion as 'deviant' techniques of individual practice and more closely related to the work of Lipsky. While this seems a logical differentiation since discretion-by-law is a central to many sections of the 2005 Residence Act, in practice the distinction between these two types is significantly blurred. In this section, I will argue that it is more useful to distinguish between discretion exercised in the handling of cases and discretion of actual decisions, complying with Variation A ('Decisions') of my findings.

There are three kinds of expel orders in the *Aufenthaltsgesetz*, the 'ought to expel' order, the regular expulsion and the discretionary expulsion. The kind of expel order to be used depends on both the nature of a committed criminal offence, the severity of the court judgement and the individual's personal background. At the Ausländerbehörde, the caseworker of the 'executive' department usually decided first if a person should be expelled and then checked which expel order to use. If neither of the other two were possible, the caseworker 'retreated' to the discretionary decision.

This practice is true of positive decisions as well. For example, in the calculation of the required income to sign an obligation for tourist visas, there is an accepted practice of still granting the obligation when the applicant misses the expected funds by less than €50. However, the decision to be generous and ignore this shortfall is not made by all, and not in all circumstances, while others go further. Some would allow for a shortfall of €80, while others would deny the obligation based on a shortfall of €8.

Both cases show that the *decision to exercise discretion itself is a discretionary practice*. The distinction between formal and informal discretion is relatively useless here: in the former case, informal discretion (deciding to expel) leads to formal discretion (the discretionary expel order), while in the latter case, 'personal' informal discretion leads to 'institutional', thus quasi-formal informal discretion. In my view, it is much more useful to distinguish between procedural discretion, thus discretion exercised in the handling of cases and decision-making process, and factual decision discretion, thus discretion in the granting or withholding of residence. A similar distinction is made by Bouchard and Carroll's study (2002), who further distinguish between a 'formal' procedural and an 'informal', 'selection grid' discretion (Bouchard and Carroll 2002: 248–51), which I have not adopted because this again rather arbitrarily introduces the formal/informal distinction.

The two examples above are examples of factual discretion. As stated in the previous chapter, the variation of decisions on comparable cases was actually rather low overall. Most potentially contestable decisions – namely these based on discretion – were done in consultation with colleagues and superiors, using the techniques of sharing knowledge discussed above. Many orders of withholding residence were in fact either written or signed by the office management, who – as both the superiors and caseworkers saw it – were, after all, better paid and thus ought to '*ihren Kopf hinhalten*', to present their head to the executioner. Most resolutions to controversial cases were thus a product of a consultative process involving different levels of the immigration office hierarchy, which helped to keep the level of variance among comparable decisions low. As Chapter 2 has shown, this was true especially in situations in which applicants had already secured residence and the complexity of the legal issue was relatively low. In more complex cases regarding more precarious residence statuses, discretion-by-law was sometimes exercised differently within and between the Ausländerbehörden. Crucially, the main difference was not this interpretation of legal consequence but the identification of the possibility of exercising discretion.

One of the most striking findings of my expert interviews with judges and lawyers was that almost unanimously, all parties involved in the appeal to decisions of the immigration offices criticised the quality of orders of withholding residence. However, this criticism seldom focused on flaws in the legal reasoning and logic of argument of these orders, but rather highlighted problems in the accurate presentation of the merits of the case and the *decision* to apply discretion. Thus even in criticising decisions based on faulty uses of discretion-by-law, in effect the other practitioners of law disapproved of 'informal' discretionary practices and deficits in the process of gathering information to make the decision. Here again, even if 'formal' discretion as identified in law is used, it is always embedded in and activated by informal practices – further illustrating the arbitrariness of distinguishing between formal and informal discretion in analysing decision-making routines. The differences in discretionary practice can thus not be estimated by a comparative analysis of a law that is applied, but has to take into consideration the organisational structures in which the implementation of legislation is embedded. Indeed, the most common uses of discretion were in the process of case handling and the prelude to decision-making, variations B (Decision-Making) and C (Handling) of my findings.

Discretion is thus a product of both the necessary vagueness of rules (Triandafyllidou 2003 and Cyrus and Vogel's – also 2003 – formal and informal discretion) as well as the individual autonomy (Lipsky 1980) of the bureaucrat vis-à-vis the legislation. It is both found in the process of handling cases and in making decisions, although in the Ausländerbehörde, the more formal discretion is institutionally controlled by superiors. With de Certeau, the subject is thus not limited to either accepting or rejecting rules, but can creatively make use of the complex and contradictory social relations by which she is bound (Certeau 1984). Consumption, the 'usage' of objects, locations, relations and constraints, is central to de Certeau. Thus neither the conditions of social reality, nor the process of becoming or not becoming, but the practices of everyday adaptation to one's own social and spatial location are crucial to social research. No position, no category is so rigid that it cannot be performed in different ways – this diverse 'acting out' of very similar institutional positions can be aptly observed in the Ausländerbehörde. Finally, discretion necessary for the application of cases and natural due to the position of the individual in the structure of the Ausländerbehörde often borders arbitrariness.

Conclusion: Law as a Challenge

This chapter has challenged the notion of one coherent black letter law that is evenly applied. It has shown that firstly, the knowledge requirements are excessive and are clearly a lot to ask from employees with a general background in administration. Secondly, since the law is constantly changing – and these changes are usually not found in the law itself – it is extremely difficult to keep up with important developments. Thirdly, law is a politicised on several levels, sometimes leading to a relegation of conflicts between state and immigrant interests to the street-levels of bureaucracy. The sociological study of bureaucracies and administration has to consider these practical issues of law. Accepting law as a process rather than a fixed set of rules (Moore 1978, West 2005) questions the possibility of a straight-forward implementation analysis. The question of formal and informal discretion is rather naive, since the boundary between formal and informal is blurred in the practice of everyday office routines. None of the studies discussed discuss the law itself or the interactions of bureaucrats and law and thus neglect that applying law is always also a process of interpretation and selection (Hiebaum 2004). The implementation of law is not only a power struggle between legislators and implementers (Bardach 1977; Lipsky 1980; Morris 1985) or between managers and caseworkers (Peters 1995), but also a constant challenge to define, manage and defend *the law*, which is a symbolic as well as substantive means (Arnold 1935).

The analysis of immigration law, exemplified by the examination of the impact of the Ankara Agreement and the decisions of the European Court of Justice, questions conceptions of law as black letter text which can form a basis of analysis or decision-making. Instead, German immigration law is shown to be *plural*, since it is based on a multitude of different types of promulgated norms from different levels of politics, inherently *ambiguous*, as its content can have multiple meanings and interpretations, and constantly *changing*, since various additional texts and interpretations of text are issued each month. Furthermore, as the study of political interventions into the work of the Ausländerbehörden in Chapter 5 will show, the interpretation of the meaning of law is dependent on one's political conviction and thus *interactive*, potentially even in conflict with other types of norms. Of course, these findings are not especially novel, and this particular perspective on law as a process is deeply indebted to the work of legal anthropologists (Moore 1978) and more theoretical legal sociologists (Arnold 1935, Ehrlich 1975, Hiebaum 2004). More recently, the work of Cotterell (2006) on the role of law opposite other norm systems in different societies as well as the comparative study of 'law in action' in courtrooms (Scheffer, Hannken-Illjes, and Kozin 2010) shows how law is a matter of interpretation and interaction, and can hold a different weight in different contexts. The findings of this study thus lend support to such an analysis of law as practice. Through this, the results point to distinctive shortcomings of previous studies on implementation.

If law indeed is not a fixed and stable set of regulations but vague and in flux, this should be recognised by studies that analyse the implementation of specific policies. This chapter stands out in comparison to all other studies on the implementation of immigration law found and discussed in that it actually considers the law itself. Indeed, most classic studies that analyse the implementation of laws in and through public administration fail to give an account of its inherent ambiguity. Thus in his seminal 'Street-Level Bureaucracy' (1980), Lipsky goes at length to discuss the autonomy of caseworkers to disobey the orders and intentions of legislators and analyses the different uses of discretion based on that autonomy, but does not consider the legal basis that allows for discretion itself. Similarly, both case studies on the – only partially successful – implementation of specific laws (Bardach 1977; Edwards 1980; Kshīrasāgara 1986; Morris 1985) and more theoretical works (March, Baier, and Saetren 1988; Peters 1995) neglect an analysis of the law as basis of implementation processes. As a result, all of these studies have found the disparity between law and implementation outcome to be grounded in the *institutional structure* of public administration (e.g. spatial and organisational distance between promulgators and implementers, cf. Edwards 1980) or *individual traits* of the bureaucrats (such as adhering to different a political ideology, cf. Bardach 1977 or normative system, cf. Arnold 1935; Kshīrasāgara 1986).

While these levels of analysis are useful and will be explained further in the course of the book (cf. chapters 4 and 6), the inclusion of an analysis of the law itself changes the overall conclusion significantly: As law is ambiguous and changing, it is inherently impossible to ever fully implement it 'according to the law'. Crucially, this does not falsify the role structural deficiencies and individual stubbornness play, but helps to qualify the expectations to the degree to which a policy can actually be implemented. Failing an impossible task is still a failure, but not quite as bad as failing something that could conceivably be achieved. Understanding that outcomes of an implementation process will necessarily differ from the original text(s) due to specific inconsistencies or ambiguities – as in the present example, the whole overall aim of German migration policy – thus directs the attention to processes of interpretation and often political debates over the meaning of a given law (Hiebaum 2004). These in turn help to explain the variations of implementation in different organisations, which can be due to different structural, individual, but also legal-interpretative reasons.

This argument to incorporate the analysis of law in the evaluation of implementation processes and the study in organisations is directly applicable in the other direction. Analyses of laws as practices have focused almost exclusively on law in the context of professional practitioner in and around courts (Banakar 1998; Lautman 1972; Scheffer et al. 2010). Very few studies (for example West 2004 on everyday Japan) actually analyse how the use of law changes once out of the hands of legal professionals. The analysis of the Ausländerbehörde caseworkers, whose work is based on law but who are not trained in law, has presented very creative and unorthodox ways of dealing with and applying legislation. In this context, law is felt and tamed rather than grasped and comprehended. There is thus a potentially fertile pasture for both theoretical and empirical enquiries in the overlapping between the sociologies of law and organisations.

Analysing the ways in which this management of knowledge happened produced two rather surprising results: very few structural responses to the difficulty of the task could be found in the immigration offices. Officials are thus very much left to their own devices, and resolve this lack of training, learning and control of knowledge by sharing the complexity of the law and working cooperatively on cases. The image of the 'black box' with unknown operational features is thus rather accurate: decisions 'happen' much more informally than following clearly structured steps. The lack of transparency towards clients is thus directly linked to the fact that with shared knowledge and informal networks of information, decisions cannot be made transparent, even if officials were willing to do so. Surprisingly, this communal sharing of knowledge and mutual support in managing the law and decision-making worked rather well in all four offices. While clearly a coping technique in order to deal with adverse work challenges (Lipsky 1980), oral knowledge networks functioned instead of or in addition to formal structures of consultation and learning.

The variations discussed in Chapter 2 can thus be explained by the fact that the law does leave substantial room for interpretation and regulation on sub-national levels. In its complexity and changing nature, the legal basis for managing migration is also very difficult to handle for caseworkers, who receive little formal support, but can share in informal oral traditions of decision-making and knowledge transfers. Through these patterns of mutual support, through together taming the legal basis of their work, officials actually manage to do their job rather well, since the outcomes of these chaotic and improvising practices are relatively similar. Thus the relatively low variation in decisions (variation A) is partially a direct result of the reliability of informal routines in which individuals develop a feeling for, not a comprehension of the law. Finally, the findings of this study concur with classic studies on bureaucracy that street-level officials do wield considerable amounts of individual autonomy and can thus use and abuse their discretion both during the decision-making process and in the decisions themselves. We can thus account for significant proportions of variation A, the decisions, and B, the decision-making process, while variation C, the style of decision-making is vested in the individual autonomy explained above. The next chapters will consider how these variations are possible by looking at the organisational structure of immigration offices (Chapter 4) and examining the political interventions that steer both structure and decision-making (Chapter 5). Chapter 6 will analyse how the officials deal with the complexity of the job and the autonomy granted. These steps will help to further understand why the management of migration happens as varied and chaotic as it does in the four cases studied.

Chapter 4

Producing and Consuming Order

This chapter will look at the immigration office as organisational entity, as workplace. Structural differences between the four case studies that account for the different levels of variation found in Chapter 3 will be examined, and attempts to increase internal coherence and efficiency considered. The somewhat chaotic and arbitrary work routines regarding the use of law and decision-making (as found in Chapter 3) are shown to be mirrored by differing and incoherent ways of work operations, and organisational change portrayed as a constant cycle of reform without ultimate goal. Rather than on a stable organisational footing, the divergent practices and unorthodox uses of law identified in the previous two chapters are presented to be situated in – and caused by – a work environment which struggles to maintain an orderly shape. However, this instability not attributed to public administration by classic accounts of bureaucracy also has a positive side. Since Ausländerbehörden have to react to the constancy of legal change identified in Chapter 2, the repetitive cycle of reform and re-reform is advantageous to an orderly and stable way of doing work as operational deficiencies and challenges are already constantly being identified and evaluated.

Structures of Bureaucracy – Structures of Inefficiency

All Ausländerbehörden distinguish between a large, general case-working department and a specialised department that focuses on the organisation of deportations, deals with newly arrived irregular migrants and is responsible for other out-of-house jobs such as the home visits in cases of a suspected marriage of convenience as discussed in Chapter 2. Within the 'general residence law' department, all offices apart from East Middlestadt had further subdivisions as discussed. These subdivisions were divided according to residence status (humanitarian migrant and everyone else), citizenship (three groups, each responsible for a number of states) and residence within the city (nine district offices). They varied in size, with a minimum of four and a maximum of 13 caseworkers directly dealing with the handling of applications and necessary documents plus two to four officials who were responsible for overseeing more difficult cases and writing the rulings on denials of residence. With a total of seven employees handling clients and a further two working on rulings, the one residence law unit in East Middlestadt is thus rather comparable to one of the subdivisions in the other departments. The subdivisions usually had a strong internal coherence – officials would often spend their lunch breaks together and turn to their group first in when questions regarding the processing of a case arose. Given the highly oral and group-based use of legal knowledge in immigration offices as discussed in the previous chapter, it should not come as a surprise that the variations within these subdivisions were substantially lower than when examining the immigration offices as a whole. This was especially true regarding the decision-making process (Variation B) and also the decisions made (Variation A). The two other variations, handling (Variation C) and self-presentation Variation D) were more influenced by the overall structure and orientation of the immigration office and the individual caseworkers themselves (see chapters 5 and 6, respectively).

Variations between Subdivisions

In Metrostadt, the case processing sections of the nine subdivisions are geographically dispersed over the whole city, with one additional section on newly arrived or exposed humanitarian migrants and the 'overseeing' sections on writing rulings concentrated in the headquarters building. In fact, due to a relatively low staffing level, some officials have to write rulings for and give advice to more than one section. As such, the section heads in the city branches, although on the same pay level as their 'writing' colleagues, wield a much greater authority over the processing of cases than anyone in headquarters. Indeed, within the headquarters, these section heads are often referred to as being their own royalty. A great sense of independence dominates within all of the subdivisions, and caseworkers are proud to be able to serve their city district locally and free from intervention from headquarters, which is seen as an almost entirely different office altogether by many caseworkers. While cases in which applications are denied are apparently handled with much less variation than in the other Ausländerbehörden due to the centralisation of the written phase of decisions, the differences found in the decision-making processes can be rather extreme. This of course has immediate consequences for the work of the 'overseeing' counterparts, because where in one district office a residence might be granted despite minor complications, another would pass it on to their writing colleague to arrange the denial of residence. Similarly, the extent of positive decisions can vary greatly, especially with regards to the step from temporary to permanent residence, but also regarding the length of a temporary residence. In one of the subdivisions, the caseworkers had decided to save their clients – and themselves – the hassle and extended temporary residence permits for immigrants with a secure status but without chances of attaining permanent residence (for example, the unemployed immigrant wife of a German citizen) far beyond the legal limit of three years. Since none of these cases ever made it to headquarters and the overseeing colleagues were not around to participate in the communal decision to take this initiative, issues like these only came up as result of my fieldwork, or through Commissioner Chance.

Steelstadt

During my fieldwork in Steelstadt, three groups handled all aspects of the law, but were differentiated by country of origin of the immigrant. In order to distribute the caseload of the immigration office as evenly as possible, the groups held responsibility over a rather arbitrary set of state citizens. Thus while citizens of Armenia and Georgia belonged to one group, citizens of Azerbaijan had been sorted to another; Syria and the Lebanon were separated from the rest of the Middle East, migrants without citizenship were part of a different group than stateless immigrants, and Sri Lanka the only Asian country distributed to the group otherwise focusing on Africa, the Americas and Eastern Europe. Since with shifting waves of immigration the distribution of states changed from time to time (Afghanistan being a recent such 'casualty'), some of the signs indicating where an immigrant had to turn to had been pasted over, only adding to the rather confusing setup. This seemingly arbitrary arrangement was due to the attempt to not only distribute the caseload equally, but also to avoid allocating all states with predominantly difficult cases to one subdivision. As a result, the subdivision dealing with Iraq and Afghanistan, the countries of origin for many recent humanitarian immigrants (and thus difficult cases) to Germany was also responsible for Turkey, with a large percentage of predominantly secure and permanent residence types and China, with a large percentage of work and study related – and thus rather straightforward – temporary residence types. However, despite these precautions, both the overall difficulty of cases and the daily caseload varied hugely.

While in Metrostadt and Middlestadt the individual subdivisions had received differentiated staffing levels, in Steelstadt, all three groups had the same number of case handlers and writer officials. As a result, while the average caseload in one group was around 25 cases per caseworker per opening period, another group often had less than 10 consultations per caseworker per day. Rather fittingly, the group within these two extremes had the highest concentration of both time consuming and legally difficult cases, with the group with the least cases also having the lowest percentages of complicated cases to handle and decide. As a result, the different groups at peak times were asked to help each other out, with mostly routine cases being delegated to another group for one consultation only. This situation leads to the groups feeling either unfairly treated as they have the most or the most difficult cases, or feeling unfairly penalised for their quick and efficient work that reduces the workload and streamlines complexities. Furthermore, the differences in workload further exacerbate the variations between the subdivisions, as these impressions of unfair treatment have a positive effect on the intragroup cohesion, even further reducing intergroup communication and exchange. Even though located in the same building, in many cases the variation between the Steelstadt groups was higher than in Metrostadt with its different district 'fiefdoms'.

Middlestadt

In Middlestadt, case working is divided into a subdivision for humanitarian and asylum issues and a general immigration law department, which is further divided into four subgroups, one of which – dealing with EU citizens, visa issues and contract guest workers – only theoretically existed, as it included cases with very limited workload and employees most of whom were on leave or on long-term sick leave during my fieldwork. The divisions between the three 'working' subgroups of the 'general' department are virtually non-existing, because the caseworkers work door to door and the writer officials even share offices, so that questions on handling cases are delegated to whoever is currently available, not necessarily the superior in charge. The real division exists between the humanitarian caseworkers and the rest, but due to the different cases and decision-making processes involved, a comparison akin to the other immigration offices is actually rather difficult. In terms of case handing, provision of service and some of the common documentary decision-making aspects, however, significant differences could be found.

The Middlestadt Ausländebehörde has no front office that buffers the stream of applicants; rather, the caseworkers have to deal with their clients alone. Since consultation happens on a first come, first serve basis without appointment schedules, the numbers of potential clients per day are not mediated. On some days, being at the Ausländerbehörde on time is no guarantee for being served. If the caseworkers in the general immigration law department feel that it is getting too crowded, they issue waiting numbers to all those who are waiting in front of their door. Whoever gets no number has to come back another day, a procedure that of course regularly leads to angry complaints, especially around closing time, which caseworkers usually let their superiors handle. In the two offices dealing with 'asylum' residences, no waiting numbers are issued. Instead, the caseworkers deal with as many as they can, and the superiors send away all other clients a few minutes before closing time. However, this leads to a quite paradoxical situation: While the caseworkers who issue waiting numbers are usually finished a few minutes before closing time, the 'asylum' caseworkers regularly work 15 to 20, sometimes 30 minutes longer. This sometimes leads to heated internal discussions on whether to try and serve as many clients as possible, or to serve as many clients as well as possible – implicitly, it is accepted that the 'asylum' caseworkers take more time to work on a case while the other caseworkers are more efficient, to the extent of sending cases with waiting numbers away because 'they are too time consuming to be handled now' (similar to Triandafyllidou 2003). Indeed, this is only one of several levels on which extremely differing views of 'service' collide.

East Middlestadt

In general, stark internal divisions make it increasingly difficult for Ausländerbehörden to react to increases in workload or the long-term absences of employees. In East Middlestadt, the Ausländerbehörde used to have a distinction similar to Middlestadt, between staff working on general residence and staff working on humanitarian and asylum issues. However, shortly before my arrival at the immigration office, the two sections were combined into one department in which everyone served all. The main reason had been a long-term absence of a caseworker, which had exacerbated the differences in case- and workload, resulting in the one remaining member of staff handling humanitarian cases not being able to manage on his own. Together, the caseworkers had decided to pool their labour in order to be able to respond to personnel shortages. This was rather striking because it meant a substantial learning obligation within the respective subfield of immigration law with which the caseworkers had not yet been acquainted and, perhaps even more importantly, an adjustment of the handling and processing of cases of two previously separate groups. The caseworkers quickly realised that this was actually much more difficult than they had thought, and involved quite a lot of stressful situations. In fact, I was asked to delay the start of my fieldwork in East Middlestadt by a couple of weeks because, as the head of the Ausländerbehörde saw it, the emotional state within the department was so fragile that she feared that an intruder might further destabilise the situation.

The tension among the caseworkers was still tangible during my fieldwork, however, perhaps exactly because of this process of debating the handling and processing of cases, comparing case working styles and deciding for a common strategy, the variation within the group was significantly lower than in the other immigration offices. Furthermore, caseload and workload were distributed much more evenly, as the caseworkers dealt with cases in sequence and without divisions by last name, origin or residence. While for the caseworkers the aftershock of having to deal with a clash in practice still reverberated, in terms of efficiency and transparency of work routines, the smallest office of the Ausländerbehörden actually had an impressive track record.

Responses to Structural Deficiencies I: Minor Measures

Apart from overall size and structure, several comparably small organisational measures had a significant impact on both Variation B, the decision-making, and Variation C, the handling of cases. While many similarities and differences in case working depended greatly on the above discussed structures, the speed and accuracy of decision-making was especially influenced by relatively minor instrument that some Ausländerbehörden or subdivisions thereof hat adopted. The three most pertinent ones are discussed below: the introduction of an information desk, of checklists for specific case types and the organisation of consultations by appointments versus a first come, first served basis.

Information Desk Duty

During office hours in both Middlestadt and most subdivisions of Metrostadt, applicants would enter the building and go straight to the individual office that was responsible for his or her case, either defined by last name, type of residence, or both. There, they would join the queue of other clients and wait until it was their turn to be called in – or until the office closed and they were told to come back another time. While long waiting times could be found at times in almost all subdivisions of all four case studies, in the offices where clients immediately went to the responsible consultation rooms, waiting could be especially frustrating. Given the complexity of providing sufficient documentary evidence as discussed in Chapter 2, not having all documents (and photocopies) needed was a rather common occurrence, and combined with people who were queuing in front of the wrong office, the wrong subdivision or altogether wrong department of city administration made up a third to half of all cases observed in each Ausländerbehörde. In Middlestadt and most subdivisions of Metrostadt, it was thus not uncommon that clients found out after waiting for up to several hours that they were at the wrong place, or missing the crucial biometrical passport photograph, printout from the national pension fund or photocopy of the last page of the tenancy agreement and thus were sent away by the official to go somewhere else or to come back another time. The level of frustration and anger expressed by the clients can easily be imagined and understood, but the caseworkers too suffered from this arrangement, as they could never be sure how many of the people queuing in front of their office actually meant work and, even more importantly, because the number of people waiting was substantially larger than in the other Ausländerbehörden.

In East Middlestadt and Steelstadt, and to some extent also in Metrostadt, an 'information desk' had been organised. This task would be rotated among caseworkers of a subsection on a weekly basis, ensuring that this workload was evenly distributed. While the effectiveness of this information desk varied somewhat from employee to employee, in most cases, the information desk would do a preliminary check on the applicant's case to see if he or she was at the right place and if all requirements had been fulfilled in order to make a decision. This included a brief review of the timing of the application (e.g. fulfilling the necessary time spent in Germany on a residence permit to apply for permanent residency), evidence presented by an applicant, and a confirmation if vital documents from other departments (such as security checks, work permits or court decisions) had been returned. Only after this preliminary inspection would the client be issued with a waiting number, or, in many cases, sent away to get more supporting documents or come back another time. Sometimes, and permitting time, the caseworker manning the information desk would also execute more menial tasks such as transferring permanent residence permits into a new passport or printing out a certificate of residence for a client's work application. Through this, caseworkers on information desk duty I observed were regularly able to resolve 30–40 per cent of daily consultations of a given subdivision. Considering that in East Middlestadt and Steelstadt, usually a total of 5–8 caseworkers were on daily consultation duty per subdivision, this signifies a considerable improvement of the speed of services provided to applicants as well as allowing the other caseworkers more time to concentrate on making decisions.

In her study of the Florentine immigration office, Triandafyllidou analysed the role of the front desk that mediated access between applicants and decision-makers rather critically, and argued that through this distancing between caseworkers and clients, migrants were not always able to state their case, and thus might not always attain the best possible residence permit (Triandafyllidou 2003). Indeed, in the case of the Metrostadt headquarters, the information desk was manned by secretarial staff without knowledge in immigration law, and subsequently avoided both by immigrants and the subdivisions that were housed in the headquarters building. However, the experiences of the version operated in both East Middlestadt and Steelstadt were very positive, since applicants were already talking to a 'proper' caseworker at the information desk.

Checklists

I have shown in Chapter 2 that the majority of cases in immigration offices are rather quick and routine affairs, while a relatively small minority of cases actually are the most difficult to decide. However, variations in case handling and decision-making occurred in almost all instances, most commonly relating to the issue of proving one's eligibility for attaining a residence permit, examples of which have been presented in Chapter 2 and Chapter 3, on the issue of national security. In the above section, I have argued that partly as a result of being forced to find compromises on ways of case working, the immigration office in East Middlestadt showed the greatest internal coherence regarding decision-making. One of the central elements of implementing the law in East Middlestadt was the use of checklists, according to which employees could assess an application and see what documentation would be necessary under normal circumstances to prove the eligibility for a residence permit. These checklists were stapled to the last page of the case file so that the next member of staff working on the application could immediately see what status the client was trying to attain and what steps had already been taken in the decision-making process. This not only dramatically reduced the time needed to read the file, but ensured that officials at least thought about the same issues and requirements during the decision-making process, and significantly reduced the internal variation.

The other three offices had generic checklists applicable to all cases that could be handed out (the practice varied considerably here) to applicants in order to show them what documents they were required to bring to the next appointment. However, despite this instrument, each caseworker still decided for him- or herself what evidence would be appropriate, so that variations in decision-making were not affected, although these lists did provide helpful as a reminder for the clients. In Steelstadt, some checklists for caseworkers existed, but were hardly ever used since all three subdivisions on general immigration law had very different opinions on documentary evidence. This was proved during my fieldwork when a special committee was formed from members of all three subdivisions to agree on a common checklist for the regular permanent residence permit according to section 9 of the Residence Act. Despite heated debates in fortnightly meetings over two months, no agreement could be reached, and when a draft was finally proposed, the employees in one subdivision informally agreed to boycott it as it did not reflect the way they worked. In Metrostadt, the head of the legal section (and responsible for overseeing due process) was rather wary of checklists because according to her, this enticed officials to 'no longer use their head', which was important in many difficult decisions. She agreed that this could be a good solution for the more systematic and straightforward decisions, but argued that since this was the domain of the different subdivisions outside headquarters it was outside her sphere of influence. Checklists thus helped to reduce the different requirements of documenting one's claim of residence and render them more transparent, but were difficult to adopt particularly in offices in which subdivisions had high levels of autonomy.

Appointments

In all four Ausländerbehörden, the dominant mode of consultation during opening hours was on a first come, first served basis. This of course offers the highest possible flexibility for applicants to choose when to visit the office. However, this also meant that the number of consultations varied greatly between opening periods – with early mornings being relatively empty and long afternoon openings (which all four offices only offered once or twice a week) often particularly full. Waiting times for migrants were thus sometimes excessively long and at other times, almost nonexistent. In Middlestadt and Steelstadt, situations occurred regularly during my fieldwork where applicants were sent away as not all clients could be served within the opening hours of the respective office. This resulted in long queues even prior to opening hours (as described in section 3.1) and some rather unpleasant scenes in the waiting areas, where different clients fought over who was next in line to be served. Many migrants, and especially German nationals who accompanied them, complained about excessive waiting times, particularly in cases where the application could not be decided immediately due to missing documents or the immigration office being forced to wait on decisions by other administrative bureaus.

In order to even out the workload and reduce waiting time, various measures were tried, but few proved effective. In East Middlestadt and by initiative of some individual caseworkers in the other offices, applicants, particularly those on a suspension of deportation that was only valid for a few weeks, were asked to apply for an extension of their residence on the day of its expiry. Some caseworkers sent clients away if they did not apply on the exact day, which often led to heated discussions and did not alleviate the problem of uneven workloads, as discussing why it was necessary for the client to come back another time often took as long as simply renewing the old permit would have taken. In East Middlestadt, the headquarters and about half of the external subdivisions of Metrostadt as well as some individual caseworkers in Middlestadt and Steelstadt, appointments could be booked in addition to the regular open consultations. This service was usually reserved for applicants who had to leave work in order to make it to the Ausländerbehörde during opening hours, for large families or groups of contract workers that took a lot of time to process, for clients that were sent away due to an overload of cases during a given consultation period, or for lawyers that represented a range of clients. Offering appointments in addition to regular first come, first served consultations allowed for a mixture in both minimising waiting times and allowing for flexibility in visiting the immigration office. In the section that wrote rulings and deportation orders in Metrostadt, consultations were based solely on appointments. However, due to the very limited overall number of cases that required direct official-client interactions in that section, it is difficult to compare the effect of this system of organising meetings to that of the other subsections and offices. Partly as a result of the discussion surrounding my findings, the Steelstadt office decided to change its opening service to a purely appointment-based system in September 2011. However, it was too early to assess any changes in the way interactions took place at the time of writing this study.

The discussion of these three measures show that while both caseworkers and office management was interested in finding solutions to the imminent structural deficiencies, habits, routines and territorial sentiments blocked the adoption of measures that might have improved the immigration office as workplace. Furthermore, the autonomy of individual subsections is considerable, even further exacerbating the differences within the offices. The next section will consider debates and attempts to altogether change the operational structure of work in immigration offices through organisational reform.

Reactions to Structural Deficiencies II: Reform and Re-reform

The short comparison of the current structures within the four offices shows that all four offices were faced with different issues, which were partly caused by the structural layouts. As the discussion of the three relatively minor measures of improvement has demonstrated, there was an ongoing debate on how to best deal with the externally enforced work conditions, with an active participation of all levels of employment. However, the bigger the office, the more top-down the decision-making process actually happened. All four offices had changed their internal structure with the introduction of the new residence act and anti-terror legislation in the early 2000s, all four offices had been forced to make temporary adjustments due to a critical low in personnel since then, and all four offices had just changed or were about to change their infrastructure again during the time of my research. Thus all offices had seen three structural reforms within less than a decade. Much of this was initially influenced by legislative changes and the political discussion that surrounded it (this will be discussed in Chapter 5), causing the establishment of specialist groups, sometimes in cooperation with other departments. However, all reform attempts also included the intention to adjust structural issues that the previous organisational change had either not been able to solve or, in some cases, that the previous reform had in fact caused.

Rather than relying on a very rigid, clearly structured and stable organisation, the bureaucratic agencies I studied were highly flexible and adaptable and in fact constantly engaged in the process of changing the structure. Indeed, many of the external experts I interviewed complained about constantly changing persons of contact and work patterns. While being dynamic is not part of the classic accounts of bureaucracy, the recent work of organisational theorist Nils Brunsson (2009) on 'Reform as Routine' analyses similar patterns of constant change. According to Brunsson, reforms are not primarily relevant to improve a structural problem of a workplace, and indeed are often rather inefficient, but rather serve as a way of managing both internal and external expectation by presenting to employees and interested public that 'something' is being done. In the context of the Ausländerbehörden, structural change was one of the main possibilities to gain access to additional funds from the city council. Merely pointing to a lack in staff or technical resources was never sufficient; instead, a detailed vision for reform had to be presented in order to improve the internal work conditions (more on this in Chapter 6). Indeed, the fact that the heads of office approved of my fieldwork in their bureaus can very probably be linked to this, since my results were used as evaluation to a structural reform (in the case of Middlestadt and East Middlestadt) and as basis of ideas and feedback for future reform in Steelstadt and Metrostadt. In addition to presenting my results, I provided all offices with a short summary of my relevant findings and was asked to give talks to high ranking city officials on reform in immigration offices by two of the cases. My results could thus be used to further the claims for more resources. Brunssons theory of routine reform is therefore rather useful in understanding the processes of constant organisational change in the Ausländerbehörden. However, in addition to being a rhetorical mode of motivating and promoting ones cause, I would argue that being receptive to structural malfunctions and flexible in adapting the structure is a necessary condition for administrative bodies such as the immigration offices that deal with such complex, constantly changing and politically charged legal issues. Rather than merely revealing reform attempts as 'bogus' due to their predominantly low effectiveness outside of political motivational rhetoric, the ability to motivate both internal and external partners through the reflection and adaptation of processes should be seen as a positive attribute of organisations.

'Performance': The Lack of Reflecting Work and Outcomes

In the discussion around structural change and improvements to the work conditions of the immigration offices, one thing was remarkably absent: a concept of good administration to pursue, or, less abstract, an idea of what good work in Ausländerbehörden should be like. As the previous section stated and as will be further discussed in the following chapter, initiatives to reform the organisational setup had to be sold *politically* as part of a legislative change or so-called sea change in the way the offices represented themselves. However, there were no discussions about how the work of the Ausländerbehörden should *function*, or to what end operational routines should be reshaped. This had rather peculiar results, as discussions I had with caseworkers on the concept of performance showed.

Many of the employees who liked their work used the opportunity to talk to an outsider about the everyday routines in Ausländerbehörden to complain not only about the work conditions, but also about the problem of not being rewarded for good performance. Instead, many caseworkers expressed their frustration and asserted that 'if one does good work and shows initiative, one is not rewarded, but merely ordered to take on more work that the do-no-gooders can't manage', as caseworker 41 phrased it. Many added that while they felt that they should be financially rewarded for performing well above the average of others, at least some form of symbolic recognition on the part of the superiors would be nice. However, when I enquired about what 'good performance' looked like or how it could be measured, hardly anyone had a clear idea.

While there was a system of keeping a statistic of consultations per opening period in all four Ausländerbehörden, it was generally accepted to be nonsensical since it was agreed that a mere counting of cases could not reflect the work people had to do given the stark differences in difficulty of applications. In addition, almost every caseworker had a different system of keeping the statistic, and many forgot to keep track of counting the number of consultations so that they estimated a number based on previous experience at the end of the opening period. The office management in all four cases admitted that the workload statistic was rather useless and that they only kept it because they were told to do so by the organisational department of the local council. Indeed, many employees expressed their bewilderment about the concept of counting cases as a measure of performance, and in one case, the head of office explicitly stated during our first meeting that he would only allow me to do my fieldwork if I refrained from such 'nonsense' like calculating the average time needed for the processing of a case.

The last 20 years have seen a rise in debates both in public and academia around ways to increase efficiency and customer service in state administration, often collated around the phrase of 'New Public Management' (Rahodi 2002; Softe 1998). This change is generally seen as linked to the marketisation of administration (Sennett 2006), referring to both the outsourcing or privatisation of public services and the drastic change in conceptualising and evaluating work in bureaucracy, focussing on measurable performance indicators and systems of internal accounting (Flynn 1997; Hood and Scott 2000; Woodhouse 1997). Woodhouse (1997:223) has identified the changes in administration attributed to New Public Management as shift from debates around concepts of duty towards the public good to concepts of contractual obligations towards customers (see also Farnham and Horton 1993; Jordan 1994). The evidence of the four Ausländerbehörden shows that while the concept of performance was used rather widely by caseworkers who felt that they outworked their colleagues, no actual definition for this existed, and ways of quantifying work were seen as rather odd and dubious. Similarly, the immigration offices had no concept of efficiency, it was not even a term used or discussed by officials. The Ausländerbehörden were thus part of cycles of change and used concepts of performance attributed to New Public Management, but without actually being affected by these new forms of quantified and economised evaluation of administration, including their negative impact as discussed by Born (2005) or Sennett (2006). Thus while there were constantly discussions on *improving* the work conditions surrounding substantial issues (long waiting hours, different workloads of subdivisions), no overall goal existed as to how the Ausländerbehörde should work, or what goals it should seek to attain, or in what way case working should be done. Thus during my fieldwork in both Metrostadt and Steelstadt, the office management circulated or discussed drafts of organisational change without any reference as to what aim the change was to pursue other than ensuring funding and alleviating shortcomings of the current structure. In short, reforms failed not only because they were not much more than managements of expectations (Brunsson 2009), but also because they were conducted effectively aimlessly. This is particularly relevant as other than the short section indication that immigration offices are to apply the law as stated in the section 71 of the Residence Act, no external guidelines were available that stated how or in what ways an Ausländerbehörde was supposed to work. The offices of my fieldwork were thus left to their own devices in making sense of their role and structure – and thus susceptible to outside interventions, as Chapter 5 will show.

The analysis of the structures of the administration of immigration law in Germany has thus helped to explain why officials are able to work so differently despite having the same job description: structures are inefficient, the impact of supervision is low, and since no overall aims or goals except surviving the everyday exist, there is no system of accountability that the employees have to apply their work to. Furthermore, all four offices found themselves in constant cycles of planning and enacting structural reform, with mixed to no improvement on the work conditions in Ausländerbehörden. While Brunssons (2009) argument about the management of expectations is persuasive and applicable to this study, the constant changes also resulted in an adaptiveness that bureaucracies are often not seen to have. Thus while failing to deliver an organisational structure that would allow for the stable, rational processing of cases that traditional analysts of bureaucracy stressed so much, the constant reproduction of the ordering system allowed for the flexibility to incorporate the most recent legal changes into the practices of work at the immigration offices. In that sense, the management of migration in German public administration can be seen as an active procedure of ordering rather than a fixed state of order, something that is also stressed in the work of Cooper and Burrell (Cooper 1986; Cooper 1987; Cooper and Burrell 1988;

Jones et al. 2005). If immigration offices are thus not stable organisations in which cases are processed in an orderly fashion and instead dynamic but aimless systems that constantly need to stabilise their own inconsistencies and deficiencies, variations such as those found in my fieldwork and presented in Chapter 2 are to be expected. The next section examines the potential impact of this for the clients of the Ausländerbehörden through an analysis of the interactions between applicants and employees.

Conclusion: A State of Ordering

This chapter has improved the understanding of the process of implementing immigration law in Germany through looking at the differences in work organisation in the four different offices as well as through analysing the impact of rather chaotic structures and ways of case working for immigrants. The chapter has thus analysed the *production* of order through the maintenance of organisational structures as well as its *consumption* through by clients through interactions between applicants and officials (Linstead 1993). Rather than being effective means of processing people, Ausländerbehörden are in a constant struggle with problems of inefficiency and consequently undergo a constant cycle of reform and structural failure. Part of this can be attributed to the changes in legislation that have added tasks to the work of immigration offices, so that the ability to reform should be seen as a necessary given and not a systemic failure. The analysis of structural change has further shown that while employees in the Ausländerbehörde care about the quality of their work, there is no conceptualisation of the goals or responsibilities of the office, partly a result of the lack of conceptualisation and structuring of immigration offices on the federal level.

In many ways, the Ausländerbehörden discussed in this book do not resemble the description of current forms of public administration. With their high proportion of *Beamte*, of civil servants on tenured contracts and a practically life-long job guarantee for all employees notwithstanding budget cuts, their lack of managerial methods of measuring performance and efficiency and the complete absence of efforts to privatise or outsource services, at least for natives of the English-speaking world, immigration offices must appear like a relic of the good old modern times of expansive public administration. While the German bureaucratic system in general has not been subject to such extensive cuts and restructurings as Britain or the United States since the late 1970s (Farnham and Horton 1993) and Australia or New Zealand since the late 1980s (Flynn 1997), the impact of New Public Management has been significant, for example in the restructuring of employment agencies in the early 2000s (Schönig and Bröker 2004). The fact that there were some efforts to measure workloads in all four offices shows that concepts of New Public Management had probably taken a foothold somewhere within the individual city councils. However, the responses of caseworkers and office management to this (see section 5.3) also indicate that there is a significant –

and successful – resistance to such measures. As a result, all four immigration offices were relatively untouched by new forms of work in administration and seem rather anachronistic compared to current accounts of bureaucracies such as that by Richard Sennett (2006). In his 'Culture of the New Capitalism', he identifies the decline of two key aspects that mark the shift from 'old' bureaucracy to new forms of marketised public administration: informal trust and institutional knowledge. In the Ausländerbehörden, both informal trust and institutional knowledge were rather dominant and as shown in Chapter 3, both were crucial to the implementation of immigration law.

While not marked by forms of organisation attributed to current bureaucracies, many of the theories of recent organisational theorists still apply to the immigration offices. Particularly the 'postmodern' accounts organisations by Cooper and Burrell (Burrell 2006; Burrell and Cooper 1988; Cooper 1986, 1987) and Brunssons critical organisational theory (1985, 2009) help make sense of the unstable and flexible aspects of the structure of the Ausländerbehörden. All four case studies had seen and prepared for both large structural reform and small-scale alterations of operational routines. This constant repair of organisational deficiencies can well be seen as part of a 'routine' reform process which is not intended to increase efficiency, but to manage outside and inside expectations (Brunsson 2009). After all, the only way for immigration offices to increase funds or to resist budget cuts and have positions refilled was to present a new plan of reform (due to a legislative or political change) and channel additional funds to new subsections or special projects. In that sense, not the structures themselves were stable but the constant attempts to improve them. As a result, the dominant and routine aspects in the work of the case studies were the case working practices and not the structures in which they were embedded. Despite the variations in expecting specific documents, being especially helpful or unhelpful, or charging for a photocopy or not, the general *patterns* of work were the same in all four offices, notwithstanding the current structure. People were processed – and in turn socialised, as discussed in Chapter 7 – through the work routines of the immigration officials, notwithstanding of structure or specific interpretation of law or requirements of a case. It is in this sense that complex organisations define themselves through their social practices (Cooper 1986) and that structure – order – is produced around these practices rather than the other way around (Cooper and Burrell 1988).

In this sense, bureaucracy can thus be seen as dynamic, procedural and defined through practice, and in its effects on clients even 'magic'. In fact, one could even state that the most 'irrational' aspect of work – the oral tradition of making sense of law – proved the most effective, since this significantly reduced the outcome variation. While it should not be suggested that the immigration offices of my study were beacons of effectiveness, they nevertheless *managed*. Rather than seeing the cycles of reform and re-reform as cynical as Brunsson (2009), the evidence of this study suggests that while not achieving any sense of stability of efficiency, by being dynamic Ausländerbehörden at least managed to stay afloat of significant legal developments, something that would be considerably much more difficult within a very stable but inflexible form of organisation. Furthermore, in a way the irrational practice of basing decisions on experiences rather than text was completely rational from the perspective of the caseworkers. Rationality is thus contextual rather than absolute (Perrow 1979), and the dynamic of always having something to improve is useful in the context of a legal basis in which something always changes.

In a way this account of organisation might appear like the total opposite of the Weberian ideal type of bureaucracy (cf. March and Simon 1958; Peters 2001; Weber 1968), however, I would argue that Weber's account is still relevant. Despite the range of criticisms that almost all scholars of organisations since Weber have lodged against the rational and effective account of bureaucracy (see section 2.5), and even despite the fact that the Ausländerbehörden of this study worked far from rational or effective, the self-representation of bureaucracies has not changed as drastic as the sociological examination of it. Crucially, the attempts of adherents of New Public Management to include *more* managerial aspects of work and work evaluation indicate if anything, the belief in rule-bound, effective and rational bureaucracy is not yet done with. Furthermore bureaucracy still is the dominant form of state administration, and the analysis of even the most drastic attempts to marketise the state (Flynn 1997; Woodhouse 1997) have shown that despite drastic cuts, the focus of Thatcherite New Public Management is not to abolish bureaucracy altogether through the privatisation of services, but rather that the focus is significantly more on the *internal* reform towards a more rational and effective – and thus somewhat Weberian – ideal of public administration. Finally, Sewell and Barker (2006) stress the historical context of Weber's analysis of bureaucracy. Indeed, it is worth reminding oneself that Weber (1968) examines the *rise* of bureaucratic forms of state organisation and thus the results of a historical sequence. In that sense, Weber is still correct today, as of course rule-governed somewhat chaotic and arbitrary decision-making in administration is more rational than somewhat chaotic and totally arbitrary decision-making not governed by rules.

Chapter 5
The Politics of Immigration Offices

The previous chapters have shown how decision-making practices in German immigration offices are shaped by the complex law and the unorthodox, practical approach caseworkers take in its application, and how these offices struggle to find an organisational structure that accommodates the important task they are set to do, leading to a constant set of reforms and reforms of previous structural changes. Furthermore, we will see in Chapter 7 how the chaotic structures and practices of the Ausländerbehörden not only influence the decisions made, but also have an impact on the way migrants are socialised into German society and how they learn behaviour and expectations towards a 'state' that at times seems extremely unfriendly and arbitrary. The two previous chapters have presented the Ausländerbehörde as if working in complete isolation from the outside world, left to their own devices in dealing with the immigrants in their vicinity. However, the immigration offices exist within a network of other organisations and actors, even if scholars of public administration and street-level bureaucracy have tended to view their case studies as if in a vacuum (Halliday et al. 2009). This chapter will show how in fact the Ausländerbehörde can be a site of intense political conflict and how the offices have to negotiate with a number of parties that attempt to exert influence over the way they fulfil their role as migration management agencies of the Federal Republic of Germany. Three main levels on which political intervention takes place will be discussed – other state institutions, the local city government and the public sphere. The different forms these interventions can take and their overlap will be discussed on the basis of two examples of a political conflict that was relevant in all four case studies and in which all levels of intervention took part: deportations and the debates around the overall direction of the immigration office.

The Ausländerbehörde: Regulatory Office or Integration Service?

With the change of the centre-right Kohl to the centre-left Schröder government in 1998, many expected a new direction in migration politics – and indeed, the coalition agreement between Social Democrats and Greens foresaw significant changes in Germany's citizenship, migration and asylum laws. The drastic change in the citizenship law has been widely discussed, some commentators (Joppke 2010), argue that with the new legislation, Germany has moved well beyond its classical ethnic *jus sanguinis* form of nationhood (cf. Brubaker 1992). However, as briefly discussed in Chapter 1, the legislative change regarding residence law was halted by the changing international climate after the terrorist attacks on New York in September 2001 and the power shift towards the Christian Democrats in Germany's upper chamber of parliament, the *Bundesrat*. As a consequence, when the residence act was finally enacted, it was notably different from the initial plans of the centre-left government (Geddes 2003; Groß 2004). The practical changes the new law entailed were thus significantly different from the rhetoric that surrounded the promulgation of it. While there was no discussion that the legal basis of work in the immigration offices had changed, it remained unclear how drastic this change actually was. This disparity between rhetoric and fact further complicated the debates around the future of the Ausländerbehörde as primary migration management agency that had been spawned by the announcements to rework the old residence act. In all four immigration offices, the issue was still hotly debated during my fieldwork, several years after the passing of the law.

Three broad lines of argument prevail and were held by different actors that surrounded the Ausländerbehörden and by different officials within the individual offices. Table 5.1 summarises the different opinions as ideal types and considers the suggested implications for immigration offices. The crucial issues here regard the overall work approach of the Ausländerbehörde, which now might be a provider of service to all or some migrant groups and the direction of migration policy that the offices have to apply. While the two are clearly linked, they focus on different aspects of this potentially new phase of migration management in Germany:

Table 5.1 Interpretations of the 2005 Residence Act

Implication of the 2005 Residence Act	Sea change	Balanced	Hesitant
… for German migration politics?	A new phase; The new law is inclusive, humane and actively encouraging immigration	A new phase; The new law actively encourages immigration of those who can positively contribute to the economy	Some changes; Implications for quite a few immigrants, but no new policy of open doors
… for the overall aim of the immigration office?	A total overhaul; Immigration offices should support migrants in their integration into German society	A readjustment; Providing a service to those who come to Germany to work or study	None; The aim always was and still is to regulate migration into Germany
… for the daily work of the immigration office?	A new structure; New approach to casework of all migrants	Some changes; Special treatment of select groups	No changes; Business as usual

The interpretation of migration politics relates to the self-presentation towards other groups and offices, while the change in approach to the work involves the everyday routines and interactions with applicants, who might now be seen as clients rather than supplicants.

The one undisputed change in the residence law is the introduction of compulsory language courses for new immigrants and the requirement of certain levels of competency in German prior to entering the country as well as prior to attaining permanent residence and citizenship. However, even regarding these so-called integration courses, the interpretation varied greatly. While especially international commentators have noted that requiring language proficiency is actually a tightening of entry requirements (e.g. Boswell and Geddes 2011), many of my caseworkers regarded it as a great opportunity and service to immigrants, since the courses are heavily subsidised by the German government. Thus the integration courses have been described as 'empowering' and 'facilitating the integration potential of immigrants' during the expert interviews I conducted. Others dismissed the regulatory values of the language requirements, since entering Germany without a language certificate and not completing the course had no negative implications apart from not being able to attain citizenship; the residence within Germany, however, was not at stake.

Deportations

Deportations, the expulsions of non-citizens through force, are arguably among the harshest coercive measures within the realm of the modern state. Often, and especially since the 'war on terror', deportations are criticised not only for the harshness of the measure but for perceived unlawful proceedings associated to the deportations, such as 'indefinite detention, suspension of due process, and torture' (Peutz 2007, 183). Indeed detention, i.e. confinement to prison-like institutions, has been effectively indefinitely extended to several years in countries like the US or the UK (Wilsher 2004). Recent studies (Coleman 2008 on homosexuals; Kanstroom 2000 on criminals) have suggested that deportations are not only removals from within and thus tools of internal border control, but rather serve as mechanisms of social control, a 'cruel power' (Gibney 2008) to remove socially 'unwanted' individuals.

The implementation of deportations has also received some interest – including an ambitious call for an 'anthropology of removal' (Peutz 2006) – and some of the studies provide interesting starting points for my own ethnographic investigation. Nathalie Peutz's study of Somali deportees (Peutz 2007) suggests that through the interaction with immigration officials through the deportation process, individuals internalise an ideology of the rule of law, even if in their own case due process has been violated – related to the arguments on 'states of exception' that operate outside the law to uphold the law (Agamben 2005; Hussain 2003). Nihawan has forcefully pointed at the crucial role of medical staff in approving of deportations from Germany, and discussed the politically contested area in which medical practitioners work both for and against immigration officials (Nijhawan 2005). Perhaps the single most important contribution to the study of the insides of immigration administration has been published by Antje Ellermann in her multi-level comparative study of deportations in the United States and Germany (Ellermann 2006, 2009), which has been discussed above. She provides a forceful argument for the need of an analysis beyond simple outcome evaluations and findings of policy gaps, and argues that the street-level implementation is the crucial element in understanding the process of deportation (Ellermann 2009, 121). Deportations are thus socially coercive measures with politically contested implementations, the actual nature of which however remains unclear – even Ellermann focuses on the management of public opinion rather than the planning and execution of deportations. While this book only considers deportations as (rather side-lined) part of the practice of Ausländerbehörde, the political debates and attempts to intervene on the work of immigration offices as well as the difficulty of executing expulsions are considered in this and the next chapter.

Of course, most supporters of the sea change interpretation of the 2005 Residence Act acknowledged that part of the work of the immigration offices was still to enable the deportation of those migrants who had no possibility of obtaining a legal residence permit. However, there were still marked differences in how the different Ausländerbehörden presented the task of deporting to the public, as well in the approach to the actual implementation of deportations. This is in line with the findings of a recent report on the execution of deportations that finds that less than 15 per cent of rejected asylum applicants are actually deported (Clearingstelle Trier 2010). Similarly, Boswell and Geddes (2011) report that the high disparity between immigrants without residence and actual deportees is a phenomenon common in all European states, with high sub-state variations. Thus while in East Middlestadt the department for ending residence was also responsible for revising cases for extreme hardship that would forbid deportation, in Steelstadt and Middlestadt, the officials working on deportations were often rather annoyed when a hardship case had been granted, as it meant a 'failure' of their attempts at doing their work, and having wasted time for 'nothing'. This variance clearly shows the different approach to 'solving' cases, and in many ways reflects the overall incoherent dealing with the issue of deportation. Given the fact that deportations are extreme measures that tear individuals and families from their social structure and remove them to their country of origin without permission to return to Germany, it should not be surprising that these measures are at times highly contested. Here again, the Ausländerbehörden find themselves under pressure from various groups.

Public Pressures: Media, NGOs and Other Interested Parties

Local activism around issues of immigration is a global phenomenon and has received some academic attention in recent years (Bosworth 2011; Burman 2006; Ellermann 2006, 2009; Varsanyi 2010). Ellermann (2009) accurately describes the notable difference between public opinion on migration issues on a general level, which is often sceptical towards what is seen to be too much lenience in enforcing residence law, and the substantial public support mobilised around cases of particular individuals and families that have long-term connections within a local community. Thus while a tough stance on immigration issues on a federal level might gain widespread support and crucial votes, immigration offices often find themselves under immense local pressure against implementing the more restrictive aspects of residence law. All four offices had experienced public opposition to the planned deportation of immigrants and consequently had begun to draw upon strategies to manage public pressure in order to avoid future escalations of conflict.

In the 1990s and early 2000s, Middlestadt rose to questionable fame as a site of several public rows over deportation cases, involving all the big public actors: politicians, public servants, churches, schools, NGOs, and the media. The Ausländerbehörde was faced with immense pressure, including large demonstrations which took place in front of the office. Several nationwide newspapers also took up these issues, and in one instance, one of the most famous political comedians made a joke about the 'brown shirts of the Ausländerbehörde in Middlestadt', which was not well received at all in the Ausländerbehörde.

Metrostadt is the site of several media enterprises with a nation-wide reach and a set of rather notorious local tabloids. Given the wealth of potential media outlets, it is relatively easy for different interest groups to attain publicity for a specific case, as a result the Ausländerbehörde was regularly faced with particularly aggressive campaigns against the deportation of immigrants, especially in the 'heydays' of humanitarian migration to Germany during the 1990s. Furthermore, Metrostadt has a quite diverse political spectrum with a tradition of radical factions on both the left and right, which have all clashed with the immigration office at one point or another. Thus in the early 2000s, a branch of the Ausländerbehörde was attacked by an anarchist group that threw eggs and bags filled with paint at the officials. More recently, a local populist right-wing association has tried to co-opt the work of the immigration office for their purposes and sent flowers to the head of office after deportations as a sign of mutual respect and support of the 'common cause'.

In Steelstadt, public debate and conflict has been focussed mostly around one particular ethnic group that has settled in significant numbers in the city. This group, whose citizen status is disputed in its country of origin and of which many members have withheld evidence in order to not be deported and lived on a sufferance since the 1980s, has been associated with organised crime in Steelstadt, causing widespread news coverage of 'gang cultures' flourishing without the intervention of the immigration office. However, individuals of that ethnic background have also been part of public campaigns organised to galvanise support for greater leniency in cases of hardship, specifically by allowing the individuals and families concerned to remain in Germany. Thus somewhat ironically, one of Germany's biggest magazines has published stories on both sides of the issue, neither of which showed much sympathy for the work of the Ausländerbehörde.

Given the low proportion of immigrants in East Middlestadt, the debates around deportation cases have been much less frequent, although there is a fully functioning support network of NGOs, lawyers, church organisations and local media dedicated to supporting the migrant community. Recently, the immigration office had to deal with cases in which Christian communities had granted refuge to immigrants, basing their claim on the right of any individual to seek sanctuary in a church. Since similar cases had caused great embarrassment for other Ausländerbehörden which had failed to handle the matter delicately, the officials in East Middlestadt took enormous care to avoid significant media attention around the issue and engaged directly with church officials to resolve the situation. The avoidance of bad press was seen as particularly important as East Middlestadt had been associated with the re-emergence of neo-Nazi movements in the former German Democratic Republic following reunification. While the actual presence of rightwing groups was actually rather low, the city was still struggling with the label of being a 'brown-infested town'.

The examples above give an idea of the great variety of public actors that can be involved in debates around immigration, and the different ways in which these conflicts take place. The two main organisations that solely focus on the issue of deportations and asylum seekers are pro Asyl, a NGO that supports asylum seekers and has offices in all major German cities – including my four case studies – and the *Flüchtlingsrat* (Refugee Council), which is a network of local interest and support groups for migrants and often partially funded by pro Asyl. Other important actors are individual church communities and the welfare branches of both the federal Lutheran and Catholic Churches, which also have offices in all major cities and provide general welfare support as well as offering specialised legal counsel for immigrants. In some cities a NGO with social democratic roots, the *Arbeiterwohlfahrt* (Workers' Welfare), also offers specialised support to migrants, often offering native language speakers as counsel and interpreters. All cities also have an elected Migrants' Council (*Ausländerbeirat*), which is consulted by the city municipal councils on issues relating to migration, but has a more passive role in the public sphere, usually endorsing positions that other organisations have brought forward. Lawyers that are specialised in the field of immigration law are usually involved in some of the organisations, sometimes providing pro bono work at regular intervals. Pro Asyl is by far the most radical of these groupings, fighting for the right of free movement for mankind, and are thus often dismissed as idealistic dreamers by the officials of the Ausländerbehörde and some of the more conservative groups who do not challenge the federal migration policy in general, and are usually only concerned with a particular individual case or group of cases. In addition to these traditional groups that are found in most cities, there are a number of ethnicity-based NGOs that focus on groups with continuous legal issues. These groups often coordinate a variety of welfare provisions from specialised education to legal assistance and the provision of housing. Examples of these include support networks for Roma, ethnic Kosovars, Kurds and sans papiers from various states of the Middle East. Often, membership of these support networks consists of both ethnic Germans with an interest in the issue and members of the particular ethnic group.

Since none of these organisations are actively involved with the decision-making process, the main aim of welfare groups and NGOs is to attract the public's attention and exert pressure on the city councils and Ausländerbehörden The most efficient means of doing this is through instigating press coverage of problematic case constellations. Thus the more immediately available media outlets were to the organisations, the more publicity contested cases received. In Metrostadt, this was the most extreme, followed by Middlestadt, Steelstadt and East Middlestadt. Apart from retaining good contacts with local journalists, a number of activities were highly successful in gaining the attention of the press. These include public demonstrations, activities involving school classes raising awareness if children were involved and displays of photographs of the abhorrent living conditions in social housing. In addition to 'going public', the interest groups would lobby potentially supportive parties in the city council, usually the left-wing parties, but given the activity of church communities and the welfare branches of the two federal church organisations, some Christian Democrats also took an interest in issues of deportation. All organisations also provided support by collecting donations, clothes or food for particular cases, and supported the individuals and families themselves if they had sufficient financial means, but given the large number of migrants with precarious status, these funds were rather quickly depleted. Many welfare workers and lawyers also accompanied their clients to the immigration office, however, this did not always achieve the intended outcome.

> Two middle-aged men enter the office, one dressed in a shabby suit, the other in street wear. The two officials roll their eyes upon recognising the former, and the interaction which now follows is accompanied by a strange tension in the room. The officials, who are normally rather cheerful in their interactions with applicants, are very formal and although the case is extremely simple – the client has a German child and thus a claim to residence – the caseworker only issues a certificate of application, claiming that some routine checks still need to be made. The man in the suit accepts this, formally shakes the hand of everyone (including me) and leaves with the client. When I ask about this rather strange encounter, the caseworker who dealt with the client tells me that the "suit" was a volunteer migrant support officer of one of the big welfare organisations and infamous for supporting hopeless cases. "We should better check this one

carefully" states the caseworker and explains that usually there is something suspicious with the cases that involve this particular welfare officer.

The bad reputation of a volunteer or a lawyer can thus have a negative impact on the handling of a case – often, officials justified their heightened scrutiny of a case by stating that 'if someone has to turn to a lawyer, something must be wrong with the case'. Rather than assisting a client in attaining residence, support from welfare organisations actually alerts many employees in the Ausländerbehörde, which automatically associate a NGO supporting migrants with irregular migrants and failed asylum seekers.

Managing Public Opinion

All four cities shared the experience of being the centre of attention regarding issues of deportation and hardship cases, and all four cities further struggled to deal with public pressure in their own ways. The change in legislation and debates that proclaimed Germany to finally be a 'country of immigration', four decades after mass immigration to Germany had started thus provided an opportunity for the immigration office to get past the negative image that Ausländerbehörden in general had attained during the early 1990s. However, once again the four offices took very different measures in reforming themselves and their images, each with their individual problems and success stories.

Metrostadt

Metrostadt underwent the most extreme change coinciding with the new residence act. Internally, a new department providing additional services was established. While general case-working and decision-making remained with the district branches and headquarters, the new department was created with the aim of improving the service of the Ausländerbehörde to immigrants seeking work and those required to attend language classes. One section of the department thus dealt with the granting of work permits, which was done in cooperation with the local employment office. After the initial application, the case of a migrant is sent to this section for consideration. This is supposed to speed up the decision-making process and thus allow immigrants to enter employment quicker than in other immigration offices. However, the internal sending of case files takes rather a long time and cases now are in danger of being overlooked by two rather than one official, effectively cancelling out the benefit in efficiency which the specialised work permit section is supposed to provide.

The second section of the new department specialises in the provision of counsel regarding the new 'integration courses', which are provided by private agencies. The section assesses the current level of proficiency as well as the specific needs of the applicant and on the basis of this is able to delegate the immigrant to the providers that offer the most suitable courses. Furthermore, the section assists migrants who voluntarily want to attend the language courses in finding funding – the German government subsidises courses for immigrants with 'exceptional integration requirements' and further offers follow-up consultations to see if the applicants successfully attended the integration courses.

The integration course section is markedly different from all other subdivisions in the immigration office. Instead of case working, the focus is entirely on providing a service to the migrant. Since the section is not involved with the decision-making process on questions of residence, migrants are not seen as cases, but as people who need assistance in finding the best possible language course. The caseworkers take pride in being seen in a different light by migrants than the rest of the Ausländerbehörde, and clearly differentiate between work practice within the section and how 'they', the rest of the bureau, work.

The section on integration courses is the beacon of the new external policy pursued by the immigration office. Of the four case studies, Metrostadt has almost completely aligned itself to the sea change interpretation of the legislation change. The self-presentation to outsiders is almost entirely focussed on the new way of endorsing migration, on being welcoming and on trying to resolve the precarious cases that are so often the issue of heated public debate. For this, the office pursues a politics of openness and interaction with the different migrant support organisations. The most drastic move towards this has been the establishment of a hardship committee in which representatives of political parties and migrant support organisations discuss the legal resolution of precarious cases with the Ausländerbehörde. Thus the immigration office not only presents itself in a different way, it actively encourages participation in decision-making through the committee. As a result, the relationship with welfare organisations has dramatically changed, and many of my interviewees in Metrostadt spoke with great enthusiasm about the new policy pursued by the office. While some contentious issues remained, the general climate between migrant support groups and immigration office was very positive. The immense public pressure Metrostadt experienced had been successfully detained.

While this clearly marks a remarkable success for the immigration office, two things are noteworthy that put the 'sea change' into context. First, the new approach to case working was only prevalent in one subsection of a department of the Ausländerbehörde, which actually was the only section that was not actively involved in decision-making. The beacon of customer friendliness was thus also the only instance of it. The second issue relates to the hardship committee. As there is no legal basis for such a committee, its decisions are not binding, but only suggestions to the work of the Ausländerbehörde. Furthermore, the cases presented to the committee are preselected by the legal caseworkers of the immigration office and are usually rather obvious – other cases are simply not accepted for the committee with reference to an 'ongoing investigation into the matter'. Thus the resolutions of the committee are premeditated by the immigration office, which either provides clear instances of hardship (such as a disability or successful economic integration) or clear instances in which hardship has to be denied (a convicted rapist). When asked about this, the head of office smiled and explained that the hardship committee was set up to be a 'playground for the politicians' of Metrostadt. In conclusion, the sea change did not actually change that much in practice, apart from successfully managing public opinion.

Middlestadt: The Ausländerbehörde as Part of the Citizens and Integration Bureau

As a result of this, and anticipating the changing climate with the newly elected Schröder government, the then head of the Ausländerbehörde decided to act and started working on a new structural basis for immigration law application in Middlestadt. The result is the '*Einwohner- und Integrationsamt*', the Citizens and Integration Bureau, which is now led by its creator.

The Citizens and Integration Bureau is rather unique in Germany in combining the Ausländerbehörde, the 'classic' implementation agency of immigration law, a new integration bureau, and a number immigrant consulting services, operated by local NGOs. The Integration Bureau includes the nationality office for applications to citizenship, a central service desk that gives advice on the language and integration classes that are now compulsory for permanent residence and citizenship, a legal advice desk, and several employees who support and are engaged in projects that the city funds to enhance integration – education courses targeted especially at women, health courses in foreign languages, Muslim counselling services, and other projects. The integration bureau has issued an integration concept, a slim 25-page booklet which sets out variables on which integration is supposed to be measured, and sets goals to be attained regarding language, education, employment, housing and living, health and care, and 'integration competence of the administration'. Every year, a report on the state of integration is issued, and in the summer of 2009, a conference was held, in which the developments were assessed five years after the integration concept was implemented.

During my fieldwork, I spent several days in the integration bureau, interviewing the employees, sitting in during opening hours of the language desk, participating in departmental meetings, and also visited a two-day seminar on 'intercultural competence for bureaucrats', organised by the integration bureau. The 'philosophy' of the integration bureau is clearly set out, and clearly communicated by all members of staff and during office hours. Services are provided in a customer-friendly and helpful way, indeed, together with the local NGOs, who share the same building, a good dozen of languages are spoken. Many of the projects seem excellently prepared, highly tailored to the needs of Middlestadt's migrants, and constantly assessed to avoid mismanagement. Having taken the NGOs – the welfare branch of the strong Catholic Church and two big federal welfare organisations – 'on board' has eased the communication in difficult cases and subsequently significantly reduced the media coverage of cases, taking the Ausländerbehörde out of continuous crossfire – a radical step of pre-empting public opposition (cf. Ellermann 2006). It is celebrated as a great success, and senior members of the integration bureau roam the city halls of Germany, presenting the 'Middlestadt model' of government-led integration policies. However, in reality, the process is not quite so smooth.

On all occasions in which I sat in or noticed the language advice office, it was very little frequented. While on a 'typical' Wednesday afternoon at the Ausländerbehörde a caseworker would deal with 25–30 cases and send away probably a handful due to time constraints, on the Wednesday that I sat in with the language advice caseworkers, there were 10 clients, which was considered a lot. The NGO caseworkers too had, according to their own counting, between eight and 10 clients per opening slot. The legal advice in the integration bureau is basically not used at all, and the responsible caseworker has now taken on other duties instead. Thus while in the Ausländerbehörde in-depth advice often was not provided, mostly with the explanation of time constraints, the advice offices were heavily under-frequented. When talking to employees on both sides about this paradox, it became evident that despite cooperation between the Ausländerbehörde and the Integration Bureau at senior levels, distrust and prejudice dominated at the level of caseworkers. Both 'sides' saw the other as 'having some really nice people, but some who just haven't changed'. The NGO caseworkers and a surprisingly high number of integration bureau workers (some of whom came from the Ausländerbehörde) saw the 'black sheep' in the Ausländerbehörde as anti-immigration and stubbornly unfair, while the Ausländerbehörde caseworkers complained about the lack of legal expertise and the unfair prejudices against their own agency. Many were also unforgiving for the other side's involvement in prior conflicts. While both complaints have some currency, they mainly show that the old antagonisms have not been settled by incorporating them into one agency. The conflict has not been solved but merely taken out of the public sphere – a sly move, but politically rather than problem-oriented, as senior officials on both sides have conceded, and evocative of how other scholars have described immigration policies elsewhere (Ellermann 2006; Guiraudon and Joppke 2001). The structures of the citizens and integration bureau certainly have the capacity to change this, but they require a good deal more political will and effort than is actually taking place.

Further to internalising, but not solving a conflict, the creation of a strong integration bureau has had a deteriorating effect for the Ausländerbehörde. Potentially consumer-friendly aspects of the work, such as the language advice or the citizenship granting, have been outsourced into the new agency. Many progressive and pro-immigrant aspects of the new Aufenthaltsgesetz have thus been effectively channelled away from the Ausländerbehörde, which can more or less work 'as usual'. The Ausländerbehörde is thus the 'bad cop' in a progressive-conservative polarisation, with the result that costumer-oriented approaches within the Ausländerbehörde have a harder time than necessary. Some employees have taken this as an opportunity to leave the restrictive aspects of the work behind, while many future employees are likely to find the new Integration Bureau with room for creativity and a positive community impact more attractive. Local political ideas – good ideas – have thus directly impacted on the ability of the Ausländerbehörde to get away from its image as a 'deportation agency', and further complicated the internal division between two goals: integrating and expelling (similar in M.D. Morris 1985).

Steelstadt

In Steelstadt, the change in legislation was met with little spirit of optimism about a change in the way immigration offices work. No new model of client-oriented case working was proclaimed, no name changes undertaken, and only two organisational changes happened in direct relation to the new residence act. A new section for security checks was installed, responsible for the execution of security interviews and follow up questionings as well as interacting with the different intelligence agencies. Further, one office (on the ground floor, where no other case working took place) was allocated to the migrant support organisations to provide in-house legal counsel. While there was a general acknowledgement that the change in legislation had been important, the office management agreed that for the immigration office, nothing much had changed. After all, the Ausländerbehörde was still bound by law to regulate migration by granting and withholding residence and as such constituted a regulatory body and not a 'welfare office'. Certificates for integration courses were handed out by the regular caseworkers along with a list of bodies that offered the classes. Interaction with migrant support groups as well as the city's cultural department that handled integrative measures were limited to meetings with compulsory attendance and handled in a manner that was neither overly friendly nor hostile, but in a matter-of-fact way.

The 'stubbornness' of the Ausländerbehörde to withstand the 'change of times' was criticised by many of my interviewees, who acknowledged that the office was working more or less appropriately and in accordance with the law but explained that 'an anachronistic spirit' still pervaded the bureau. However, due to a relatively small media interest in Steelstadt and a general sense of the immigration office and city council being 'thick skinned' regarding public pressure, the Ausländerbehörde was under relatively little public scrutiny despite being by far the most actively deporting bureau of all four cases, even when adjusting for size.

East Middlestadt

With migration still being a relatively new – and relatively minor – topic, the Ausländerbehörde in East Middlestadt had a rather different historical relationship with migrant support organisations. Contact was generally good, since the city administration had been an active part in taking a stance against right-wing movements during the 1990s. With the legislation change, the immigration office sought to intensify good relationships with public actors. Within the organisation, two caseworkers responsible for naturalisation were transferred from the registration department and another new position was created to liaise with different committees involving migration and to provide assistance with finding suitable integration courses. Since most new immigrants to East Middlestadt are students, asylum seekers or EU citizens, all of whom are not eligible for integration courses, the demand for counsel on this matter was rather low, as a result of which the new caseworker was also made responsible for handing out certificates of free movement to EU citizens. Similarly to Steelstadt, an office was provided to migrant support organisations, which used it on a rotating basis on two days of the week. However, very few migrants actually consulted this service, especially since the sole purpose of the in-house consulting was to refer the clients to the different support opportunities available at the local welfare organisations.

The cases of Middlestadt and Metrostadt are clearly the most remarkable in their stark difference between the official presentation and the practical impact on the everyday practice of the Ausländerbehörde. In Metrostadt, a 'playground' was established to shift debate among pressure groups into an organised, controllable space. Similarly, the inclusion of welfare organisations meant that criticism was now issued informally and much less in open confrontation through the press. Both cases show extremely efficient ways of dealing with public opposition, something which Ellermann's work has also focussed on (2006, 2009). Many of the other techniques discussed by her – such as enforcing deportations quickly and at inconvenient hours during 'dawn raids' (see also Boswell and Geddes 2011) – were part of the routine behaviour of the Ausländerbehörden; the main difference, however, was the successful cooptation and integration of previously opposing forces into the structure of migration management. Through token participation in the case of Metrostadt and effective subsidising of services through the provision of offices and work equipment in the case of Middlestadt, public opposition in many instances was left to the radical organisations that would not participate in such a truce – but which on their own lacked both resources and, crucially, legitimacy.

Are these two examples mere instances of successful spin then, prime cases of the differentiation between official facade and organisational routine, as Rowan and Meyer (1977) or Goffman (1959) identified several decades ago? Are the different opinions discussed in Table 5.1 correlated to different levels of public deception? The evidence from the immigration offices suggests a rather more nuanced reality: While clearly the management of public opposition is one of the primary driving forces behind the turn to incorporate organisations in the public sphere more closely – something which, after all, had been implemented to a lesser extent also in East Middlestadt and Steelstadt – it is not the sole reason for change. Indeed, even proponents of the most cautious of interpretations of the 2005 Residence Act agreed that the times had changed significantly from the heyday of immigration and asylum seeking of the late 1980s and early 1990s. With the change in the asylum clause of the basic law in 1993, the probationary residence permit offered to migrants on long-term sufferance and the eastward extension of the European Union in 2005 and 2007 had all but diminished the number of contested cases and deportations and thus solved a lot of the conflict on its own. The cooptation of welfare groups and cooperation on any level was primarily possible because the number of potential conflicts has drastically decreased. This gradual change occurred without the Ausländerbehörde having to intervene, which is one of the reasons why the officials in Steelstadt have not felt the need for an integrative turn – the public pressure is much lower than in the 1990s.

In addition, it would be far too simplistic to reduce the debates in Middlestadt and Metrostadt to mere spins on public perception. The impact of the integration course section for the migrants who actually consulted these services is likely to be profound. A new way of case working has entered the immigration office; and while even this has not yet had any significant influence on the way the immigration offices work in general, it constitutes an irreversible shift towards a service-based client interaction. It is not, as the official facade would have us believe, a turn towards social welfare, but a different method of social control aimed at creating a different type of 'migrant'. Specifically, the focus is shifting away from the archetype of the migrant who is denied settlement and integration and whose future lies outside of Germany to the well-behaved denizen who adheres to the conditions set by the host state in order to remain.

City Politics and Administration

Since, institutionally, the Ausländerbehörden are part of the city administration, all of the changes within the offices structures have to be approved by and arranged in accordance with the elected city parliament as well as the executive management. In many ways, both parliament and management enacted immediate pressure on the immigration office as a result of successful lobbying of the welfare organisations and migrant support NGOs. Castles (2004) has argued that as a result of this, local initiatives rather than federal policies have furthered issues of integration and multiculturalism in Germany. In Steelstadt, this delegated pressure is most remarkable in the debates surrounding the establishment of an integration office.

Since the change in legislation and the rhetoric surrounding the sea change of immigration policy in Germany neither translated into a significant structural reform nor resulted in a new phase of self-presentation and interaction with the public sphere, many of the old conflict lines remained in place in Steelstadt, despite the overall improved relationship between Ausländerbehörde and welfare organisations. During my fieldwork, Social Democrats and Greens had arranged a series of expert hearings with speakers from both the state ministries and other city councils that had already established integration departments. The Ausländerbehörde was invited to these hearings, and allowed to voice their concerns about setting up an integration department with the participation of the Ausländerbehörde. The head of office was extremely worried about these meetings and feared that he would lose support within the city council over the way in which the Ausländerbehörde was currently operating. In defending his case, he turned to the source of expert knowledge that he believed could turn the debate in his favour: me. While requiring me to stay out of the debate and delay many of my expert interviews until after the hearings (possibly – rightly – fearing that I would end up on the opposition's side), he consulted me on my insights into the work of the integration departments of the other Ausländerbehörden. I shared my concerns over the actual impact of the integrative structures in the other cities, explained my hesitant attitude towards intercultural competence trainings and briefly described my take on the socialisation process of migrants in immigration offices (see Chapter 7). With this in mind, he went on to defend his office from the 'threat' of having to be an integration office. After my stint in Steelstadt, I presented my findings to the head of office and other senior department figures. In the following discussion, we spent well over an hour looking into structural changes that could improve the issues I had highlighted in my talk. The outcome of this debate in turn formed the basis for a wide-ranging reform of the office, which won the support of the city council partly because it had been based on my 'expert consultation' and helped to defeat the voices that tried to persuade the city council for a more integration-focused solution.

While negative publicity and difficult relations with the local public sphere can be waited out and dealt with, the threat of losing the support of the city administration was a different matter altogether. This clearly indicated the influence communal politics and management wield over the Ausländerbehörde, who went out of their way to appease and persuade them. However, the local political and administrative elite were much more than an influential ally of either migration support groups or the immigration office. In many ways, they shaped the ways the Ausländerbehörden could function, most obviously through providing the means to structure and fund the offices. Table 5.2 shows the differences in pay levels and caseloads, which I have already indicated in Chapter 4. As the comparison shows, the main difference in structure seems to be between many employees with a relatively low pay level and less, but better paid and qualified personnel. However, while the difference in pay for comparable positions sometimes varied by a few hundred Euros per month, it is questionable if this adequately redeems the doubling of caseloads in Middlestadt or East Middlestadt compared to Metrostadt. The variations are a rather good indication of the overall appreciation of Ausländerbehörden by the respective city councils. In Metrostadt, while there was an acceptance that workloads were intense, the city management had declared that the majority of tasks in the Ausländerbehörde amounted to simple routine administrative tasks. In Middlestadt, the head of office had managed to persuade his superiors that the job of case handlers was in fact as difficult as positions that usually required employees with an administration degree from a college of applied sciences. However, in Middlestadt and East Middlestadt and in some departments of Steelstadt (see Chapter 6), there was a constantly high workload, while in Metrostadt, workloads were drastically lower.

Beyond providing the structural means for work, city management sometimes actively influenced the work of Ausländerbehörden. A good example of this

Table 5.2 Pay levels and caseloads

	Metrostadt	Steelstadt	Middlestadt	East Middlestadt
Number of migrants	170,000	66,000	50,000	9,500
Number of positions excluding citizenship	250	60	35	17
Employee: Migrant ratio	1:680	1:1100	1:1428	1:1357
Comparative pay level of caseworkers	Medium-low; Extreme variations among low level caseworkers,	Medium; High for senior officials	High; Pay levels of case handlers as high as pay level of ruling officials in other cities	Medium; Many career changers with qualifications exceeding their pay level
Low level caseworkers involved in writing of rulings	In some cases	No	No	In some cases
Vacancies filled within a few months?	No	No	Yes	Yes

was the lack of support by high levels of the city administration of Metrostadt for the local immigration office in dealing with public pressure. While usually the public relations branch within the major's office in a city deals with criticism and press campaigns, in Metrostadt, this was usually delegated to the Ausländerbehörde, where the head of office directly had to engage and respond to public enquiries. Similarly, rather than taking a protective stance and supporting the Ausländerbehörde like any other branch of administration, senior officials of the immigration office often had to defend the work of the Ausländerbehörde in front of the city council and committee meetings. A similar example of refusing support could be found in East Middlestadt, where the relations with the city's legal department – employing trained lawyers and responsible for consulting all branches of the administration in legal matters – were rather strained. For example, the preparation of cases going to trial was often extremely superficial, and as a result the legal officials could not provide useful support in court.

Interventions on Individual Cases

In all four cases, the city management took an active interest in the organisation of deportations by the Ausländerbehörde. In particularly controversial cases, often those involving the deportation of children and young adults as well as sick or elderly people, lawyers and migrant support organisations would try to rally public support and influence the position of senior city management and influential politicians. To pre-empt this, immigration offices would inform the mayor's office in advance on impending deportation cases, thus trying to gain their support prior to the intervention from outside groups. In some cases, senior figures in the city government would dictate terms under which the deportations had to take place, or command the halting of deportations altogether. Interventions to halt the controversial deportations and thus prevent public conflict were extremely common. This was true especially in the lead-up to local elections, since regardless of their political alignment, the governing parties and mayor standing for re-election feared a detriment in their chances to succeed if restrictive measures taken against migrants became known by the public. This usually caused great frustration among the officials preparing the deportations, who felt curtailed in their power and distrusted in their judgement of cases and law.

After another deportation was cancelled due to the 'current delicacy of politics' (a by-election was imminent), one senior official did not care to hide her frustration at not getting 'these people out'. She states that in situations like these, she felt as if her division was seen as a bunch of murderous barbarians who could only be let out of confinement on select occasions. In reality, all deportation cases had been through various phases of appeal and retrial and been finally approved by courts, thus 'rather than committing crimes against humanity, we are merely doing our job, which is applying the law as it is written!'

In Metrostadt, intervention in the affairs of the Ausländerbehörde went beyond case-by-case interventions. Seeing themselves as in charge of an internationally renowned city of trade and commerce with top tourist attractions and one of the finest culture scenes in Germany, the city council and government had decided that this should be reflected in the way in which the immigration office works, and passed several memorandums and resolutions to that matter. Not surprisingly, one of the aspects of the Ausländerbehörde's work that did not fit with this openness to the world was the organisation of deportations. As a consequence, the city management had advised the immigration office to refrain from using night raids and other surprise measures as much as possible. These measures allow the officials to execute deportations unannounced and thus without forewarning for the immigrant and thereby significantly improving the success rate of removal attempts, since many migrants attempt to avoid deportation by going into hiding during the time of an announced deportation. Without these instruments, the number of successful deportations decreased drastically in Metrostadt. As a result, both Middlestadt and Steelstadt had higher deportation rates than Metrostadt, which has a migrant population that is almost five times bigger than that of Middlestadt and treble that of Steelstadt.

Thus city officials have a number of means of influencing the work of the Ausländerbehörden at their disposal, and frequently use them. Since publicity surrounding immigration offices is mostly negative, many senior figures in the city management see the offices as ballast that can greatly damage a city's popularity. As one senior employee of an Ausländerbehörde put it, 'more often than not, they simply wish they could make us go away'. The provision of resources was scarce in all four cases, with manpower lacking especially in the two smallest bureaus and highly qualified and adequately paid employees missing in Metrostadt. Given the strong influence city officials can have, the attempts to win them over by both migration management and migrant support organisations are only a logical consequence. However, the vanity of attempting to improve the city's image also causes city officials to take matters into their own hands, trying to steer the immigration offices away from damaging the public image of the general administration.

Institutional Pressures: Courts and State Ministries

The third main factor of political influence is perhaps the most obvious: after all, both state ministries and courts are tasked to exert control over the work of Ausländerbehörden by steering the interpretation of the law and evaluating decisions during trials. I have already discussed the 'flood of decrees' immigration officials see arriving from the state ministries in Chapter 3, which can be seen as an indication that the state ministries take their role in steering legal implementation rather seriously. This section will show that publishing decrees was not the only means of influencing the work of Ausländerbehörden; more informal practices were also available to the representatives of the state. However, the interest in internal affairs of the immigration offices further than intervening in controversial cases was actually rather limited. As a consequence, the state officials cared little about the heated debates surrounding the overall orientation of Ausländerbehörden and accepted the immense variation in practice and decision-making as given.

Powerful, but Disinterested Ministries

Immigration law sections of state ministries – in all but one German state situated within the interior ministry – are tasked to direct the interpretation and application of the residence act and associated legislation. This interpretation is of course politically controlled by the current state government and a particularly popular instrument when a political party is ruling a state but not part of the federal government. Decrees, the most common promulgation of these interpretations, are thus clarifications of issues, updates of implementation practice, for example as a result of court decisions or changing world politics – a war breaking out making deportations to that nation inhumane – or political measures to counteract federal legislation. Thus the variation of legal application from state to state is rather substantial, especially regarding the most controversial matters: dealing with precarious legal situations and deportations. In general, states with stable Social Democrat government tend to have rather lenient interpretations of the law, while states traditionally governed by Christian Democrats tend to have restrictive policies towards immigration.

These different instances of interpretation of guidance are illustrated by the reaction of the different states to the decision to extend probationary residence permits for migrants who had lived in Germany without legal residence but who could not be deported for many years. The original agreement to allow these migrants to receive a probationary residence and work permits to improve their situation and get out of their precarious state ended with the turn of the 2009, and since no political compromise could be found on that issue on a federal level, the Bundesrat decided to extend the measure by another two years, but to leave the legal details to the individual states. As a result, most states governed by the centre-left decided to allow residences to be renewed even when attempts to find work had been unsuccessful if the applicant could prove they had 'sufficiently' tried to find employment. Other states, however, ordered their Ausländerbehörden to renew residence permits if the immigrants were able to support themselves without relying on social welfare, and only allowing other renewals in exceptional circumstances. Similarly, in 2008, five years after the start of the Iraq war, many states reviewed their assessment of the security situation. While one state government decided to refrain from deporting to Iraq and extend the residence of Iraqis who had fled the war but did not qualify for asylum by another two or three years, another state government issued decrees ordering the resumption of deportations to Iraq.

Ausländerbehörden in traditional 'swing states' consequently experience the most upheaval in political direction, sometimes with rather extreme outcomes. Thus in one of the states I researched in, a conservative government faced being ousted from office by the opposition in the upcoming election and consequently took last minute measures to make a political impact. One of the last acts was the chartering of a passenger jet and ordering the immigration office to 'get as many old cases aboard as possible', as one state official told me during an interview. Sure enough, a few weeks later, when the new government had been elected, one of the first measures taken by the state ministry was to issue an order to review the human rights situation of that case and to take special precautions when deciding to deport immigrants to that particular nation.

Other than decrees, state ministries were often involved in the management of very controversial or delicate cases, either because the Ausländerbehörde needed the ministry's expertise or because the support network of the migrant had petitioned to the state for an acknowledgement of hardship and granting of an exceptional residence permit. State ministries also lend their expertise during court trials that had been identified as 'lighthouse cases', which could potentially have a significant effect for other cases and be detrimental to a particular political interpretation of the law a state ministry had pursued. Thus both formally through decrees and informally through consultations and interventions on individual cases, state ministries shaped many of the decisions made in the immigration offices, and indeed much of the variation in decisions found between the different offices can be traced to different state decrees. More striking that the attempts to influence the work of Ausländerbehörden, however, was the complete disinterest ministries took in the internal affairs of the offices

While very active in promulgating legal interpretations, the sections on immigration law in state ministries were not very concerned with the actual implementation of their decrees. Similarly, when I described my research project and some of the initial results, most interview partners on state level acknowledged the striking differences in applying the law, but did not see it as 'their problem'. Indeed, according to law, state ministries are supposed to provide expertise and guidance on the implementation of immigration law, but not tasked to supervise the implementation process. Supervision of implementation is the task of the Bezirksregierungen, the primary administrative divisions of the states. The employees of the Bezirksregierungen (also employed by the state, which funds these meso-level administrations) are so badly understaffed that my interviewees admitted that the evaluation of individual immigration offices happened less than once in a decade, and usually consisted of a few interviews and a review of a handful of randomly selected cases. Crucially, the Bezirksregierungen lack both funds to exercise their supervisions properly and the political power to enforce changes, since they can neither issue state-wide decrees nor change the structure of Ausländerbehörden, who are funded by the individual city councils. Due to this division of interpretative and supervisory powers, Ausländerbehörden are left to their own devices in all but a few cases, and remain at the mercy of the individual city council to receive sufficient funds to function properly. Thus no regulations regarding the staffing, pay levels, organisation, or work processes exist that could help to ensure an equal treatment of immigrants and just process in the different cities. The only bodies which regularly review cases from different immigration offices and can ensure due process are courts.

Administrative courts: Concerned

Similar to the responsible sections of the state interior ministries, the administrative courts are formally involved in the process of implementing immigration law as they review and decide on appeals that migrants have issued against the rulings of Ausländerbehörden. Their influence is thus usually retrospective through approving or reversing decisions made. However, court judgements were actually rather rare, because most cases were settled by the conflicting parties during the trial period. Rather than enforcing the correct interpretation of the law, judges saw their role primarily as mediators between the parties.

> "Finding a decision out of court is the best possible solution for all parties involved", one judge tells me. "None of the two parties lose face and we do not have to write a long justification of our decision", he adds, smirking. When asked why so many cases get to court if the parties can agree on a compromise in the end after all, the judge pauses to think for a while, and then states that "in many cases, court is the first time applicant and Ausländerbehörde see eye

to eye. The problem is that immigrants do not trust the officials, and vice versa and that in the Ausländerbehörde things get overlooked that might cause them to compromise in the first place".

There was a general consensus among judges that while the legal appreciation of a case was more often than not accurate, the main problem lay with the evidence decisions were made on. Thus in almost all instances, judges had to request additional evidence in order to appreciate a case fully. On occasion, judges would provide informal 'feedback' on the adequacy of a ruling to the representative of the immigration office during trial. Further informal exchanges were done in short phone conversations and sometimes, judges would meet with senior figures of the Ausländerbehörde. In one of these occasions in Metrostadt, the judges enquired about the newly set up hardship committee, for which they saw no legal basis. While evaluating the general work practice of immigration offices is not part of the court's job description, the judges were genuinely concerned and interested. In providing feedback and showing interest in internal matters of the Ausländerbehörden, it was thus the administration judges, not state officials, who exerted more influence over the practice of law implementation. Furthermore, in three of the four offices, employees would orient their work more towards it holding up in court rather than following state decrees closely, similar to results Halliday (2009) found when analysing the interactions between social welfare officers and courts. Contrary to Halliday, however, the officials in this study were less anxious about their professional capital in a different 'field' of practice. Instead, efforts of working properly for the court were more grounded in the much closer relationship with judges and administrative court officials and the 'care' judges showed for the immigration office.

Conclusion: Unsupervised Political Minefields

Doing and writing ethnography shows a 'case' embedded in its context (Scheffer 2007). While the previous chapters have focused on the internal practices that influence the different application of immigration law, this chapter has served to consider institutional constraints and challenges to the work in the Ausländerbehörde. With high levels of public interest and attempts to intervene in the work of the immigration offices and a laissez-faire attitude on the state level, the different forms of practice and organisations become entirely understandable. Subsidiarity, the principle of delegating responsibility to the smallest possible political unit, greatly increases the potential for variation and thus depletes the chances for migrants to receive equal treatment. The implementation of law in Germany is thus not simply a question of more or less working 'by the book', but heavily influenced by local politics. It is a 'weak' process, easily influenced by outside factors that minimise the role of the bureaucrat as service provider (Scheffer et al. 2008). As this chapter has shown, the dangers of being deported thus vary immensely between a city like Metrostadt, where controversial deportations are seen as stains to the reputation of the city, and Middlestadt, where the Ausländerbehörde is left to work in its own ways behind a facade of integration. The implementation of law requires both integration and deportation, and the 2005 Aufenthaltsgesetz has clearly stressed the former over the latter. Ironically, the progressive efforts of the Middlestadt council and administration have effectively deflated the effects of this for the Ausländerbehörde, since service-oriented aspects of the work, such as language and integration course advice, are done by the integration bureau. For both Metrostadt and Middlestadt, incorporating NGOs has been successful in pre-empting public opposition (Ellermann 2006), but only internalised, not resolved the conflict, and further enhanced the polarisation of work objectives in the Ausländerbehörde, which now have internal or external branches that work completely differently to the rest of the office.

The political intent of a legislation change can thus be completely sidelined as in Steelstadt or used for one's own intentions as in Metrostadt and Steelstadt. Section one of the 2005 Residence Act is thus rather ironic. An Ausländerbehörde 'enables and organises immigration with due regard to the capacities for admission and integration and the interests of the Federal Republic of Germany', but given the principle of subsidiary, lack of interest on state level and the interventions on city level, this enabling and organising of migration differs greatly from city to city, as does the definition of the interests of the FRG. One answer to the question of why immigration offices work so differently is thus because there is so little control on the state level and so much intervention from the immediate community.

Indeed, the discussion of the politics in the Ausländerbehörde has shown how much of the intent and execution of immigration policy is left to the lowest level of administration, where intense debates and conflicts are carried out over the overall role and nature of migration management in Germany. Similarly, since there is no structural given, requirement or suggestion, the conditions and organisation of work in immigration offices are left to the generosity of the local city council. Finally, the implementation of residence law in these agencies is under no regulation since the body that has supervising powers lacks the capacity to enact these and is almost completely cut off from political debates and power. Granted, immigrants have the power to appeal and courts take their role as instruments of Rechtspflege, as 'caretakers of the law' rather seriously. However, the fact that offices can be held accountable for faulty decisions cannot alone justify the complete lack of engagement with the implementation process by superior branches of the executive.

Germany is a *Rechtsstaat*, a state of and governed by law, in which the executive is constitutionally bound (Schuback 2002: 73–7). One of the central aspects of the '*Rechtsstaatsprinzip*' – the principle of the state governed by law – is due process (*Rechtssicherheit*), ensuring fair and equal treatment as well as fair and comparable results: equality before and after the law. The case of uneven application of law, based on the (itself constitutionally enshrined) principles of federalism and subsidiarity might well be found to be in severe conflict with the principle due process, but is in effect systemic, an outcome of two opposing normative goals (Schuback 2002: 86–90). It is this line of argument that state officials would adopt when discussing the different ways immigration law is implemented and interpreted in the immigration offices I studied. While they tended to agree that the chaotic handling of discretion found in my fieldwork surely is no adequate representation of a *Rechtsstaat*, and some officials expressed concerns over the overall organisation of immigration offices and endangered state of due process regarding the management of migration, in the end, the matter was shrugged away as an issue for which they could not be held responsible, since it was endemic. And true, no single state ministry can change the structure of residence law application. However, it was striking that in an environment fraught with informal practices and political pressures, the significant leverage superior ministries did hold was only rarely used to edge immigration offices towards greater conformity. Instead, ministerial interventions focussed on the handling of outlier cases that could potentially damage or benefit the state government. Executive-internal mechanisms of discipline through techniques of observation and holding accountable were almost non-existing. Rather, immigration offices were left to their own devices, leading the management who did struggle with keeping a tight ship within their agencies frustrated and under the impression that superior ministries simply did not care and had no sense of the kind of guidance street-level bureaucracy requires.

In addition to not caring, engaging or intervening except in the most politically lucrative or threatening situations, there is no overall direction, aim or outcome immigration offices can work towards or orient themselves to. The fact that migration policy is disseminated through a federal parliament to a federal ministry, 16 state ministries with some 30 subsidiaries to over 400 different local councils that host the immigration offices only exacerbates this, but the central issue here is federally. The 2005 *Aufenthaltsgesetz* is a watered-down compromise including measures to ease migration and residence (regarding highly skilled migrants and hardship cases), to restrict immigration (regarding citizens of predominantly Muslim populations) and sections that could either be seen as restrictive or inclusive (compulsory but state-funded language classes). Since its promulgation, the law has been changed to incorporate residences based on international human rights statutes and at the same time further restricted the access to Germany and eased deportations. The probationary hardship residency has been extended in late 2009, but simultaneously left at the whim of the individual state governments. Crucially, German migration policies are even lacking a coherent rhetoric and expression of intent, since with the 2005 legislation change, structural reform on federal level has resulted in three different institutions competing for claims to voice policy: the federal interior ministry, a newly founded section on integration within the chancellor's office and the *Bundesamt für Migration und Flüchtlinge* (BAMF, Federal Bureau for Migration and Refugees), formerly only responsible for asylum law and now also managing the provision and financing of language courses. Thus neither in text nor rhetoric or intent is a direction that immigration offices can emulate. Instead, it is up to the local political domain to fight over the direction of federal migration policy – surely a victory for the public sphere of local communities, but a stark defeat for due process and rule of law.

Indeed, the BAMF is an intriguing case of how migration policy can work completely differently even in Germany. While the bureau has several outposts all over Germany in which case working takes place (Scheffer 2001 studied one of these), the overall management of knowledge, examination of legislation, orders on decision-making, training programs, and even social science research (Boswell 2009) takes place at the headquarters in Nuremberg. The local subdivisions are directly accountable to Nuremburg, with state legislation playing only a very minor role. In comparison to the Ausländerbehörden, the management of asylum seeking is thus a rather streamlined process that cuts out two and a half middle men: state ministries, their subsidiaries and local councils. While regionally dispersed offices will surely result in substantial levels of autonomy and variations of practice, having less political interventions and less legal material will have a significant impact on the work of the BAMF. Granted, the yearly numbers of asylum seekers is a mere percentile of the overall immigrant population and roughly comparable to the 'active' immigrants that are in the process of application in Metrostadt. But the new role as administrator of language course coordination and financial support to participating immigrants has increased the caseload of the BAMF exponentially – at least in theory, as the case working is still done in the immigration offices. It could be argued that the centralised organisation is related to the fact that asylum law is far too important to give away to sub-state administration, however, even if that were true and notwithstanding my argument about residence in premise two, surely the access to citizenship would be considered at least as important. Again, this is not the place for a genealogy of the management of migration in Germany, but the differential and frankly confusing set up is rather striking.

Chapter 6
Immigration Officials

During his adolescence, Caseworker 157 played football with the youth teams of the city's first division club. However, his hopes of turning professional were shattered after a car accident caused irreparable damage to his hip when he was 17. Not knowing what else to do, he started an apprenticeship with the city council. In 20 years as a city official, 157 has worked in three different administrative branches, and has been at the Ausländerbehörde since 2003. Although he often complains about his work, his supervisors and the applicants, it is evident from the way he engages with clients that he cares greatly. When off-work, 157 coaches the youth team of his local club, and we spend a lot of time discussing football and the dreams one has when growing up. For him, the security of employment still is the greatest appeal of the job, although he frequently states his frustration that employees are not rewarded for good work, but rather only asked to take up greater workloads.

Caseworker 85 is clearly uncomfortable with the job. Still relatively new, she struggles with the legal basis of her work and often seeks advice from more experienced staff. Before taking a few years off work to care for her twins, 85 used to work with the culture department of the city, and greatly enjoyed the atmosphere and "dealing with all these creative people". Here in the Ausländerbehörde, consultations make her nervous and she is overwhelmed with the pressure of the job. While she tells me that she is determined to "make it" and manage, when I return to the office a few months later, her colleagues tell me that she has transferred to another department.

211 is always the first at the office, regularly starting her work at six o'clock. While she says that she is an early riser and likes working in the quiet time of day, it often seems as if she mainly starts early to be able to leave the office as early as possible, just after lunch. With only two years to go before early retirement, her main objective is to sit out the next few years. During consultations, she avoids making decisions as often as possible and is highly effective at finding a piece of documentation that is still missing so that migrants will have to come back another time, when another colleague will deal with the decision. Since she talks very fast and with a strong regional accent, many applicants struggle to understand her, to which she usually retorts that "this is Germany, the official language is German, and if that is a problem, get an interpreter". The only time when 211 smiles is when she talks about her family, having recently become a grandmother for the first time.

As there are individuals behind the cases the immigration office deals with, caseworkers have a real life, hopes and dreams, a personality. This chapter considers the people that make up the office, examines how they deal with the at times extremely stressful job, looks at their attitudes towards immigration and analyses the responsibility deciding on immigrants' life chances in Germany entails. Following Carole Satyamurti's (1981) work on social welfare workers, this chapter is thus on 'organisational survival'. The first part of the chapter analyses the difficult work conditions in immigration offices and points to the high levels of stress that working in Ausländerbehörden can entail. Following from this, an account of how caseworkers cope with stress and adverse work conditions, highlighting individual solutions since Chapter 4 has shown the relative unsuccessfulness of structural reform to work deficiencies. Coping and a lack of structure both directly relate to the next section, which deals with questions of responsibility in the work of immigration officials. As conclusion to the chapter, different definitions of success are accounted for.

Working Conditions in Ausländerbehörden

In addition to working in a particularly difficult administrative field without proper preparation or training for the specific job, caseworkers had to deal with sometimes rather adverse working conditions, which were exacerbated by the structural misalignments discussed above. All of my caseworkers both within and outside the Ausländerbehörde agreed that in comparison to other sections of the city administration, even low-level caseworkers in immigration offices had to deal with rather complex legal issues. Furthermore, employees often had to deal with difficult interactions with clients due to the particular importance of the immigration law for it applicants as well as due to language and cultural barriers. The pay levels of employees in the four immigration offices differed quite dramatically for both case handlers and the officials responsible for rulings, with variations of up to four pay categories and several hundred Euros monthly. In one case, the head of the immigration office had been able to persuade the city council to increase the pay level of caseworkers to reflect their difficult task; in all others, there was no financial recognition of their sometimes extremely complex and challenging work. Furthermore, as immigration offices retain a very negative public image, employees often find themselves in a defensive position, having to explain either why 'they' were so harsh in their migration management – or so lenient. Even employees who enjoyed working in their position admitted that there was a dual lack of recognition of their work, both financially and publicly. As a consequence, Ausländerbehörden are not seen as an attractive employer and all offices struggled to find qualified and motivated staff. All immigration offices included a rather large percentage of career changers who sought the stability of city council employment in difficult economic times and could not be 'picky' about the job they accepted, as well as many young employees who had been sent to work at the Ausländerbehörde after their vocational training.

> Caseworker 138 is particularly vocal in his criticism of the way his work place is run and organised and sees my interest in the topic as an opportunity to unload his frustration as well as to provide quite fascinating insights into the local political debates around the Ausländerbehörde. One of his colleagues, who overhears our conversation intervenes and half-jokingly warns 138 that I am taking notes of all this and will be using the information for my final report to the head of office. We all laugh, and I quickly remind everyone that every source is kept confidential so that no negative consequences were to be feared. 138 laughs again, shakes his head, and replies that I should realise that this was the Ausländerbehörde. He was not afraid to express his opinion as "there is nothing worse they could transfer me to".

The same official, when overhearing a co-worker remarking that with a degree from Cambridge at my age I probably had great chances for a big career in academia, stated that he was not so sure, as 'maybe doing research on Ausländerbehörden is in his line of work what working in an Ausländerbehörde is in ours': a dead end. This attitude and the sarcasm about having reached the lowest point in the administrative food chain was widespread amongst caseworkers, many of whom either tried hard to get a job in another branch of the city council or resigned to the fact that the immigration office would be the end point of their career. Even many of the employees who did not mind or actually enjoyed working in the immigration office remarked that probably in a midterm perspective, they would want to transfer to somewhere 'quieter', where both the legal complexity and the daily stress level would be lower. The relative unpopularity of the immigration office as a work place resulted in a rather large fluctuation of employees and given the difficulty to find a replacement, this resulted in higher workloads for all remaining officials, increased stress levels and an even greater incentive to leave the Ausländerbehörde.

Given the time that new caseworkers require to gain a level of competence in which they can be fully operational in their job, a high fluctuation of employees is of course detrimental to the overall performance of the office. In Middlestadt, an internal memorandum from 2003 stated that this 'almost caused the complete breakdown of services in the department' and remarked that 'the [level of] expert knowledge decreased with every leave. Unless necessary steps are taken, there is an imminent danger of a situation in the short- or medium-term which neither allows for an orderly running of service nor for legally adequate case work'. Furthermore, with rather severe budget constraints, city councils often save money by leaving positions vacant, thus not replacing employees who moved to other departments at all. The other Ausländerbehörden had been in similar situations, East Middlestadt very recently with the near-implosion of the subdivision on humanitarian immigrants. In Metrostadt, one of the subdivision heads remarked that there was often a thin line between 'walking on crutches and completely collapsing', while in Steelstadt, it was of course in the two groups with high workload and complex cases where caseworkers tended to fall ill.

The subdivision heads as well as the heads of the Ausländerbehörden were of course aware of the difficult working conditions that permeated the offices and continuously tried to counteract the deteriorating situation. Overall, the great majority of superiors seemed honestly concerned about the situation, and took their leadership role seriously, which in turn has been acknowledged by the caseworkers and in itself has helped to defuse the situation.

Thus employees in Ausländerbehörden are faced with very important, but also very difficult tasks for which they receive little training and support, which happens in a structural setting that hinders the circulation of employees and equal distribution of workload, is rewarded with public disdain and a relatively low monetary compensation and is often further aggravated by high workload due to unmanned or vacant positions. It is thus important to recognise this enormous strain that is placed on the employees of the immigration offices in Germany.

Stress – and Coping

> I am late for work, and arrive after the first applications have been handled. As I enter the office of caseworker 166, I realise that the door to the adjacent office is closed, which is unusual because colleagues like to stand in the doorway and chitchat while one is handling a case. A few minutes later, one of the caseworkers from next door comes in and tells 166 that "she has left now, she is dead beat. I guess she won't be in all week after this". 166 nods, pauses, and then replies that "it's obvious that she can't do this any longer. This is just not working out". They agree that their superior should help "her" to get reassigned to a different branch of the city council. When I ask what happened, the colleague from next door replies that it was "the usual. They don't understand why they cannot get what they want, they suspect that you do it because you hold a grudge against them, they accuse you, you're having a bad day anyway, things go bad". 166 adds "She yells at him, he threatens to sue her for malpractice, she orders him to leave, he calls her a racist and refuses to leave. You have to be thick skinned to deal with it". The colleague they were talking about never returned to work in the immigration office again.

> One of the physicians that assess the health of potential deportees I interviewed explains at length how some migrants refuse to take their medication and hurt themselves in order to be declared unfit and not be deported. He talks about the smell of fear and about the distrust migrants have against anyone who is "of the state". When I suggest that his job must be tough, he agrees, but says that he only has a couple of cases like this in a year. The employees in the Ausländerbehörde dealt with this every day! He tells me that already a couple of times, caseworkers

> came to him to seek counsel on a case, but ended up pouring their heart out about their job. "They must have a lot of people on sick leave or requesting transfer", he quite rightly suspects.

Through the presentation of the work practices and organisational structures, the previous chapters have shown some of the challenges that accompany working in an immigration office. The basis of the work is ever changing and highly complex; interactions with clients can be very difficult as immigrants come to consultations fraught with expectations and fears, and the work conditions in which the everyday takes place are far from ideal. Chapter 4 has considered the efforts to improve work conditions through structural reform, and concluded that the effects of these organisational changes are rather small. Many employees complained about the difficulty of the task, and voiced their hope that I would 'understand what they had to deal with', which was apparently not understood by clients or the general public. Indeed, many officials felt misrepresented by public representations of the Ausländerbehörde, and complained about 'bad press', although many admitted that this had been significantly reduced in past years – due to the more permissive immigration law, and at least in Middlestadt and Metrostadt also due to institutional changes (see Chapter 5). Nevertheless, the main difficulty in the implementation of immigration law is not so much the dealing with adverse working conditions but the difficulty of the work itself, and we have seen strategies of knowledge transfer and collaborative decision-making have in the discussion of law and its implementation in Chapter 3. This section is less concerned with group strategies to improve practice, but with the ways in which individuals deal with their situation.

Through making decisions on residence, officials at the Ausländerbehörde have an enormous impact on individual lives, indeed; often on the lives of whole families (cf. Bouchard and Carrol 2002).While this is true of other aspect of street-level bureaucracy as well (Dubois 2010), Scheffer (2001) rightly argues that the impact on residence law on most other legal decisions – concerning welfare, work, citizenship, trade, or crime – assumes a social priority in immigrants' lives. Even health insurance and pension funds enquire about the legal status of migrants, and employers are heavily fined for employing immigrants without permit (Castles and Miller 2009; Sieveking 2001). The officials in the Ausländerbehörde are of course aware of this enormous responsibility. All of them have made a negative decision, and all of them have seen the impact of their negative decision: people unable to move freely within Germany due to residence restrictions to Middlestadt, people barred from full welfare benefits or entering the job market, people not being able to bring their spouses and children into Germany. Most of them have been involved in a case which resulted in a deportation or expel order. Both result in an indefinite ban from re-entering the German state. Understandably, these responsibilities weigh heavy on the officials' shoulders – even when they have years of experience with denying residence applications.

Coping

Deportations are surely the most extreme and emotionally stressful tasks immigration offices have to fulfil. Here it is impossible to turn away from the fact that there is a deeply personal aspect to each case. Caseworkers responsible for executing deportations regularly force entry to the immigrants' domiciles and literally snatch people from their homes; they take them away from their family, their friends, their belongings, put them in the back of a van and drive them to an airport where a plane takes the migrant on a one-way trip far away. The total vulnerability of migrants and the immense power immigration officials wield is nowhere more obvious, more frightening.

> On the second day of my fieldwork, caseworker 23 took me to the police detention centre, where an irregular migrant had been imprisoned. We were accompanied by an interpreter, a Jordanian woman who had worked for the Ausländerbehörde previously. Not having been to a working prison-like institution before, the visit had a lasting impression on me: windowless cells, a tiny outside court with a "fenced" sky, an interrogation room with a one-way-window, and the stale smell of fear and cheap cleaning utensils. The young man "we" are interviewing about his identity – in order to get a temporary passport and deport him – is almost exactly my age. He looks scared, lonely and forlorn. He has crossed the Mediterranean on a boat, and worked on a construction site since 2006. The interpreter is exasperated about his "uneducated" Arabic; he only speaks slowly, has a slight stutter. He can hardly spell his name, let alone fill out the forms 23 gives him. His handwriting is shaky and untrained. During the interview, he asserts that he wants to go home and is willing to cooperate in any possible way. 23 agrees to let him phone his mother in his North African home, where he left his identity card. In what follows, we are witnesses of the dramatic conversation between a mother and her child, who is in prison for the first time of his life, and cannot but notice the universal language of exasperation and fear, tears. The mother promises to help and finds the identity card, while children seem to be crying in the background. Being illiterate herself, the mother rushes off to find a neighbour to read out the identification number on the identity card, while 23 and the detention guard discuss the payment details of the phone call (it is deducted from the detainee's pocket money). When she is back, the line breaks down, and a few chaotic minutes follow, reconnecting across the Mediterranean Sea. After the interpreter has noted the identification number, she spends five minutes trying to explain to the neighbour how to find and use a fax to send a copy of the identity card to the Ausländerbehörde. Later, the detainee tells us that he has saved €800, and that he would like to ask a friend to bring it to the detention centre so he can take it home, but 23 tells the interpreter to tell the detainee to never mention it again. Otherwise, 23 would have had to confiscate it and use it as a means to cover the costs of detention and deportation to come.

> As we leave, we agree that the detainee will never see his money again. I am exhausted from the experience, and secretly regret having started this study. But 23 is quiet too. As we pass the gates of the police station, he exclaims what a "poor s–ker" the detainee was, and that "these cases are always hard, when you see what's behind all this". He asks me about how I experienced the interview, and when I tell him, he advises me not to get to close to individual cases. "You only lose from empathising. It only gets harder, and doesn't change anything."

Distancing is a well-known and widely used technique found in bureaucracies. When individuals become cases and lives become files, the emotional attachment to decision-making is minimised, and responsibility made bearable (Blau and Meyer 1987; Peters 1995). Scheffer's analysis of the asylum granting process finds similar techniques (2001), and Bouchard and Carroll (2002) show the 'automated' ways in which immigration officials deal with immigrants. Impersonality is a traditional part of the analysis of bureaucracy since Weber (see Chapter 4), however, as scholars like Katz et al. (1973) have maintained, a balance between impartiality and sensitivity is crucial. At the Ausländerbehörde, the former is usually a given, while the latter far too often missing. Most employees are distrustful of 'tales' of need and personal problems, and often are preventively suspicious of immigrants (cf. Rousseau et al. 2002). Indeed, there are a few cases in which the Ausländerbehörde has been tricked by migrants, and even two lawyers agreed that there were 'some sly foxes'. However, the complete distancing and distrust often does not help the immigrants, and, as they become frustrated and aggressive, this creates even more stress for the bureaucrats, who sometimes simply cannot see the personal circumstances of a 'case'. Distancing thus is a normal and often useful technique to prevent the official to become individually entangled with a case and reduce stress. This process is similar to the techniques of neutralisation that Matza and Sykes (1957) have found with young delinquents who downplay the relevance of their crimes. However, this had its clear downside in cases where empathy and sensitivity were direly needed.

> The first actual deportation I accompany is that of an elderly man, a skinny, ashen faced failed asylum seeker. We knock on the door of his apartment at dawn, and one of the caseworkers has already picked the lock before his wife opens the door. A wife? There was no mention of a wife in his case file! Will she be deported as well? There is no time to ask, because the three caseworkers have already entered the small flat, handed out the deportation order and court approval, checked all rooms for potential threats, and identified and searched the deportee, who is in the painstakingly slow process of dressing himself. I will later find out that the pair was "merely" married according to the customs of their culture, something that is not legally accepted as marriage in Germany and thus making it legal to tear this couple apart. Meanwhile, one impatient caseworker commands the man to speed up, while another official orders the

> wife to pack a suitcase – the only thing the migrant will be able to take with him. During this, the two residents are not allowed to speak to each other, not allowed to touch, not allowed to exchange last words when we lead the man out of the flat, down the stairs and towards the van. Within 15 minutes, I had been witness to the breaking up of a marriage and the end of residence, all without so much as goodbye or a hug. On the way out, the officials joke about the lock-picking skills one of them displayed just now, apparently totally oblivious to the consequences of their action.

Months later, during the discussion of my results, I retell this episode and stress that while the fact that the deportation could be done based on a legal technicality was disturbing enough, my greater shock concerned the utter lack of compassion and sensitivity during the situation. After the talk, one of the caseworkers who had participated in the deportation takes me aside, and tells me that he agrees with me and that when he started to work in deportations, he tried to make things more humane. However, he quickly stopped allowing for goodbyes and last words, because 'you can't bear it. You cannot bear it. No one can, not even the most hard-hearted among us hard-hearted bunch. It a tough job as it is … It cannot be done'.

Another means of creating a distance from private and professional life was spatially differentiating the two. 'I stop talking and thinking about my job when I leave the city limits', caseworker 6 told me. Many employees of the Ausländerbehörde lived outside their city, and many told me how they avoided contact with clients outside office hours as much as possible. 'Another place I won't eat again', 17 told me when he filed away the case of an applicant who had found a new job at a restaurant. Many employees stated that they avoided going shopping with their family, as they disliked being recognised with their family. In Middlestadt, many employees expressed concern that I had rented a room in the shabby but friendly 'West' area of town. 'I couldn't live there – everyone knows me there!' one exclaimed. None of them asserted that it would be dangerous to live there, but many explained to me that they wanted to avoid any personal contacts with their clients – immigrants – as much as possible. In a similar vein, an official in East Middlestadt told me how she had stopped using public transport, because for some reason, she would always bump into a 'case' of hers.

Difficult cases and long procedures dominate the employee's imagination of work at the Ausländerbehörde. Even though more than half of all migrants in Middlestadt have a permanent residence, they only visit the Ausländerbehörde when they have a new passport issued to have their visa label transferred and thus are outside the imagination of 'immigrants' when the employees speak about them. One way of dealing with the difficulty of the job was to make jokes, often about individual cases and to share 'funny' anecdotes. Some comments outside opening hours were also rather rude, and in the first few weeks of my stay, the employees were hesitant about it in my presence, or would later apologise and maintain that this was nothing personal or general, just 'had to come out' at this point. For them, cursing, laughing, complaining about a case was 'natural', 'human', in short, a normal way of letting off steam and dealing with stress and frustration (again, cf. Matza and Sykes 1957). It was usually expressed when clients were away and in a circle of insiders, who could understand the problem.

Extremely different handling of cases, grumpy, stubborn officials, opaque decision-making processes and negative decisions in the context of immigration law have often brought about claims of anti-immigrant sentiments and institutionalised racism against certain groups (cf. Juss 1997 on the UK; Leun 2006 on the Netherlands; Nijhawan 2007; Mandel 2008 on Germany; Töpfer 2002). Indeed some of the 'jokes' made in the Ausländerbehörde were on the border of being unabashedly racist, and the fact that many employees tried avoiding immigrants in their free time would further support such an interpretation. However, there were no signs of any systematic mistreatment of certain cultural, ethnic or racial groups. Despite their sometimes severe criticisms, all lawyers and NGO workers agreed that the Ausländerbehörde was not xenophobic, although some singled out one or two employees who they charged with more-or-less openly holding such views.

> One of the employees in the "executive" department, and surely a hardliner on the restrictive side of the immigration law, identified himself in one of our first meetings to be "probably more on the right side of the political spectrum" and told me that in his view, there were many "assholes who exploited the welfare system, rapists and drug dealers" who he wanted convicted and deported. However, he also maintained "you cannot be a Nazi and work here", since there were just too many positive decisions which a "true" racist surely could not handle. Furthermore, he added that Germany has greatly profited from migrant workers and would probably continue to rely on migration forever.

Similar 'immigration necessary, but out with criminal immigrants' positions were shared by quite a few employees. Drug-related offences were especially seen to be problematic, which one of the lawyers confirmed in his interview. However, he also added that this was in line with legislation, which eases the deportation of drug offenders in §53 Aufenthaltsgesetz. In addition, many employees in the Ausländerbehörde have a migrant background or immigrant spouses. Migrant 'involvement' does not predict the treatment of clients in any way. Thus while there surely are officials with moderate right-wing political alignments and restrictive attitudes on immigration, this has no systemic effect. Furthermore, these attitudes do not predict particularly unfriendly behaviour. One lawyer, who had once been a client of the immigration office himself, told me that in his view, the employees of the Ausländerbehörde were not anti-immigrant: 'They just totally lack any sense of service.' I would agree with this statement. While institutionalised racism would be too big a claim, there are many employees with a generally unfriendly attitude towards their clients (Juss 1994, 1997; Rousseau et al. 2002). In fact, often (ethnic) German clients fare worse off than immigrants. Instead of xenophobia, some officials seem to be nurturing a healthy misanthropy. In order to protect themselves from being overwhelmed with emotional attachment, they have become cynical, cold, and excessively unfriendly.

Responsibilitiy

> Caseworker 30, with whom I regularly went to court hearings, often admitted his surprise after leaving the court, when another "pretty sure" case had been turned into a mutual agreement between the parties. "Things just look differently in court, when the applicant is there and explains himself", he stated more than once, and in one instance criticised the caseworkers for not having been sensitive enough. A mentally disabled immigrant had been ordered to be expelled despite not having any family left in his country of birth and despite medical certificates stating that the immigrant would not be able to live by himself and medical facilities in the home country were not equipped for proper treatment. During the court hearing, the applicant's sister and (German) husband had explained in a convincing and moving statement how they cared about the brother, to which the judge had only exclaimed "finally, an intact family", and asked 30 about his opinion.

I have analysed the importance of courts as spaces of mediation in Chapter 5, and mentioned that on many cases, a compromise can be found that both applicant and office find agreeable. Part of the explanation to this phenomenon certainly lies with the difficult interaction between officials and immigrants as discussed in Chapter 6, and the techniques of distancing that officials use to not have to bear the emotional burden of a case are certainly also influential. While the deflection of stress is understandable as part of a coping process, the collective failure of taking responsibility and the lack of common sense and compassion surely are not. In his seminal essay, Dennis Thompson (1980) has called this 'the problem of many hands' since in any complex organisation, many officials contribute to a decision-making process, the overall responsibility is often difficult to determine. Indeed, as Bovens (1998, 48f) pointed out, it is possible that a false decision or failed outcome is produced not by willingly wrongful behaviour, but the sum of neutral actions, so that no one might be guilty.

In the Ausländerbehörde, a lack of both awareness of responsibility and responsible behaviour clearly was not a mere unintended consequence of the division of labour, but something employees actively enforced and used to avoid having to be responsible. Thus many case handlers would dismiss their responsibility for the overall history of a case since they 'merely' collected evidence and prepared negative decisions, the rulings and legal appreciations of which were done by the more senior staff. Employees working on rulings in turn dismissed their responsibility for an overall case because they never actually met the migrant and would thus rely on the evaluation and evidence of the case handlers. Also, even if a decision was made it often did not mean that migrants had to leave Germany, that was up to the 'executive' department dealing with deportations. Furthermore, controversial decisions were supervised by the office management anyways. Heads of department, legal specialists and heads of office all stated that they had so much to do with organising work, keeping the office on track with legal development and dealing with public pressures that they hardly ever saw enough of a case to make a full judgement over the issue and could only assess the logic or reasoning employed by the writers of rulings. While the senior officials did have a sense of representing the immigration offices and protecting their staff from harm by positioning themselves between them and public criticism, they also denied their responsibility for a case gone wrong. They caught the bullet for someone else, were martyrs, not those responsible.

> On a stakeout in preparation for a deportation, I accompany caseworker 319, a relatively new member to the "executive" team in a number of surveillance exercises. Since there is not a lot to do, I use the time to engage 319 in a conversation about his views on the job, the other employees, the office, hoping that since we are alone, he will be more reflective on the issue and curtail his answers to the expectation to the team in which he normally works and interacts with me. He tells me that he enjoys the work as there is a huge variety of tasks and no case or workday are alike, that he deals well with the fact that he regularly has to work early mornings (for deportations) and late (for stakeouts and check and search activities in bars, brothels or on public transport) and that the compensation for this is rather good, that he gets along with most of his team mates and that overall, the job is an immense improvement on the one he had before. "It's a shame for the people, though", he adds after a few minutes of silence, and, when probed further, tells me that he could understand why people would come to Europe illegally and try to avoid deportations. "That's human nature, wanting to lead a better life", and, with a crooked smile, adds that it is "too bad for them that we are doing such a fine job here". I ask him if it was sometimes difficult to fulfil the tasks set to him because he immediately saw the consequences, and how he deals with that big pressure of responsibility. 319 affirms that "emotionally, it is hard, especially when there are families involved and all that. But you know, they knew they were breaking the law when they came here, they were taking a risk and they knew it. And they had a chance, right; I mean the law sometimes gives you a chance". And after a pause "I think it must be hard for the colleagues who make the decisions [to deny residence] on these cases".

On all levels of the immigration office, employees would deny their responsibility through two related mechanisms that the previous example displays. Firstly, officials shift the responsibility to another department: case handlers to decision-makers, the decision-makers to the case handlers, the deportation section and the office management, the office management to all caseworkers, the deportation section to the decision-makers. No one denied that they were involved in the management of migration in some way, but many contested being actually responsible for the fate of a migrant's case and instead shifted the weight of responsibility to another office. The second technique of denying responsibility consisted of denying the ability to act responsibly. Caseworker 319 clearly states that his job is a reaction to the conscious decision of a migrant to act in contradiction to the law. Thus really, he is not responsible for the deportation to happen because firstly, the migrant committed an act that caused his deportation and secondly, there is an existing and valid law that tells him what to do, so he has to, emotional attachment aside. While in their everyday practice, employees wield considerable discretion in handling and deciding a case as Chapter 3 has shown, in their justification of their actions, they deny having leverage and present themselves as merely executing and following orders. This line of argument would often be used when confronted with applicants that 'bothered' employees with questions about their file, about delays, decisions, or required documents, and also by senior management who liked to present the immigration office as totally bound by the set, rigid law and without space for discretionary practice. However, as chapters 3 and 5 have shown, the interpretation of law and its political meaning are much less predetermined as the employees of the Ausländerbehörde would like outsiders to believe.

Avoiding Responsibility

In addition to denying responsibility when held accountable for their actions, some employees in the immigration offices would also avoid being in a situation in which responsible behaviour was necessary. The easiest way for this was for case handlers – and in Metrostadt, decision-makers – to postpone making the decision to another consultation in the hope that another colleague would have to deal with the case then. Difficult cases could thus take excessively long not only due to their complexity, but also because caseworkers would pass the buck around from colleague to colleague. While far from prevalent, this technique occurred frequently, most in Steelstadt, where cases were rotated across different offices, and least in East Middlestadt, where case working took place in one big office so that colleagues would pick up on such behaviour more quickly. Further than the threat of detection, the case handlers in East Middlestadt had a much stronger sense of community and togetherness, which meant that the social cost of delegating cases was higher. Further than the postponing of decision-making, caseworkers could utilise the well-established informal network of knowledge exchange to share the responsibility by consulting others, and to avoid acting responsibly altogether if they managed to pass the case or decision on to a superior employee as a result of the consultation process. While the use of networks of knowledge was prevalent in all immigration offices, there were substantial differences in the possibility to get rid of the decision or case by involving a superior. Again, most occasions of this were found in Steelstadt, and particularly excessively in one group.

One of the three sections on general immigration law had hit particularly hard by sick leaves and transfers, as a result of which many new employees were assigned to work in the group in the past three years. Since familiarisation with the tasks take a rather long time (as discussed in Chapter 3) and the remaining caseworkers struggled with simultaneously training the new arrivals while doing their own work, the decision-makers were crucial to assisting case handling. When the previously new employees were fully inducted, the practice of consulting the immediate superiors regularly continued, so that rather than one or two questions per consultation period, case handlers would seek advice on even the most menial matters. This often happened instead or before asking their immediate colleagues and resulted in a knowledge exchange pattern that was formed like a star, with knowledge transfers only between case handler and decision-maker rather than a web, in which everyone can rely on everyone else. As a result, the decision-makers complained about not being able to do their own work, while the case handlers were annoyed that their superior was often already in consultation with another colleague and complained about an often inclement attitude towards their peers.

The avoidance of responsibility thus has actual implications for the efficiency and quality of service. Satyamurti (1981) has called these forms of behaviour organisational deviance and described ways of cutting corners and being less than efficient in ones the practices of social workers. These practices present a challenge to the work of the Ausländerbehörde and of course increase frustration as well as adding to the internal variation of work, especially relating to variation C, the style of case working. Indeed, Barnard's famous quote is directly applicable to this study: 'The practical difficulties in the operation of organization seldom lie in the excessive desire of individuals to assume responsibility for the organization action of themselves or others, but rather lie in the reluctance to take responsibility for their own actions in organization' (1938, quoted in Bovens 1998: 45). However, it would be too simplistic to blame for irresponsible behaviour exclusively on the individual caseworkers. Bovens' (1998) work on responsibility in complex organisations rightly points to the fact that acting responsibly requires both the possibility to assume responsibility and the expectation of being held accountable. Drawing on George Herbert Mead's work on the 'generalised other' (Mead 1967), Bovens suggests that if virtuous behaviour is not expected or encouraged within an organisational culture, people are more likely to not act responsibly (1998, 27). With the exceptions of East Middlestadt, these conditions for responsibility were all but lacking in the Ausländerbehörden.

Success?

A central problem of the work of the Ausländerbehörde is that due to the nature of its duties, it has to deal with two totally divergent sets of goals (cf. Guiraudon and Joppke 2001: 11). On the one hand, its employees are held to always examine the possibility of the best possible residence permit, while simultaneously, caseworkers have to obey orders to screen applicants for involvements with terrorism and be as proactive as possible in 'convincing' migrants to cooperate in the efforts of their deportation.

Success I

Paragraph 104a of the Aufenthaltsgesetz, introduced in 2007 to comply with EU regulations, holds that migrants who have been living for eight years or more at least partially on a suspension of deportation (Duldung) can receive a residence permit if they have not committed any grave criminal offences. The state ministry had issued a rather permissive decree in support of this, and in the Ausländerbehörde, this has been considered a 'coup' ('*Befreiungsschlag*'), as most senior officials have named it. As a result, the decree has been used to grant most immigrants a residence permit in record time, which has been widely publicised and boasted, as the head of the state immigration law department sarcastically stated. However, this has been acknowledged and positively mentioned by all lawyers and NGO workers I interviewed, as well as being a reason for pride for many employees.

Success II

> Four a.m., Wednesday morning. I stand, freezing, in front of the Ausländerbehörde and wait for the deportation team to arrive. Today, four people are supposed to be deported simultaneously, a couple, the husband's father and a cousin. The three men are involved in different aspects of organised crime, in drug trafficking, racketeering and street violence. Since they are expected to hold illegal weapons, there is a threat of things "turning sour", and the officials have asked for police support. By 4:15, the official in charge has already sweated through his shirt; by 4:45, we meet the three dozen police officers allocated to today's deportation. Three teams are going to access the three different locations simultaneously, while one team stays behind as backup and another team circles the streets of the city district, looking for signs of trouble. Due to the potential risk of the situation, the official in charge has decided I am not allowed to enter the immigrants' homes with the teams and that I have to wait outside with the staff that keeps watch on the windows and side exits. Not owning a bulletproof vest, I am wearing my leather jacket, which makes me look like a dandy lost in the middle of preparations for battle. At 6 a.m. sharp, a piledriver smashes the front door of the residential home that houses the couple and in-laws and sure enough, by 6.10 two hand-cuffed men, one in pyjamas, the other in his underwear are brought out, laid onto the street, searched, and put into one of the waiting vans. Shortly afterwards, a woman in a tracksuit appears, followed by a scolding elderly women and three visibly frightened children. Everything went

> smoothly, the operation was a success. By noon, all four immigrants have left German territory.

After a big operation like this, there was a sense of achievement among many officials, who had spent weeks to plan an important deportation like this. The official in charge was 'glad' that he was able to 'offer' me such a spectacular deportation, and 'one that mattered' at that. Other than in the cases described above, here it was much simpler to find meaning in the accomplished work, after all, Germany was now rid of convicted criminals, local mobsters.

> A caseworker of the "executive" department is visibly pleased, and talks about something which is "smooth as oil". As I enquire about what pleases him, he tells me that he has just received the temporary passport for an immigrant he has long been trying to deport. Until now, the consulate had not been cooperative ("weren't feeling like it", as he explained), but finally, three years after the expel order and 18 months after finally having identified the immigrant, who had used five aliases, he had been successful – the deportation is now a mere matter of booking a flight. "This was the first case on which I had to write the expel order", he tells me, "and now this. This is going to be a successful month".

On another occasion, I sit and talk with two caseworkers, when a senior official comes by and asks mockingly if we had nothing better to do than chitchat. One of the caseworkers retorts that he has already fulfilled his deportation quota [of one] for the month, which causes the superior to smile, sit down, and suggest playing a round of cards instead.

With the exception of the 'executive' department, all officials are engaged in both integrative and restrictive activities. When asked about 'successful' work, few can clearly define what they perceive success or good work to be in the Ausländerbehörde. For some, it is simply 'not having too much to do', for others, 'finishing a work without complaints'. While there were only a few instances in which 'getting work out of sight' was considered successful (cf. Triandafyllidou 2003), there was no commitment to perfect decision-making either. Perhaps goals and definitions of success are especially unimportant in an environment in which performance is neither measured nor rewarded (Peters 1995), as in the German civil service, where most positions are permanent and effectively irredeemable (cf. Hague and Harrop 2007). However, many employees were harsh critics of 'inefficient' or 'lazy' colleagues, and actually complained about not being rewarded for performance – a strange turn towards new public management (cf. Hague and Harrop 2007). Mostly, 'unsuccessful' workers – at least in the eyes of their colleagues – were those who were ill for long periods of time, as well as new colleagues who struggled with getting to grips with the law. Conversely, one might argue that 'being there' and 'doing one's thing' sufficed for being a successful employee at the Ausländerbehörde.

Conclusion

By examining who the caseworkers are, how they are trained and under which conditions they work, we can gain an understanding of some of the surprising ways in which immigration officials work as well as some of the shortcomings attributed to them as discussed in the previous section. Both this chapter and Chapter 4 have introduced the reader to bureaucratic excesses that appear to come straight out of a Kafka story. Immigration offices are often the workplace of unmotivated officials with little training and understanding of migration in Germany, who exercise vast amounts of power over individual lives without being properly supervised, paid, or socially recognised. Indeed, immigration offices are not only the lowest end of the immigration legal system in Germany, they are often also socially stigmatised agencies within the city councils. Yet, decisions made in these offices have an immense impact on all aspects of migrants' lives and, in turn, also influence the work of other branches of city councils. In addition to being an unpopular workplace, potential frustration levels are kept high by a usually uneven distribution of workloads over the offices, the difficult legal basis on which decisions have to be made as well as difficult interactions with clients who are willing to (sometimes physically) fight for their residence rights.

Through distancing themselves from the emotional difficulty of their jobs as part of the coping process discussed above, officials also deny their responsibility for their actions. While many acknowledge that very important decisions on individual lives are made in 'the office', only very few feel to be the responsible party for the decision. This is partly the problem of many hands (Thompson 1980) which is inherent to complex organisation in which the division of labour also entails a division of accountability for faulty work, but, as Bovens' (1998) analysis has shown, also due to a lack of structural enticement of responsible behaviour. However, in the Ausländerbehörden, responsible actions as well as taking responsibility for bad decisions was almost entirely dependent on the individual employee.

The final part of the chapter has shown that conflicting goals often result in a division of the agency into a section that values costumer orientation and tries to accommodate individual circumstances into the legal framework and a section that is solely interested in removing individuals from Germany and acts as a rogue police force trying to uncover the machination of criminal immigrants. Successful work in Ausländerbehörden is thus not clearly defined or divergent, indeed, caseworkers sometimes feel as if they are working against each other by simultaneously trying to find a way to allow for residence and attempting the deportation of a migrant. It is thus hardly surprising that caseworkers focus on the few aspects of their job that are rewarding notwithstanding diverging policy goals: job stability and protection.

Chapter 7
The Impact of Migration Management: Immigrant Socialisation and the Magic of the State

This chapter will move away from the four different immigration offices and consider the wider implications of this research project. How can examining the ways and wises of managing migration in Steelstadt, Metrostadt, Middlestadt and East Middlestadt enhance our understanding of issues beyond the realm of visas and photocopy wars? What are the implications of studying the legal implementation, organisation, political context and individual agents of four cases of German street-level administration? I will argue that previous works on migration policies and management have underestimated the complexity of the issues involved and ignored or mystified the socialisation process that happen during the interaction between client and state officials. In addition, the focus of interest within academia appears to be somewhat removed from what matters to its objects of study. Hence rather than citizenship or asylum, residence should be a more central concern for the study of migration and migration policies.

This chapter looks at the consequences of incomprehensible practices and structures for the interactions between employees and applicants, and considers the concept of 'illegibility' and the impact on the socialisation process of migrants, arguing that immigration offices make a contribution to the integration of immigrants to society. The previous four chapters have provided in-depth evidence into the four factors that influence the practice of migration management. All follow a similar line of argument: it is more complex than it seems, issues are more controversial, less clearly defined, 'grayer' than an analysis of policies would suggest. Despite an overall trend towards greater harmonisation, the complexities of law, organisation, political interference as well as individual coping strategies mean that there are great sub-national variations in the management of migration. These are surely exacerbated by the German federalist system, but can be expected to be found in all kinds of offices that implement policies.

The question one could ask, and indeed one that is often asked with regards to implementation studies, is why we should care. Yes, there is some friction at the bottom of the institutional hierarchy, but is this not negligible considering more general political developments? Indeed, Chapter 2 has shown that only a limited part of cases, mostly among the most marginal types of residences, is decided differently. Do we need to care how many photocopies applicants have to provide in order to attain their residence? One obvious answer to these questions is that indeed, gaining an inside look into the administration of migration does not completely alter our understanding of state responses to immigration. This book does not claim to overthrow migration theory, but to fill a gap in the existing literature, to complete the academic description. It would be nice if policy analyses would recognise that the texts they examine will never be fully implemented – as indeed recent studies do (Boswell and Geddes 2011).

However, there is a case to be made that implementation practices have a greater impact. My findings suggest that due to different advice given to clients, many improvements in residence status (regarding length of possible residence, employment rights, and access to citizenship) are never decided because clients are *discouraged from applying*. There are thus differences in the decision-making process due to the fact that as a result of the face-to-face interaction, no decision-making process is started. This is especially relevant since immigrants cannot appeal decisions that were never made, and given the high complexity of the law and opaqueness of the process, many immigrants have come to simply accept the officials' advice and refrain from consulting a lawyer. Since officials are not legally bound to advise their clients, but solely to decide on their applications, it is up to the institutional culture and the individual if they see cases of unfounded discouragement as a problem – or as a successful deflection of work.

Given the fact that many social rights depend upon a certain residence status, implementation practices influence official perceptions of immigration. The following case concerning work permits illustrates this. According to §10 and 11 of the *Beschäftigungsverfahrensverordnung,* the decree on the process of allowing immigrants to work, migrants on a sufferance can work after a year if the Ausländerbehörde grants its permission. This permission can be withheld if the applicant has failed to collaborate with the immigration office in solving their inability to deport. As discussed in Chapter 5, 'collaboration' is interpreted with great variation, as is the application of §10 and 11 of the *Beschäftigungsverfahrensverordnung*. In all four cities, however, it was agreed that these cases should only be reviewed upon application, and that the possibility to work for migrants with a sufferance ought not to be advertised. As a result, many immigrants who legally could and would like to work continue to rely on welfare. The higher level of welfare recipients among immigrants in Germany (and resulting debates about 'freeloaders' in the system) are thus partly a result of administrative decisions not to tell migrants that they could work. While in the eyes of some officials the German state is too poor to make photocopies of documents, it is completely logical to retain immigrants on welfare benefits by not informing them and discouraging the application for work permits. Statistical representations aside, it should be clear that these variations in practice matter because they matter to immigrants. The following section will discuss aspects of the face-to-face interactions in Ausländerbehörden, and analyse the impact of these interactions.

Official-Client Interactions: The Making of Migrants?

Perhaps unsurprisingly, the patterns of interactions between immigrant applicants and Ausländerbehörden officials mimicked the relative structural chaos in the agencies' organisation. While autonomy is already one of the key concepts of Lipsky's work on street-level bureaucrats (1980, see section 2.4), the autonomy of caseworkers in relatively unstable and unsupervised subsections was further exacerbated. This was apparent in almost all stages of the consultation, and is perhaps best illustrated by the different first encounters between officials and immigrants.

Encounters of a Different Kind

> The door to the office of caseworkers 3 and 16 is always open. 16 explains that this is so no one can threaten or try to bribe the employees. After a client case is finished and the client has left the room, the next client has to wait until called – usually by a loud "NEXT!" Once the client has taken a seat (if he stands, he will usually not be encouraged to sit) and either 3 or 16 is ready, the official asks "*Worum geht's denn?*" ("what's it all about?"), often in a manner-of-fact-like, let's-get-down-to-business tone. Greetings are almost never exchanged, or answered. If the client starts talking before the official has made his opening query, she is shut up with the phrase "*Zeigen Sie erst mal Ihren Pass*" ("Present your passport first").
>
> The office door of caseworkers 243 and 334 is usually shut. After a client has left the room, they usually close the door behind themselves. When they are ready, 243 or 334 walk to the door, open it and ask for the next customer in a friendly tone. After the client has entered the room, usually greetings are interchanged, the applicant is asked to sit, followed by a few sentences about the weather, the bad state of public transport or the giant teddy bear that adorns the desk of 334, whose son won it at the local fair. After this, the responsible caseworker would usually open the consultation with asking what they "could do" for the client.
>
> The office door of 17 (next to 3 and 16) is usually ajar. After a client has left the room, the next client can enter. If no one enters, 17 usually shouts "Is there nobody who wants to come in" with a sarcastic undertone in his voice. When I was sitting in the office, 17 would usually make a comment about the client entering, often loud enough so the client could hear it as well. As the caseworker has a tendency to be annoyed about his work, remarks were usually rather negative and rather harsh, for example regarding potentially work intensive types of residence ("I bet this is another f–ing obligation for tourists", "See that plastic bag? That's all work for us to go through. Twenty Euros he is applying for permanent residence", "You're bad luck, kid, you're a magnet for shitty cases,

> and here come another"), sometimes accompanied by "it's nothing personal" directed at the client. Greetings are answered.
>
> As her colleague has been on sick leave for over a year, caseworker 79 has an office to herself and complains to me about the "loneliness". During consultation hours, she likes to chitchat with applicants about almost everything. Given her phenomenal memory of faces, 79 often immediately recognises many clients from previous visits and enquires about the family or work, often providing unasked advice to younger applicants ("Make sure to finish high school"; "You have to be a role model for your siblings since your dad is nothing but trouble"; "You would get a job if you started wearing something other than sweat pants") or warning older applicants about younger relatives ("That nephew of yours was caught drunk driving again. You have to do something about it"; "You have such a pretty daughter, can she not find a better match than her do-no-good fiancée?").
>
> Caseworkers 278 and 109 like to take their time between cases and keep their clients waiting before calling them in through the open door. No matter what the queue in front of their office, they drink coffee and discuss the quality of public radio (in decline), make jokes about the previous case (altogether hopeless), and talk to me about my haircut (too long) or my last name (which translates as "owl" in German, which is, of course, hilarious, especially if I married someone named Snow and adopted a double-barrelled name, etc.). When an applicant politely enquires if it was alright to enter or when the next applicant would be considered, 278 and 109 regularly shout the client down with remarks such as "You cannot barge in like this", "Do YOU want to work here instead of us", "We're not at *Wünsch Dir Was*" ("Make a wish", a popular game show in the 1980s and 1990s) and complain to me or themselves about the "damn impoliteness" and impatience of applicants (only referred to as *Die*, "them"). 109 also had a collection of particularly "stupid-looking" passport photos, and he and 278 would regularly judge whether someone had the "potential to join the album".

While officials who shared an office usually employed similar routines, the discrepancies between workplaces were significant and relatively stable. Even though all employees were aware of the enormous differences of consultation practice, the constancy of their own approach caused them to act surprised to outright annoyed by breaches in the patterns of interaction. Clients thus had to adapt to these informal rules of engagement or face snide remarks, brash rejections or patronising explanations of 'how things work around here'. In many instances, disregard of the informal interaction rules had a negative impact on the lenience which caseworkers applied their discretion. Additionally, these breaches of conduct would also influence the upcoming consultations with other immigrants. Patterns like these continue throughout the official-client interactions, and thus impact on the degree to which applicants can explain their situations or the time officials take to explain legal implications. Furthermore, they broadly correlate with the 'generosity' displayed in informal or procedural discretion, but not necessarily with factual discretion (see Chapter 3). Thus caseworkers who tended to have reserved attitudes towards applicants would often be tougher in requiring proof through documents, but not necessarily tougher in their decision if the applicant had been judged credible.

Some officials regularly behave in a moody, grumpy or unfriendly way, while others are usually open and friendly. Busy periods and personal circumstances certainly impact the attitude towards clients, but mostly friendly officials retain their friendliness in stressful periods, while grumpy bureaucrats remain untouched by even the nicest of weathers. Since the rotation of cases or stand-in duties are common in all four cases, immigrants hardly know what to expect, let alone how to behave. Even 'regulars' that had to come to the immigration office frequently can find themselves in surprising situations where routine patterns of behaviour – even the matter of leaving the door open or closed – result in strongly negative reactions by caseworkers. These elements of variations of approaching interactions and the resulting unpredictability of expected behaviour combined with the complexity of the law and lack of transparency in decision-making are at times almost incomprehensible to outsiders and (rightly) lead to accusations of arbitrariness and chaos. This closely resembles the 'illegibility' of states that the anthropologist Veena Das has identified in her work (Das 2004). Das argues that state power 'oscillates between a rational mode and a magical mode of being' (ibid.: 225), with this 'magic' originating in everyday regulatory practices that are unpredictable and with real and potentially dangerous outcomes to the subject. Given the impact of decisions in immigration offices on migrants' lives, this analysis, while deriving from practices of the certainly even more unpredictable Indian state system, applies directly to the management of migration in Germany.

Applicants are thus subjected to a form of state rule that is additional to and enhancing the authority executed through the implementation of law in an ordered administrative process. While the impact of this cannot be measured within the scope and through the methodological lens of this present work, there are several indicators worth mentioning at this stage. First of all, during the expert interviews, both lawyers and NGO workers stressed the anxiety applicants felt when visiting the Ausländerbehörde, even when deportations were not imminent or not even discussed. Almost unanimously, my interviewees would tell of instances in which they had been asked to confront the immigration office instead of the clients, who were said to express fears of 'being taken away' and denied their rights. Furthermore, lawyers and NGO workers complained about caseworkers leaving applicants 'in the dark' about both the necessary requirements of attaining residence and the likely outcome of the decision-making process. Indeed, this was something I frequently observed during my fieldwork, for example regarding the necessary income needed to secure ones livelihood (see Chapter 2, variation B). While the calculation is indeed a rather complicated process, caseworkers regularly defended their refusal to respond to migrants' questions by explaining that in their view, immigrants ought not work just to attain residence – a (to me) rather bewildering normative stance shared by many.

The 'denial of rights' and allegations of arbitrariness were common features of conflicts between applicants and immigration officials, often expressions of the desperation of immigrants who could simply not understand what was going on or angry accusations shouted at officials by frustrated clients who perhaps also did not want to understand. Also, this was a common suspicion voiced by German nationals (with or without migrant background) who interacted with the immigration office in cases of family reunifications and relational residences. Further common features of client-official interactions that indicate an awareness of both the impact and illegibility of decisions include extremely apprehensive and timid behavioural patterns often exhibited by sole female applicants or the overly brash and almost thespian self-presentation of young males who seemed constantly on the edge and suspecting maltreatment in the every move of the officials. Also, in many cases immigrants voiced great relief when being told that the application would be relatively easy to process, was decided positively, or when the employee made any attempt to positively engage with the client. Those caseworkers with a rather friendly attitude towards the consultations would express their confusion over this, since, 'We aren't that bad' or 'That was such a clear cut matter' that any anxiety would be unwarranted. In all four agencies, anecdotes were passed around over mostly single, middle-aged men who needed to 'drink themselves some courage' prior to entering the immigration office. This was considered as amusing as unnecessary, because again the employees did not see the potential danger of their office. Within the staff of the immigration office, there was thus a lack of awareness – or denial – of the impact of their work beyond mere rule-bound administration.

Residence and Citizenship Compared

It is worth comparing these findings with the impressions of the work of the nationality law sections of the immigration offices. While not systematically considered in this study because in Middlestadt, citizenship issues were handled by another agency and in East Middlestadt, the caseload was extremely low; there is a remarkable pattern that was clearly found in all three cities that included sections that decided on the attainment of German citizenship. Despite having structural and, importantly, practical problems similar to the residence law sections, the interactions between clients and officials were much more relaxed and less pervaded by tension and the suspicion of malpractice. During my – admittedly comparably few – observations of nationality law case working, no conflicts arose and there were no instances of heated debates. Contrary to the residence sections, applicants would usually turn up unaccompanied by a supporting friend or family member to consultations on citizenship. While still seeing their work as stressful, caseworkers in the nationality law sections unanimously exclaimed relief not to be working with 'residence', since 'They have to deal with all the [emotionally] difficult issues'. In contrast, the employees maintained that 'it's not about as much here', implying that the decision to attain citizenship was seen with a more relaxed attitude. Further stressing this disparity, in one city, officials of the nationality section uttered their disapproval about the 'unfortunate' fact that their clients had to share a waiting area with (mostly asylum-related and thus precarious) residence applicants. The lawyers I interviewed agreed to these observations, stating that in citizenship cases, the issue of leaving the citizenship of another country was often more problematic than dealing with the German offices. Significantly, welfare organisations did not have specialised sections that supported applicants for German citizenship. The only issue lawyers, applicants and immigration office regularly quarrelled with was the speed of decision-making on citizenship. Arguably, this is much more closely related to classic complaints lodged by citizens than the procedures in the immigration offices, where such complaints were relatively few and mostly related to secure residences, especially related to work permits. Regarding residence, both lawyers and caseworkers expressed the attitude that without a decision, people could at least not be deported.

The stark difference between the emotional underpinnings of the interactions between officials and applicants to German citizenship indicates two important issues: firstly, becoming a German citizen is not seen to be as important as becoming a secure and permanent resident by either caseworkers or immigrants. This is further supported by the relatively low numbers of naturalisation after the sea change in nationality law in 2000 (Geddes 2003; L. Morris 2000, 2002). Especially among long-established immigrants with secure residence, there appears to be no demand for Germanisation – especially at the expense of losing one's original citizenship (Mandel 2008). Thus secondly, the effort to gain citizenship happens in a completely different context. While the attainment of residence or fight against deportation often happens through a struggle with a system that is incomprehensible and overly powerful, the attainment of citizenship is a process initiated and undertaken by someone who is already used to dealing with the state and who knows his rights, for example regarding the unnecessary delay of decision-making. In other words, the findings indicate that the status of citizenship is of less relevance to the immigrant than the status of resident, and that prior to becoming German, the applicant has already become a member of German institutional life. If membership of German society is thus in practice not primarily associated with German citizenship, and residence is such an emotional issue, it is worth considering the ways in which immigrants might arrive at this stage of non-citizen membership, and the role the interactions in the immigration office might play in this through mechanisms of socialisation.

A Lasting Effect: Mechanisms of Socialisation

Beyond individual interactions, there are several factors that allude to the lasting effect of the interactions with the immigration office. As precarious cases are both immensely more complex and handled with greater variation than secure residences, immigrants without permits and new arrivals were subjected most to both unpredictable ways of case-working and immediate effect of the decisions made. As a result, it is on them that the impact of the immigration office could be assessed easiest.

In a few cases, I was 'fortunate' enough to observe applicants at different stages of the decision-making process and thus get to know them and their cases a little better. One of these clients was even more memorable by the fact that he was born on exactly the same day that I was, something I realised during a trip to the embassy of his country of origin where he is presented by the immigration office in order to get a temporary passport for his deportation. As I shared this information, he, the two caseworkers that accompany him and I started talking, reflecting on our very different lives and migration experiences. He explained that he understood why he was being deported, since he had gotten on the wrong track of things and been convicted several times. However, he also argued that he had never had a fair chance, and recounted his difficult relationship with state institutions. In this, he interchangeably used Germany and *ihr*, 'you'. When I ask who he meant by 'them', he replied 'well you Beamte (bureaucrats), the state, like the Ausländerbehörde. You never wanted me to get my rights (to residence), always found a reason to not allow me to stay'. He then told us that once, he had almost tricked 'you immigration office people' by finding a German girl who was willing to marry him, resulting in 'Germany' being unable to reject him any longer. The relationship had not worked out; he had been 'too stupid'. A few weeks later, I accompanied him and his caseworkers again, this time driving towards the airport, towards a 'home' that he has not seen for over a decade.

Two things stand out here: Firstly, the migrant felt that he had been denied a 'fair chance' that he thought he ought to have had. While laying the blame on others is perhaps understandable in such a situation and reflects 'techniques of neutralisation' among youth deviants (Sykes and Matza 1957, see also Chapter 6), the recounting of new hurdles always emerging once the last has been passed does reflect some of the practices in immigration offices. Throughout the process, the migrant claims to have felt unwanted, so that he could 'as well' not care about the law since he was on the wrong side of it anyway. Secondly, in his reflections on his case history, individual officials, the immigration office and the German state all become one, moulded into one massive – and malevolent – thing, 'Germany'. This pattern was confirmed in many cases during my interviews with lawyers and representatives for migrant support organisations, many of whom were first-generation migrants themselves. The Ausländerbehörde, in the imagination of immigrants, represents the state that acts unwelcoming, confusing, or with open arms towards them.

All offices had specific 'problematic groups', groups that shared an especially precarious legal situation to such a great extent that membership of that particular ethnic group was almost immediately associated with 'trouble' by caseworkers. Examples of these include Roma groups from Romania or the former Yugoslav

Republics, Iraqis, state-less immigrants from Syria or the Lebanon, or Vietnamese child migrants. Within these groups in particular, interactions with the immigration offices had had a lasting effect, as the precarious status of one generation of migrants was often inherited by the younger generations. In such cases, often a kind of stalemate of predicament had been reached, wherein an immigrant had no legal right to reside, but could also not be deported. In failing to obey their duty to cooperate as ascribed by section 82 of the Residence, migrants effectively waived every possibility of attaining a legal residence status in order to not be deported and remain in Germany. As reprimand, immigration offices regularly used their full rights to cut the social benefits of these migrants to less than €200 per month, deny any right to employment or further education, and arrange for housing in specific blocks that often lay isolated and without public transportation to the city centre. While not detained as in other European states including the UK, the 'problematic groups' were effectively cut off from the social life of the rest of the local community for years, and in some cases, for decades. Fortunately the number of such cases has been reduced drastically by the introduction of the 2005 Residence Act and its probationary residence permits; however, Middlestadt, Steelstadt and Metrostadt each still had a few thousand remaining cases to deal with. More importantly, even if members of these groups received a residence permit, their distrustful attitude toward the immigration office as well as their label as 'problematic' within the office remained.

In Steelstadt, the council department of youth welfare started an initiative to act as mediator between the Ausländerbehörde and members of a specific ethnic group with precarious residencies. Due to the stalemate between the immigration officials and migrants, almost no member of that group had been able to benefit from the change in residence legislation since the responsible caseworkers had decided that the prolonged failure in their duty to cooperate had made the migrants ineligible for residence permits. As well as taking part in some of these negotiations, which were dominated by distrust and reiterations of past wrongs both parties thought the other had committed, I interviewed the youth officers who had initiated the mediation. During the interviews, the officers explained the difficulty of 'breaking the ice' between the two parties, but also told me of their struggle to establish a relationship of trust with members of the ethnic group in their own work, since, as one officer put it, 'they think that every part of the administration is like the Ausländerbehörde', potentially malevolent.

The interactions between immigration office and migrant thus had a lasting impact not only over time, but also influenced the ways in which migrants approached other state institutions. While the above example is admittedly extreme, the evidence suggests that at least for precarious cases with regular contact with the Ausländerbehörde, the offices have a socialising impact that bears on the way in which immigrants interact with state institutions, with 'the state' in general.

That individuals are 'othered' through their status as immigrants and thus non-members of a national society has been a central theorem of the analysis of migration at least since the work on identity formation by Stuart Hall (Hall 1992). Similarly, regarding citizenship, Rogers Brubaker's work (1992) has analysed issues of belonging as both being inclusive (to members) and exclusive (to non-members). However, through the processing of individuals as cases, immigrants are not merely othered or excluded, but also subject to and part of the state apparatus. Through the lengthy process of interacting with officials in Ausländerbehörden, it is not only the outcome, the legal status that matters, but also the process of becoming, of being socialised into a migrant with a specific status. The sociological work of Elias Canetti (1962) has shown that any order or command does not only immediately force the person subjected to the order to react, but also impacts beyond the context of the command itself – the 'sting' reverberates. Since in immigration offices the orders issued are extremely far-reaching, allowing or disallowing the stay of an immigrant, it could be argued that the sting – the impact – of these commands is particularly enduring. This type of political or systemic socialisation – migrants retain their cultural, religious or gendered formations of identity – has received little academic attention so far, since for most social psychological approaches, political socialisation happens during childhood and adolescence (D.C. Schwartz and S.K. Schwartz 1975) and the sociological literature on the interaction between immigrants and state has mostly focused on issues of multiculturalism (Kymlicka 1997), stopped at the recognition of difference and analysis of exclusion (e.g. Hall 1992, Agamben 2005) or did not apply their concepts of hybridity to legal categories (Bhabha 1994). Czarniawska-Joerges (2002) has made a similar point regarding the making of communal identities in the advertising campaigns of city councils. The two most helpful approaches to explaining these mechanisms of socialisation are those of Erving Goffman on total institutions (1962) and Michel Foucault on discipline (1979) and biopolitics (2008).

Both Goffman and Foucault shared an interest in the institutionalised power of the modern state over relatively powerless subjects. While surely the totality of institutionalisation is significantly lower even among the most precarious immigrant groups of this study compared to the prison inmates of Foucault's Discipline and Punish (1991) or Goffman's inmates in Asylums (1962), they share a key characteristic: the power to intrude into and determine almost all aspects of life (Goffman 1961: 17). However more important are the mechanisms at work as identified by the authors. Although interested in the 'abnormalisation of the margins' (Bigo 2008), in both studies, institutions not merely impose an example to deter outsiders, but change the subject beyond the stay at the institution (Goffman 1961: 25, 336). Furthermore, while these subjects are socialised by an organisation, the socialisation does not necessarily take place as a result of an all-encompassing, conscious plan of a specific individual or group of people, but rather through individual interactions as well as a specific configuration of organisational order. Goffman (1961: 24–37) identifies five mechanisms that are formative to the mental career of a patient (see also Silverman 1975), all of which apply to the case of immigrants in the Ausländerbehörde: the office acts as barrier to full participation within society, revokes a sense of a full identity through the making of a 'case' that is interested in only very specific aspects of identity, includes interactions which can feel humiliating and in which the power of officials is enforced, and intrudes into the privacy of individuals. Goffman's concept of a career is similar to the internalisation process described by Foucault (2008), who also stresses techniques of delimitating access to full social life, intrusion of privacy through surveillance and representations of omnipotent institutional power (1991).

Through the varied, incomprehensible, sometimes arbitrary and often changing practices and patterns of order in the Ausländerbehörde, a migrant could be given the impression of being a burden, of being unwanted or troublesome. In return, office and thus the state is presented as inflexible, not understanding or caring for the individual's situation, as omnipotent beyond the limits of the law. The evidence suggests that at least for those immigrants who had regular exposure to the immigration office through regular interactions with officials, clients can 'get the impression', might internalise, that they count very little in the German administrative system, that they do not attain their right through due process but through fighting for it or resisting the pressures of the duty to cooperate. As individuals with a precarious legal status, they are on the margins of society, through interacting with the Ausländerbehörde, they appear to learn their place, and to behave accordingly: either with total deference, enduring the sometimes humiliating interactions with caseworkers, or resisting, because, as the deportee at the start of the section stated, they never had a chance anyway.

If this argument is true, immigration offices have a responsibility beyond determining who can stay, and why. If the effect of the official-client interactions goes beyond determining a legal status and includes a socialising or educating experience, immigration offices and their employees act as significant others to immigrants. The officials are thus representatives of the state as a whole, since the presentation of order and due process will greatly impact the immigrants' expectation of order and due process in the whole of the German state system.

In the light of this, and the 'representative' nature of the work of immigration offices as usually the first and main contact points immigrants have with 'the state', both the behaviour of some employees vis-à-vis their clients as well as the variations in decision-making between subdivisions appears relevant beyond a mere technical assessment of process. In many ways, the four Ausländerbehörden of this study are not institutions of service, but an opaque agencies of sometimes Kafkaesque proportions. A stark hierarchy of power perpetrates the Ausländerbehörde: a hierarchy between the autocratic bureaucrat and the powerless migrant dependant on the official's mercy. However, this hierarchy is not part of a racist or intentionally malevolent system, although it may well feel that way. Negative socialisation experiences are much more a product of a lack of conceptualisation than a conspiracy to subjectify.

A Call for a Shift of Attention: Residence Takes Precedent over Citizenship

Without going astray into an analysis of the social psychology of belonging, the findings of this work indicate that the emotions attached to the attainment of secure residence outweigh those of becoming a citizen of Germany. The fear and anxiety, desperation and anger expressed by immigrants in the interaction with caseworkers during consultations on residence law as well as the lasting effect these interactions have are clear signs that point to the fact that both the status of residence and the process of attaining it hold significance for the persons that attain and undergo it. This appears to be especially true for immigrants that remain in a precarious legal status over long periods of time. While the specific impact is not part of this study, two related conclusions can be drawn from the findings on the interactions between clients and applicants in residence and nationality law administration. Either, it could be that staying and participating in a national society is more relevant than belonging to its imagined community of fellow nationals. Or, it could even be that through staying and participating in a national society, belonging to it is attained as much or more than through attaining the status of fellow national. While the institutional role of shaping belonging in the context of immigration offices will be discussed separately in assertion three below, it is worth considering the impact of both conclusions for the study of integration and identity in multicultural and yet uni-national societies.

In the discussion of belonging, rights and minority groups, the legal status and thus access to belonging and rights is more often than not neglected, mostly because, following the great T.H. Marshall (T.H. Marshall 1950), the focus is on internal differentiations within national communities (Gilroy 1987; Kymlicka 1996 on Canada; Parekh 2008; Phillips 2007 on Britain) or, alternatively, because globalisation and human rights disperse national legal categories (Soysal 1994). If they do consider status, they tend to focus on citizenship as main means of organising belonging, following Brubaker's (1992) finding that citizenship both unifies (the nationals) and segregates (the non-nationals). Sassen's work on 'Guests and Aliens' (2000) is thus a great treatise on how immigrants are not equals because they are not full citizens, and other studies, too, follow the analysis of the lowly status of the denizen or metic (Kivisto and Faist 2007). Indeed, many studies on immigration and minority groups focus on the excluding effect techniques that labelling and differentiating have (Agamben 2005; Mamdani 1996; Hall 1992; Sadurski 2008). Unfortunately, very few studies move beyond the simple dichotomy of 'us' and 'them', of member and non-member. The evidence presented in this study suggests that within the German migration management system, the distinction is at least threefold: between us, those who are similar and the others. Indeed, even the most right-wing polemical nonsense is almost exclusively directed at new arrivals and not at the established descendants of guest workers (Eatwell and O'Sullivan 1992). However, the studies that allude to this point of stratification of rights and resident positions are rather few and tend to be very legalistic and avoiding of the issue of belonging, as well as often being relegated to the sidelines of academic debate (Gibney 2008; L. Morris 2002).

One of the few notable exceptions is Joppke, who rather accurately argues that 'citizenship' actually means very different things to very different academics and distinguishes between three key aspects, status, rights and identity, respectively referring to the legal position, to the access to liberties and protections of a state and to belonging (2010). In his discussion of recent developments in nationality he rightly argues that despite specific additional hurdles to individuals of Islamic background, there has been a move towards the liberalisation of attainment of a nationality in the West. Following Soysal (1994), he sees improved access to rights for residents, resulting in 'approximations of aliens to citizens' (Joppke 2010: 32), although recognising the stratified nature of these improvements in rights. Regarding belonging Joppke argues that citizenship remains a tool for both inclusion and exclusion and holds that access to citizenship is among the key issues for immigrants seeking to become full members of their host society. On this last issue, my results differ from Joppke's argument, and his first two points lend support to this perspective. Certainly in Germany, the liberalisation of citizenship came as a result of the – much belated – realisation that the immigrants who had settled in the state since the 1960s were there to stay, members of what constitutes 'Germany' and should attain the possibility to be recognised as such. The sea change in nationality law was thus a reaction to already existing social reality.

Secondly, exactly the approximation of denizens to citizens in their access to rights explains the low levels of naturalisation that followed the new legislation. The sea change was symbolic and, as Mandel (2008) argues, not far reaching enough since it does not allow for dual citizenship. In a Western block of societies where citizens seem to care less and less about their political rights of electing and being elected, it cannot be surprising that denizens are for the most part content with access to every other right. Indeed, as immigrants are increasingly allowed to participate in local elections and since 2005, there is an EU permanent residence permit that allows almost exactly the same freedom of movement to all EU citizens, one could argue that naturalisation will remain unattractive where dual nationality is not attainable. This could be true beyond Germany, as none of my fellow EU aliens residing on Thames or Tyne are considering becoming British in addition to their home citizenship, not even when they have realised that they are stuck with bland food and strong ale.

Belonging to the society of a nation state might thus simply be sufficient for many permanent residents, furthermore, the fact that issues of belonging do not stop after the change of passports might also explain the hesitance to and relative disregard of naturalisation. This is the lesson that the scholars of multiculturalism within relatively coherent societies of citizens point to, perhaps nowhere as vividly as in Gilroy's 'There ain't no black in the Union Jack' (1987). In the case of Germany, the phenomenon of not belonging despite being citizens is best illustrated by the case of ethnic German re-settlers from the former Soviet

Union, who immediately attained citizenship upon arrival in the late 1980s and early 1990s and yet struggle with being recognised as Germans (Bade and Oltmer 2003; Mandel 2008; Hüttermann 2010), feeling *fremd im eigenen Land*, 'foreign in one's own country', as vocalist Frederic Hahn of Advanced Chemistry rhapsodised in the early 1990s.

It is thus possible to have attained the status of citizen without belonging to the national community and also to belong without the proper status. I am not arguing here that due to certain esoteric globalising forces the state has lost its ability to decide over inclusion and exclusion, access and denial of rights; in fact, this book shows that the state still wields considerable power. Instead, the argument put forward here is that the focus on citizenship in much of academic engagement on the status of belonging is misleading, since it is the attainment of secure residence that has the most implications of rights and emotional attachment to it. For immigrants, 'can I stay' is more pressing and relevant than 'can I be part of your imagined community', especially since residence guarantees rights, while citizenship cannot guarantee belonging

Conclusion: Beyond People Processing

As the status of secure resident seems more important than the status of citizen, there is evidence that the process of becoming a resident holds an important and lasting impact and in many ways defines both the migrants' perception of the state and his role in relation to it. The findings indicate that the immigration office represents 'the state' to migrants. It is worth reminding oneself of the significance the Ausländerbehörde has for immigrants and the chaotic practices one finds within institutional structures. The impact of decisions made in the Ausländerbehörde is sometimes difficult to assess for people for whom – including the author – visa applications are part of an exotic holiday experience. Scheffer (2001) rightly argues that in countries with low naturalisation rates such as Germany, residence law is superior to all other non-constitutional laws, since it directly affects and regulates all aspects of life. The study has shown how procedural discretion often leads applicants on significant detours on the way to a residence permit, causing and enhancing unnecessary anxieties and prejudices. In order to secure a legal status that determines work and education, social welfare and family unification, applicants often have to participate in a labyrinth of arbitrariness of absurd dimensions. The Ausländerbehörde is in itself not racist or xenophobic – but it is far from being a provider of services. Veena Das' (2004) concept of illegibility helps to understand and contextualise this: what immigrants experience in the immigration office is thus more than chaos, it is an additional intransparent or 'magic' source of institutional power. In addition to holding a (relative) monopoly of power over means of normative violence, the dominance of states is thus expanded by practices that – often unintentionally – create illegibility and uncertainty. A state that by law can control one's life has a certain authority, a state that can legally overstep this law and which is unpredictable in its execution of order is worth fearing – and resisting. As in Kafka's stories, the autonomy to be arbitrary is not merely annoying, it is intimidating and, sometimes, humiliating.

The management of migration in German immigration offices is just more than mere 'people processing' in the way used by Prottas in his paradigmatic work (1979) or the edited volume of McKinley (1975). Clients are not merely turned into cases by bureaucracy in order to be categorised and thus processed according to set rules of modern stable rational administration, the turning into cases of residence has an impact beyond the actual decision made, as it also changes and defines the client vis-à-vis bureaucracy and hence, the state. Van Maanen (Maanen 1978) and Schwartz and Schwartz (1975) both allude to importance of the role of organisations as workplace in socialising or processing its members, but fail to expand these notions to the interaction between client and organisation. Building on Foucault, Gilroy (1987) has identified mechanisms of categorising race as technique of othering (Alderson 2009), and a similar argument can be made for categorisations within the legal management of migration. Agamben's work on marginalised groups and the state of exception (2005) further shows ways of containing unwanted elements and ruling beyond the rule of law. However, in immigration offices, migrants are not only excluded and made different, but also processed into resident-subjects. The comparison to Goffman's account of mechanisms of creating the inmate in total institutions (1962) has shown great similarities in the way the interactions between officials and clients in immigration offices drastically shape and alter the applicant's life and life possibilities. In addition, employing the work of Foucault (1991, 2008) has provided similar insights into the disciplining of unruly migrants, into the making of ordered, 'docile' subjects, but also trained our eye to acts of resistance to this ordering by stepping outside the framework of legal residence and accepting one's position as precarious other. A further similarity to both Goffman and Foucault is the fact that the impact of the Ausländerbehörde is greatest on those with the most precarious status.

Thus immigrants that are not 'wanted' for their skill and have misbehaved by irregularly coming to or staying in Germany are disciplined most, subjected to formal and informal techniques of dominance until – ideally, from the perspective of the immigration office – they are either docile and self-governed and ready to join the majority of denizens or successfully excluded and deported. The offices' great focus on *Mitwirkung*, the duty to cooperate as well as the expectation of reverence to due process and 'how things are done here' is symptomatic of this. Recent arrangements of probationary hardship residences might be more lenient in their allowance of residence, but the mechanism remains the same: the applicant can get a taste of 'proper' residence if he complies with the correct behaviour expected of a client to German state bureaucracy and continues to comply during his period of probation. Rather than the actual securing of livelihood, punctuality, proper documentation and self-identification as well as proof of successful interaction with other agencies – especially the employment centre – are decisive in passing for a hardship residence.

The immigration office is thus a total institution with open doors – since immigrants are always welcome to leave. The one thing that remains unclear in this account is the question of intentionality. My results show mechanisms of subjectification and discipline as outcome of the chaotic and 'magical' structures of immigration law administration that allow for both the increased importance of process in comparison to outcome and the stark variations in procedure found in Variations B, C and D of this study. Is the making of orderly immigrants an accepted or not reflected unintended consequence of mismanagement and federalism, or an intentional means of creating adequate members of German society? Not being a fan of conspiracy theories beyond Anglo-American pulp fiction, I tend to lean towards the former explanations, but do not have the means to prove this within the scope of this study. Perhaps, a genealogy of the management of migration would be timely.

Chapter 8
Understanding Policies from the Inside – A Summary

After queuing among strangers, being allocated a number, waiting in forlorn corridors and several barely comprehensible discussions with caseworkers, the five migrants of the introductory chapter leave the immigration office with mixed feelings and mixed results.

> Amira, the child that grew up in Germany without residence, was told that there was nothing the immigration office could do for her, and that she should consider leaving Germany voluntarily. This way, she would get monetary support from the German government, and be enlisted into a program that cares for repatriated immigrants like her, providing accommodation and assistance in finding a job in her country of birth. While this was not what she had wished for, a ray of hope had appeared in the form of a social worker, who, while accompanying another client, had talked to her about the possibility of appealing to the state ministry for a recognition of hardship. She has agreed to come and see the social worker in her office in the next few days.
>
> Yu, the chemistry student, was luckier. While legally, an internship would not suffice for him to attain a work residence, he qualifies for a probationary residence permit for one year that allows students to find a proper job while doing part-time work. After handing back his passport, the caseworker advises Yu to come back as soon as he has a job offer and not wait for the full year, as upgrading to a better residence status is always possible, and preferable.
>
> After his consultation with the Ausländerbehörde, Hassan finds himself in a catch-22 situation. He could get his work residence renewed, but only upon provision of a valid work contract – something his boss is only willing to supply once Hassan's residence is settled. The caseworker was quite adamant that while she could understand the dilemma, procedure had to be followed correctly and that no permit was granted in Germany on good faith alone. Now Hassan has to try to persuade his boss to give him a preliminary contract, which will not be easy as his boss is never pleased with the special arrangements he has to make for the only non-German employee in the firm. When he gets home, Hassan realises that with all the trouble over his own residence, he has forgotten to ask about the possibility of his wife and children joining him in Germany.

> In her attempt to stay with her daughter and grandchildren, Ursula was told that without securing her livelihood, she would not be able to attain a residence permit and would thus have to leave Germany after the expiration of her visa. However, having just become a grandmother for the first time herself, the caseworker is sympathetic, and suggests to Ursula that she could apply for residence and get a certificate of application which would be valid for three months. Since deciding such "difficult cases" usually took "a long time", who knew, maybe the immigration office would have to extend this certificate for another three months afterwards, and so on. Not sure if this is the best solution, Ursula is nevertheless happy to be able to stay in Germany longer.

> Saidi, Amira's brother, had to leave the immigration office after a quarrel with a caseworker. As a consequence, he is barred from entering the immigration office for a year and has to send a friend to renew his permit in the meantime. When he tells his lawyer about this, the lawyer fumes, and tells Saidi that this has not helped his situation as his reputation was now likely to cause the officials to decide against his application for residence.

In the past seven chapters, I have attempted to explain the 'inside' of immigration law: the processes and practices through which it is applied to individual cases as well as the structural and political factors that impact this implementation. I have shown that differences in application vastly exceed differences in interpretation of the legal basis, and that the paths to residence can vary greatly even when the same permit is obtained in the end. Ausländerbehörden, the focus of this study, have been revealed to be the site of political contest and structural derangement, of migrant formation and employee frustration and, most of the time, of a positive answer to the initial question asked in this study. Yes, people can stay, but under unclear conditions and as a result of non-transparent administrative procedures.

As the 'failure' of migration policies in their implementation is apparent, the mechanisms that lead to this failure are measurable and comparable. However, this requires us to go beyond the subfield of migration studies. When doing so, it becomes apparent that taking policies or the rhetoric surrounding the promulgation of legislation at face value is as naive as seeing the 'implementation game' (Bardach 1977) as a black box in which political intentions are 'somehow' lost. Similarly, scholars of law have to acknowledge that not all those who practise law are trained in the highbrow art of jurisprudence, but that law is also managed and coped with, felt and tamed rather than grasped and comprehended. As for bureaucracy, this study has shown that the most disorganised and informal practices – sharing information to gain a feeling for an appropriate solution – provided the greatest means of establishing accuracy and similarities in decision-making. To view people-processing organisations as mechanistic institutions of categorisations might thus be a gross oversimplification, since an ordered structure of work was not simply given in the Ausländerbehörden, but constantly had to be stabilised and produced. Furthermore, the ethical component required in making a human judgement should be stressed more in both academic analysis and practice.

Making Sense of the 'Black Box': Four Factors to Explain Implementation

This book has followed a specific ethnographic mode of enquiry: the key concern was to analyse law as practiced, cases as processed and organisations at work. Thus not so much the outcomes of social action, but the process of acting itself has been the focus of investigation and is at the heart of this work. I suggest a framework includes five elements, one mode of examination and four dimensions of explanation. It is useful to comparatively examine the levels of variation, not only regarding decisions made, but also regarding the patterns, interactions and processes that lead up to the decision. Moving beyond identifications of more or less discretion or more or less direct implementation, it is further necessary to consider four elements, namely a) the *legal basis* and its use, b) the *structures of offices* and interactions between officials and clients therein, c) outside actors' attempts of exerting *political influence* and internal responses to them, and d) the *strategies of coping* and dealing with responsibility adopted by officials themselves. Each of these have been discussed in a separate chapter, which will be briefly reviewed in the now following section.

Chapter 2 introduced the reader to what decision-making in Ausländerbehörden looks like and how differently the four offices went about their work. While it has been shown that much of the work in immigration offices is formulaic and repetitive, the example of 'marriages of convenience' has shown on how many different levels an application can be judged, handled, evaluated and decided differently. Thus implementing immigration law should be seen less as a straightforward process and more as a set of divergent practices which lead applicants on very different routes to residence. The second part of Chapter 2 addressed this issue and formulated four levels of variation that capture the essence of these different routes and routines. This study thus proposes that further than in measuring different outcomes (Variance A), the differences of work in immigration offices can be assessed through examining the process of making decisions (Variance B), the ways in which cases are handled in general (Variance C) and the political environment in which the decision-making process takes place (Variance D). Regarding the predictability of outcomes, the evidence suggests that in the majority of routine cases, applicants can be expected to receive the same decision notwithstanding the office they applied to. However, in cases in which migrants have insecure or precarious legal statuses, the variance in outcomes is rather high. Combined with the findings on Variations B, C and D, it appears that while most immigrants can count on a relatively reliable decision on their application, this is not a result of due process, since, as stated above, the routes to residence differ significantly both within and between offices.

Chapter 3 analysed both the legal basis of decision-making and the learning and use of law in immigration offices. It was found that in the case of German immigration legislation, the concept of 'the' law as a single document on which decisions are based and from which outcomes can be estimated is misleading. Instead, officials had to base their decisions on a great variety of sources with partially conflicting interpretations and directives, which were further undergoing constant change. This was illustrated by looking at two examples, the role of EU legislation and decisions by the European Court of Justice regarding the Ankara Agreement, and security checks as a measure of preventing terrorism. The second part of the chapter examined how officials – who were not trained law practitioners – dealt with this complex decision-making basis. Rather than institutional measures of managing knowledge – trainings or information databases – employees relied almost exclusively on oral and communal ways of learning and applying law. Not knowing the legal solution to a problematic case was not sanctioned, but regarded as normal. Instead of looking up an answer themselves, caseworkers shared their problems and found a solution in cooperation with their colleagues. In the four Ausländerbehörden studied in this book, the challenge posed by the multifarious and changing legal basis was met by experience, not in-depth textual analysis. This was also apparent in the use of discretion, which was always informal because the decision to exercise discretion was triggered through practical considerations and only seldom by specific legal formulations. Analysing law as challenge and its implementation as creative and communal thus explain both the low level of outcome variations in the majority of cases and the high level of variations in especially unsecure cases. Given that a collective knowledge based on experience governs decision-making in Ausländerbehörden, decisions are more reliable when many previous cases exist to refer to and, related to this, when the legal constellation is simple enough to make cases inherently comparable.

Chapter 4 provided an account of the structures of Ausländerbehörden and the ways in which clients were affected by them. A comparison of the four case studies, focusing on their overall structures as well as specific attempts to improve work routines, highlighted two findings: one, that subdivisions produced a high internal cohesion of practice within themselves, but also significant resistances to attempts to increase office-wide standards of procedure. The second finding showed that all four offices were undergoing continuous efforts of structural adjustment as a response to both organisational deficiencies and outside pressures. These cycles of reform and re-reform were not based on conceptualisations of good practice or performance indicators as modern accounts of new public management would expect, but rather directed at improving insufficiencies of the previous reform and phrased as part of a politically dictated programme in order to attain the necessary funds for structural change. Case working was thus not standardised partly because it did not take place in a stable environment.

Chapter 5 showed the Ausländerbehörden within their institutional and political context, and discussed ways in which different actors tried to intervene in the work routines and decision-making processes. Based on the examples of discussions around deportations and integration, attempts to exert political clout were examined on three levels: local public pressures, the influence of the city council and interventions from state ministries and courts. All three spheres of influence have been shown to be able to challenge both work routines and decisions made in the Ausländerbehörde, and particularly local alliances of NGOs, church organisations and the wider public have damaged the reputation of the offices and pressured the city councils to control the work of immigration offices. As a result of this, two of the four case studies have undergone a drastic structural and ideological renewal, supposedly to signify the new way in which immigrants are welcomed and treated by the German state. However, a closer analysis of the impact of these changes has shown that the main effect – and to a significant extent, also the main intention – of these renewals was not to actually change the practices within the offices, but to manage public opinion and reduce negative press coverage of the city administration. State ministries have been shown to be rather removed from the everyday problems and needs of immigration offices. Not being directly responsible for an oversight of due process, ministries tend to intervene mainly in delicate political situations, either to reduce damage or win public support. It was thus members of courts – as 'caretakers of the law' – who showed the most interest in Ausländerbehörden working properly and predictably, and who in their discussions of cases offered practical as well as legal support. The work in and of immigration offices is thus politically contested and susceptible to quite astounding local interventions, which help to explain the overall difference of the self-presentation of Ausländerbehörden as well as specific difference in Variance A, the outcomes of the decision-making process.

Chapter 6 analysed the final explanatory dimension suggested at the outset of this study: the officials. Through giving an account of the testing working conditions and the high levels of stress experienced by employees of the Ausländerbehörden, the first part of the chapter has contributed to an understanding of the difficulty of the task faced by officials on a daily basis. The subsequent analysis of coping strategies argued that the emotional distance and lack of empathy shown by officials were not primarily indicators of malice and anti-immigrant sentiments, but rather techniques of organisational survival. This argument should not be seen as an attempt to defend the brash and unpleasant conduct and attitude displayed by some caseworkers, but as an explanation of behaviour that is not necessarily inhumane and definitely human. Unfriendly conduct can thus be seen partly as a reaction to stress and difficult working conditions, but also explained by the lack of organisational stability that would sanction such actions. The discussion of the denial of responsibility that was widespread among officials confirms this claim: lacking mechanisms that held individuals accountable for their actions, responsibility evaporated as a result of 'problem of many hands'. Since a decision usually involved more than one caseworker and more than one level of hierarchy, questions of liability could be handed up or down, or blamed altogether on 'the system' and 'the law'. The few instances in which responsible behaviour was encouraged were based on informal group pressures and individual initiative or work ethics. The final section of the chapter focused on yet another outcome of the uncertainty imposed by both complex law and instable organisation: caseworkers had very different and usually very personal conceptions of success and accomplishment in work. Similar to the lack of a conceptualisation of 'performance' discussed in Chapter 5, caseworkers had to define their measures of self-worth and success in work themselves. Thus for many, the central issue was to get by.

As a result of my getting access to four different immigration offices and gaining the trust of their employees, this study has thus managed to gain a deeper level of understanding into the process of implementing immigration law than any of the previous efforts discussed. The framework of analysing law, structure, political context and individual actors has proved useful in accounting for the differences in practice found in the four Ausländerbehörden as presented in the four levels of variation in Chapter 2. A high level of triangulation was possible through the long period of fieldwork, its comparative design and the external validations through expert interviews and reports to the objects of study, who had the opportunity to react to and challenge my representation of their work. The findings and their explanations are thus subject to a high level of internal validity. The reader should be able to attain a clear insight into how and under which conditions immigration law is applied to individual cases in the German state administration system. Decisions are made in a somewhat chaotic and creative process that sometimes borders arbitrariness, but nevertheless predictable results are delivered most of the time. This process is influenced by the complexity and changing nature of German immigration law and communal techniques of applying it, by a weak internal coherence caused by ineffective and unstable organisational structures, by attempts to exert political influence from different levels, and by different coping strategies and abilities to deal with stress of individual officials.

It should thus not come as a surprise that through analysing practices, the author has come to the conclusion that practices matter. In addition to the issue of perspective and distance, the meagre sum of four case studies of course does not lend itself to be the basis of an overhauling of all there is to say about migration, law, or bureaucracy. Furthermore, the very particular offices (dealing with immigration) in a very particular administrative system (at the lowest end of German federalism) clearly cannot do justice even to the most 'typical' of complex organisations. However, they can help to question existing knowledge and open new pathways to analysing and explaining the complex system of migration management and state administration.

Conclusion: It is More Complicated

In Chapter 1, a definition of the task Ausländerbehörden have to fulfil was given; arguing that based on the job description included in section 71 of the 2005 Residence Act, the role of immigration offices was to execute the migration policy of the Federal Republic of Germany. Based on the findings of this study, this can be somewhat elaborated. The role of immigration offices is not only to execute a federal migration policy, but to take part in the interpretation and making of it. In them, law is not simply applied to cases, but also managed and defined. Similarly, applications are not simply processed through routine technical steps, but these routines have to be formed, and their measures of success defined.

The findings of this study show that examining only national documents when analysing migration policy is lacking in at least three ways. First, national legislation and the issuing of policies by federal governments are not the only origins of policies regarding migrations, and at least in the case of Germany, not always the motors of innovation. EU integration might not have replaced the nation state as prophets of regionalisation and globalisation foresaw in the 1980s and 1990s, but nevertheless wields an increasing influence over the policies of its member states. Especially the European Court of Justice, arguably the EU institution most freed from national ties, has forced national governments to change their approach especially regarding association law like the Ankara Agreement and human rights codes like the European Convention on Human Rights (Boswell and Geddes 2011). With the Lisbon Treaty granting the European Court of Justice even more say in even more issues, this court-based policy making is likely to stay for good.

The second complication of a narrow national policy view is the need to differentiate between rhetoric, intent and text. Taking policies or their political discussion at face value neglects the fact that legislation is always a compromise of different political opinions that has to be 'sold' to the public and contextualised within a greater political project (May and Winter 2009; Maynard-Moody 1989). The analysis of the German immigration law shows that while the intention of the 2005 Residence Act within the project of the centre-left Social Democrat/Green government was rather clear, political reality forced substantial amendments between its first draft in 2002 and its promulgation in 2004. As a result, the law had changed and been watered down by compromise so much that for practitioners, the actual direction and amount of change it brought is still debated, as Chapter 6 has shown. Nevertheless, it has been sold as the very same 'sea change' it was intended to be. Castles (2004), in examining why migration policies often seem to fail, alludes to this point by referring to the 'hidden agendas' of policy, implicating that text, rhetoric and intent can differ greatly. Thus in Germany labour migration continued despite the 'recruitment ban' of 1973 (Castles 2004), as the law actually still allowed for it. Similarly, the introduction of compulsory language courses can be seen as a means of integrating and welcoming immigrants or raising the barrier to new arrivals (Boswell and Geddes 2011). Without considering the different and often contradictory elements of 'policy', scholars are thus in danger of being misled.

Finally, as this and many other studies have shown, a policy is hardly ever fully implemented and almost always unevenly applied by different organisations. Indeed, the findings from the fieldwork show that the current Residence Act and administration system leave significant freedom to the local councils and their immigration offices both in interpreting the intention of the law (see Chapter 5) and applying it (see Chapter 3). Overall, most decisions might be congruent with the legal basis on which it is based. However, even for these cases, the way towards and the experience of attaining residence can differ greatly. This matters because it is more than a nuisance to applicants, as the interactions with immigration officials are likely play a major role in the socialisation of migrants into a state. Furthermore, these findings explicitly show the failure of federal migration policy to dictate a course in state-immigrant relations. Thus without an analysis of implementation, it is unclear just how much and where policies fail. This should not mean that the sole power to examine policies should lie with the ethnographers of their implementation, but that the lessons from such studies can assist other authors to adjust their wider, comparative perspective and that an awareness of and a sense for deviations through implementation can help to reduce the fallacy of representing national policy as an unqualified given.

Bibliography

Agamben, G. 2005. *State of Exception*. Chicago, IL: University of Chicago Press.

Alderson, C. 2009. 'Border Security/Border Securité'. In *A Foucault For The 21st Century: Governmentality, Biopolitics and Discipline in the New Millennium*, edited by S. Binkley and J. Capetillo Ponce. Cambridge: Cambridge Scholars Publishing.

Alexander, M. 2007. *Cities and Labour Immigration: Comparing Policy Responses in Amsterdam, Paris, Rome and Tel Aviv.* Aldershot: Ashgate.

Anderson, B. 2008. 'Migrants and work-related rights'. *Ethics and International Affairs* 22 (2): 199–204.

Anderson, B. and M. Ruhs 2010. 'Researching Illegality and Labour Migration'. *Population, Space and Place* 16 (3): 175–9.

Andrijasevic, R. 2006. 'How to Balance Rights and Responsibilities on Asylum at the EU's Southern Border of Italy and Libya'. Oxford: University of Oxford, COMPAS Working Papers. Available online: http://www.compas.ox.ac.uk/publications/Working%20papers/wp-06–27.shtml.

Armbruster, W. 2003. *Ausländerrecht für das Assessorexamen und die gerichtliche Praxis*. Villingen-Schwenningen: Neuer Medienverl.

Arnold, T.W. 1935. *The Symbols of Government*. New Haven, CT: Yale University Press.

Bade, K. and Jochen Oltmer 2003. *Resettlers: German Immigrants from Eastern Europe*. V&R Unipress.

Banakar, R. 1998. *The Doorkeepers of the Law: A Socio-Legal Study of Ethnic Discrimination in Sweden*. Aldershot: Dartmouth.

Bardach, E. 1977. *The Implementation Game: What Happens after a Bill Becomes a Law*. Cambridge, MA: MIT Press.

Behr, R. 2006. *Polizeikultur: Routinen, Rituale, Reflexionen: Bausteine zu einer Theorie der Praxis der Polizei*. Wiesbaden: VS Verlag.

Benz, M. and H. Schwenken 2005. 'Jenseits von Autonomie and Kontrolle: Migration als eigensinnige Praxis'. *Prokla* 140 (35 (3)): 363–78.

Bhabha, H.K. 1994. *The Location of Culture*. London: Routledge.

Blau, P.M. and M.W. Meyer 1971. *Bureaucracy in Modern Society*. 2nd edn. Random House studies in sociology SS12. New York: Random House.

Bloch, A., N. Sigona, and R. Zetter 2011. 'Migration Routes and Strategies of Young Undocumented Migrants in England: a Qualitative Perspective'. *Ethnic & Racial Studies* 34 (8) (August): 1286–302.

Bojadžijev, M. and S. Karakayalı. 2007. 'Autonomie der Migration. 10 Thesen zu einer Methode'. In *Turbulente Ränder. Neue Perspektiven auf Migration*

an den Grenzen Europas, edited by Transit Migration Forschungsgruppe, 2. Aufl., 203–10. Bielefeld: Transcript.
Bommes, M. 2003. 'Der Mythos vom transnationalen Raum'. In *Migration im Spannungsfeld von Globalisierung und Nationalstaat*, 90–116. Opladen: Westdeutscher Verlag.
Boswell, C., and A. Geddes 2011. *Migration and Mobility in the European Union.* European Union series. Basingstoke: Palgrave Macmillan.
Bosworth, Mary 2011. 'Deportation, detention and foreign-national prisoners in England and Wales'. *Citizenship Studies* 15 (5): 583–95.
Bouchard, G., and B.W. Carroll 2002. 'Policy-making and administrative discretion: the case of immigration in Canada'. *Canadian Public Administration* 45 (2): 239–57.
Bovens, M. 1998. *The Quest for Responsibility: Accountability and Citizenship in Complex Organisations*. Cambridge: Cambridge University Press.
Brochmann, G. and T. Hammar 1999. Mechanisms of Immigration Control: A Comparative Analysis of European Regulation Policies. Oxford: Berg.
Brubaker, R. 1992. *Citizenship and Nationhood in France and Germany*. Boston, MA: Harvard University Press. Available online: http://search.ebscohost.com/login.aspx?direct=true&db=ioh&AN=1114092&site=ehost-live&scope=site.
Brunsson, N. 1985. *The Irrational Organization: Irrationality as a Basis for Organizational Action and Change*. Chichester: Wiley.
Brunsson, N. 1989. *The Organization of Hypocrisy: Talk, Decisions, and Actions in Organizations*. Chichester: Wiley.
Brunsson, N. 2009. *Reform as Routine: Organizational Change in the Modern World*. Oxford: Oxford University Press.
Bundesamt für Migration und Flüchtlinge 2009. *Ausländerzahlen 2008*. Nürnberg: BAMF.
Burman, J. 2006. 'Absence, "removal", and everyday life in the diasporic city: antidetention/antideportation activism in Montréal'. *Space and Culture* 9 (3): 279–93.
Buruma, I. 2007. *Murder in Amsterdam: The Death of Theo van Gogh and the Limits of Tolerance*. London: Atlantic.
Calavita, K. 1998. 'Immigration, Law, and Marginalization in a Global Economy: Notes from Spain'. *Law and Society Review* 32 (4): 529–66.
Canetti, E. 1962. *Crowds and Power*. London: Gollancz.
Carling, J. 2007. 'Migration Control and Migrant Fatalities at the Spanish-African Borders'. *International Migration Review* 41 (2): 316–43.
Carr, M. 2012. *Fortress Europe: Dispatches from a Gated Continent*. London: Hurst & Company.
Castles, S. 2004. 'Why migration policies fail'. *Ethnic and Racial Studies* 27 (2): 205–27.
Castles, S. and M.J. Miller 2009. *The Age of Migration International Population Movements in the Modern World*. 4th edn. Basingstoke: Palgrave Macmillan.

Certeau, M. de 1984. *The Practice of Everyday Life*. Berkeley: University of California Press.

Coleman, M. 2008. 'US immigration law and its geographies of social control: lessons from homosexual exclusion during the cold war'. *Environment and Planning D* 26 (6): 1096–114.

Collyer, M. 2010. 'Stranded Migrants and the Fragmented Journey'. *Journal of Refugee Studies* 23 (3): 273–93.

Cooper, R. 1986. 'Organization/Disorganization'. *Social Science Information* 25 (2) (June 1): 299–335.

Cooper, R. 1987. 'Information, Communication and Organisation: A Post-Structural Revision'. *The Journal of Mind and Behavior* 8 (3): 395–416.

Cooper, R. and G. Burrell 1988. 'Modernism, Postmodernism and Organizational Analysis: An Introduction'. *Organization Studies* 9 (1): 91 –112.

Cotterrell, R. 2006. *Law, Culture and Society: Legal Ideas in the Mirror of Social Theory*. Law, justice, and power. Aldershot: Ashgate.

Council of Europe 2013. *Handbook on European Law Relating to Asylum, Borders and Immigration*. Luxembourg: Publications Office of the European Union.

Cyrus, N. and D. Vogel 2003. 'Work-permit decisions in the German labour administration: an exploration of the implementation process'. *Journal of Ethnic and Migration Studies* 29 (2): 225–56.

Czarniawska-Joerges, B. 2002. *A Tale of Three Cities: Or the Glocalization of City Management/Barbara Czarniawska*. Oxford: Oxford University Press.

Das, V. 2004. 'The Signature of the State: The Paradox of Illegibility'. In *Anthropology in the Margins of the State*, edited by V. Das and D. Poole. School of American Research advanced seminar series. Santa Fe: Oxford: School of American Research Press; James Currey.

Davy, U. 2008. 'Einbürgerung in Deutschland – blinde Flecken in einem Rechtsstaat'. *Die Verwaltung* 41 (1): 31–62.

De Genova, N. and N. Peutz 2010. *The Deportation Regime Sovereignty, Space, and the Freedom of Movement*. Durham, NC: Duke University Press.

De Haas, H. 2008. *Irregular Migration from West Africa to the Maghreb and the European Union: An Overview of Recent Trends*. 32. International Organization for Migration. Available online: http://www.starappeal.unhcr.org/49e479ca0.pdf.

Dienelt, K. 2009. 'Ist die Visapflicht für türkische Staatsangehörige durch die Rechtsprechung des EuGH entfallen?' Available online: http://www.aufenthaltstitel.de/fremdinhalte/20090416_Einreisebestimmungen_Tuerkei.pdf.

Dienelt, K., ed. 2010. *Deutsches Ausländerrecht*. 2. Aufl. München: Deutscher Taschenbuchverlag.

Dollinger, F. and S. Speckmeier 2007. *Ausländerrecht: Eine fallorientierte Darstellung für Praxis und Ausbildung*. Heidelberg: Müller.

Doomernik, J. and M. Jandl, eds 2008. *Modes of Migration Regulation and Control in Europe*. IMISCOE reports. Amsterdam: Amsterdam University Press.

Dubois, V. 2010. *The Bureaucrat and the Poor Encounters in French Welfare Offices*. Burlington, VT: Ashgate.

Durkheim, E. 1915. *The Elementary Forms of the Religious Life: A Study in Religious Sociology*. London: George Allen & Unwin.

Düvell, F. 2006a. 'Crossing the Fringes of Europe: Transit Migration in the EU's Neighbourhood'. *COMPAS, Centre on Migration, Policy and Society* Working Paper 33: 1–33.

Düvell, F. 2006b. *Illegal Immigration in Europe: Beyond Control?* Palgrave Macmillan.

Eatwell, R. and N. O'Sullivan, eds 1992. *The Nature of the Right: European and American Politics and Political Thought since 1789*. Themes in right-wing ideology and politics series. London: Pinter.

Edwards, G.C. 1980. *Implementing Public Policy*. Washington, DC: Congressional Quarterly Press.

Ehrlich, E. 1975. *Fundamental Principles of the Sociology of Law*. New York: Arno Press.

Ellermann, A. 2006. 'Street-level democracy: how immigration bureaucrats manage public opposition'. *West European Politics* 29 (2): 293–309.

Ellermann, A. 2009. *States against Migrants: Deportation in Germany and the United States*. Cambridge: Cambridge University Press.

Extraterritorial Immigration Control Legal Challenges 2010. Immigration and asylum law and policy in Europe vol. 21. Leiden: Martinus Nijhoff Publishers.

Fahrmeir, A. 2000. *Citizens and Aliens Foreigners and the Law in Britain and the German States, 1789–1870*. New York: Berghahn Books.

Farnham, D and S. Horton 1993. *Managing the New Public Services*. Basingstoke: Macmillan.

Fauser, M. 2012. *Migrants and Cities: The Accommodation of Migrant Organizations in Europe*. Farnham: Ashgate.

Feldman, G. 2012. *The Migration Apparatus: Security, Labor, and Policymaking in the European Union*. Stanford, CA: Stanford University Press.

Fischer, R. 2012. *The Europeanization of Migration Policy: The Schengen Acquis between the Priorities of Legal Harmonization and Fragmentation*. European university studies. Series 31, Political science Vol. 616. Frankfurt am Main: Peter Lang.

Fisher, H.D. 2009. *The German Legal System and Legal Language: A General Survey Together with Notes and German Vocabulary*. 4th edn. London; New York: Routledge-Cavendish.

Flynn, N. 1997. *Public Sector Management*. 3rd edn. London: Prentice Hall/ Harvester Wheatsheaf.

Foucault, M. 1979. *Discipline and Punish: The Birth of the Prison*. Harmondsworth: Penguin Books.

Foucault, M. 2008. *The Birth of Biopolitics: Lectures at the Collège De France, 1978–79*. New York: Palgrave Macmillan.

Geddes, A. 2003. *The Politics of Migration and Immigration in Europe*. Sage politics texts. London: SAGE Publications.

Geiger, M. and A. Pécoud, eds 2010. *The New Politics of Migration Management: Actors, Discourses and Practices.* 1st edn. Springer.

Geyer, F. 2009. 'EU-Türkei: Stillhalteklausel bewirkt Recht auf visumfreie Einreise für Dienstleister, egal was in der EU-Visum-VO steht'. *Anwaltsnachrichten Ausländer- und Asylrecht* No 2/2009: 11.

Gibney, M.J. 2008. *Who Should Be Included? Noncitizens, Conflict and the Constitution of the Citizenry*. Basingstoke: Palgrave Macmillan.

Gilroy, P. 1987. *'There ain't no black in the Union Jack': The Cultural Politics of Race and Nation*. London: Hutchinson.

Goffman, E. 1962. *Asylums: Essays on the Social Situation of Mental Patients and Other Inmates*. An Aldine library edition. Chicago, IL: Aldine Pub. Co.

Groß, T. 2004. 'Germany'. In *Migration and Asylum Law and Policy in the European Union: FIDE 2004 National Reports*, edited by I. Higgins and K. Hailbronner. Cambridge: Cambridge University Press.

Gruszczak, A. 2012. 'Immigration control and securing the EU's external borders'. In *The EU's Shifting Borders Theoretical Approaches and Policy Implications in the New Neighbourhood*, edited by E. Stadtmüller and K. Bachmann. Routledge/GARNET series: Europe in the world 16. London: Routledge.

Guild, E. and S. Peers 2001. 'Deference or Defiance? The Court of Justice's Jusrisdiction over Immigration and Asylum'. In *Implementing Amsterdam: Immigration and Asylum Rights in EC Law*, edited by E. Guild and C. Harlow. Oxford: Hart.

Guiraudon, V. 2000. 'European Courts and Foreigners' Rights: A Comparative Study of Norms Diffusion'. *International Migration Review* 34 (4): 1088. doi:10.2307/2675976.

Guiraudon, V. and C. Joppke 2001. 'Controlling a New Migration World'. In *Controlling a New Migration World.* London: Routledge.

Hague, R. and M. Harrop 2007. *Comparative Government and Politics: An Introduction.* 7th edn. Basingstoke: Palgrave Macmillan.

Hailbronner, K. 2008. *Asyl- und Ausländerrecht.* 2., Óberarb. Aufl. Stuttgart: Kohlhammer.

Hall, S. 1992. 'The question of cultural identity'. *Modernity and its Futures*, edited by T. McGrew, S. Hall and D. Held, 273–326. Cambridge: Polity Press.

Hess, S. and B. Kasparek 2010. *Grenzregime Diskurse, Praktiken, Institutionen in Europa*. Berlin: Assoziation A.

Hess, S. and V. Tsianos 2007. 'Europeanizing Transnationalism! Provincializing Europe! – Konturen eines neuen Grenzregimes'. In *Turbulente Ränder. Neue Perspektiven auf Migration an den Grenzen Europas*, edited by Transit Migration Forschungsgruppe, 2. Aufl., 23–38. Bielefeld: Transcript.

Hiebaum, C. 2004. *Die Politik des Rechts: eine Analyse juristischer Rationalität.* Berlin [u.a.]: de Gruyter.

Hobbs, D. 1988. *Doing the Business: Entrepreneurship, the Working Class and Detectives in the East End of London*. Oxford: Clarendon Press.

Hofmann, H. and R. Hofmann 2008. *Ausländerrecht: AufenthG, FreizügG EU, AsylVfG, StAG: Handkommentar*. Baden-Baden: Nomos.
Hood, C. and C. Scott, eds 2000. *Regulating Government in a 'Managerial' Age: Towards a Cross-National Perspective*. Discussion paper no. 1. London: Centre for Analysis of Risk and Regulation; London School of Economics and Political Science.
Hruschka, C. 2011. "Dublin' und seine Auswirkungen auf das Asylwesen'. *terra cognita* 18: 102–5.
Hussain, N. 2003. *The Jurisprudence of Emergency: Colonialism and the Rule of Law*. Law, meaning, and violence. Ann Arbor, MI: University of Michigan Press.
Hüttermann, J. 2010. *Entzündungsfähige Konfliktkonstellationen: Eskalations- und Integrationspotentiale in Kleinstädten der Einwanderungsgesellschaft*. Weinheim: Juventa Verlag Gmbh.
Janis, I.L. 1972. *Victims of Groupthink; A Psychological Study of Foreign-Policy Decisions and Fiascoes*. Boston, MA: Houghton, Mifflin.
Jones, C., R. Munro, P. Hancock, and M. Tyler, eds 2005. 'Gibson Burrell: Diabolical architect'. In *Contemporary Organization Theory*. Sociological review monographs. Malden, MA; Oxford: Blackwell Publishing/ Sociological Review.
Joppke, C. 1999. *Immigration and the Nation-State: The United States, Germany, and Great Britain*. Oxford: Oxford University Press.
Joppke, C. 2010. *Citizenship and Immigration*. Cambridge: Polity Press.
Jordan, G. 1994. *The British Administrative System: Principles Versus Practice*. London: Routledge.
Juss, S.S. 1997. *Discretion and Deviation in the Administration of Immigration Control*. Modern legal studies. London: Sweet & Maxwell.
Kanstroom, D. 2000. 'Deportation, social control, and punishment: some thoughts about why hard laws make bad cases'. *Harvard Law Review* 113 (8): 1890–935.
Katz, E., ed. 1973. *Bureaucracy and the Public: A Reader in Official-Client Relations*. New York: Basic Books.
Kivisto, P. and T. Faist 2007. *Citizenship: Discourse, Theory, and Transnational Prospects*. Key themes in sociology. Malden, MA: Oxford: Blackwell.
Klepp, S. 2011. *Europa zwischen Grenzkontrolle und Flüchtlingsschutz. Eine Ethnographie der Seegrenze auf dem Mittelmeer*. Kultur und soziale Praxis. Bielefeld: Transcript.
Koslowski, R., ed. 2011. *Global Mobility Regimes*. New York: Palgrave Macmillan.
Kshīrasāgara, R. 1986. *Untouchability in India: Implementation of the Law and Abolition*. New Delhi: Deep & Deep Publications.
Kymlicka, W. 1996. *Multicultural Citizenship: A Liberal Theory of Minority Rights*. Oxford: Clarendon Press.
Lahav, G. and V Guiraudon 2006. 'Actors and venues in immigration control: closing the gap between political demands and policy outcomes'. *West European Politics* 29 (2): 201–25.

Lautmann, R. 1972. *Justiz – die stille Gewalt*. Frankfurt am Main: Athenäum-Fischer-Taschenbuch-Verl.

Lee, R.A, and P.A. Lawrence 1985. *Organizational Behaviour: Politics at Work*. Hutchinson management studies. London: Hutchinson.

Lemberg-Pedersen, M. 2012. 'Forcing Flows of Migrants: European Externalization and Border-Induced Displacement'. In *The Border Multiple. The Practicing of Borders Between Public Policy and Everyday Life in a Re-Scaling Europe*, edited by D. Jagetic Andersen, 35–53. Farnham: Ashgate.

Leun, J. 2006. 'Excluding illegal migrants in the Netherlands: between national policies and local implementation'. *West European Politics* 29 (2): 310–26.

Linstead, S. 1993. 'Deconstruction in the study of organizations'. In *Postmodernism and Organizations*, edited by J. Hassard and M. Parker. London: Sage.

Maanen, J. van 1978. 'People processing: Strategies of organizational socialization'. *Organizational Dynamics* 7 (1): 18–36.

Mamdani, M. 1996. *Citizen and Subject: Contemporary Africa and the Legacy of Late Colonialism*. Princeton studies in culture/power/history. Princeton, NJ: Princeton University Press.

Mandel, R.E. 2008. *Cosmopolitan Anxieties: Turkish Challenges to Citizenship and Belonging in Germany*. Durham, NC: Duke University Press.

March, J.G., V.E. Baier, and H. Saetren 1988. 'Implementation and ambiguity'. In *Decisions and Organizations*, 458. Oxford: Basil Blackwell.

March, J.G, and H.A. Simon 1958. *Organizations*. New York: John Wiley & Sons.

Marshall, B. 2000. *The New Germany and Migration in Europe*. Europe in change. Manchester: Manchester University Press.

Marshall, T.H. 1950. *Citizenship and Social Class, and Other Essays*. Cambridge: Cambridge University Press.

Martin, P. 2003. *Bordering on Control Combating Irregular Migration in North America and Europe*. ION migration research series No. 13 (2003). Geneva: IOM.

Massey, D.S. 1998. 'March of folly'. *American Prospect* 37: 22.

May, P.J. and S.C. Winter 2009. 'Politicians, Managers, and Street-Level Bureaucrats: Influences on Policy Implementation'. *Journal of Public Administration Research & Theory* 19 (3): 453–76.

Maynard-Moody, S. 1989. 'Beyond implementation – developing an institutional theory of administrative policy making'. *Public Administration Review* 49 (2): 137–41.

McKinlay, J. 1975. 'Clients and Organizations'. In *Processing People: Cases in Organizational Behaviour*, edited by J. McKinlay. London; New York: Holt, Rinehart and Winston.

Mead, G.H. 1967. *Mind, Self, and Society: From the Standpoint of a Social Behaviorist*. Works of George Herbert Mead v. 1. Chicago; London: University of Chicago Press.

Menz, G. 2011. *The Political Economy of Managed Migration Nonstate Actors, Europeanization, and the Politics of Designing Migration Policies*. 1st paperback edn. Oxford: Oxford University Press.

Moore, S. Falk 1978. *Law as Process: An Anthropological Approach*. London: Routledge & Kegan Paul.

Morris, L. 2000. 'Rights and Controls in the Management of Migration: The Case of Germany'. *The Sociological Review* 48 (2) (Mai 1): 224–40.

Morris, L. 2002. *Managing Migration: Civic Stratification and Migrants' Rights*. London: Routledge.

Morris, M.D. 1985. *Immigration: The Beleaguered Bureaucracy*. Washington, DC: Brookings Institution.

Niederberger, J.M. and N. Wichmann 2004. *Prävention irregulärer Migration*. Forschungsbericht/Schweizerisches Forum für Migrations- und Bevölkerungsstudien 34. Neuchâtel: SFM, Schweizerisches Forum für Migrations- und Bevölkerungsstudien.

Nijhawan, M. 2005. 'Deportability, medicine, and the law'. *Anthropology and Medicine* 12 (3): 271–86.

Oezcan, V. 2004. *Germany: Immigration in Transition*. Berlin: Social Science Center.

Parekh, B.C. 2000. *Rethinking Multiculturalism: Cultural Diversity and Political Theory*. Cambridge, MA: Harvard University Press.

Patton, M. Quinn 2002. *Qualitative Research and Evaluation Methods*. 3rd edn. Thousand Oaks, CA: Sage Publications.

Pécoud, A. and M. Geiger 2011. *The New Politics of Migration Management: Actors, Discourses and Practices*. London: Springer.

Perrow, C. 1979. *Complex Organizations: A Critical Essay*. 2nd edn. Glenview, IL: Scott, Foresman.

Peters, B.G. 2001. *The Politics of Bureaucracy*. 5th edn. London: Routledge.

Peutz, N. 2006. 'Embarking on an anthropology of removal'. *Current Anthropology* 47 (2): 217–42.

Peutz, N. 2007. 'Out-laws: deportees, desire, and the law'. *International Migration* 45 (3): 182–91.

Phillips, A. 2007. *Multiculturalism Without Culture*. Princeton, NJ: Princeton University Press.

Prottas, J. Manditch 1979. *People Processing: The Street-Level Bureaucrat in Public Service Bureaucracies*. Lexington, MA: Lexington Books.

Rahodi, C. 2002. *Influence & Accountability*. London: One World.

Rinus, P., K. Kraal, M. Martiniello, and S. Vertovec, eds 2004. *Citizenship in European Cities: Immigrants, Local Politics and Integration Policies,* edited by R. Penninx et al. Aldershot: Ashgate.

Rubin, A. and E.R. Babbie 2009. *Essential Research Methods for Social Work*. Stamford, CT: Cengage Learning.

Sadurski, W. 2008. *Equality and Legitimacy*. Oxford: Oxford University Press.

Sassen, S. 2000. *Guests and Aliens*. New York: New Press.

Satyamurti, C. 1981. *Occupational Survival*. Oxford: Basil Blackwell.

Scheffer, T. 2001. *Asylgewährung*. Stuttgart: Lucius & Lucius.

Scheffer, T. 2007. 'Event and process: an exercise in analytical ethnography'. *Human Studies* 30 (3): 167–97.

Scheffer, T., K. Hannken-Illjes, and A. Kozin 2010. *Criminal Defence and Procedure: Comparative Ethnographies in the United Kingdom, Germany, and the United States*. Basingstoke: Palgrave Macmillan.

Schiffauer, W. 2006. 'Enemies within the Gates – The Debate about the Citizenship of Muslims in Germany'. In *Multiculturalism, Muslims and Citizenship: a European Approach*, edited by T. Modood and A. Triandafyllidou. London: Routledge.

Schmahl, L. 1995. 'Die deutsche Einwanderungspolitik'. In *Festung oder offene Grenzen*, edited by M. Piazolo and K. Grolsch. München: Akademischer Verlag.

Schönig, W. and A. Bröker 2004. 'Evaluation of employment promotion in co-operation projects – Re-integration, fiscal benefit and personal advantage'. *Sozialer Fortschritt* 53 (5): 126–30.

Schuback, M. 2002. *Die Ausweisung nach dem Ausländergesetz in der Rechtsprechungskonzeption der Gerichte: unter besonderer Berücksichtigung verfassungsrechtlicher und völkerrechtlicher Maßstäbe*. Frankfurt am Main: Lang.

Schuster, L. 2011. 'Turning Refugees into 'Illegal Migrants': Afghan Asylum Seekers in Europe'. *Ethnic & Racial Studies* 34 (8) (August): 1392–407.

Schwartz, D.C., and S. Kenyon Schwartz, eds 1975. *New Directions in Political Socialization*. New York: London: Free Press; Collier Macmillan Publishers.

Sciortino, G. 2004. 'Between Phantoms and Necessary Evils. Some Critical Points in the Study of Irregular Migration to Western Europe'. *IMIS-Beiträge: Migration and the Regulation of Social Integration* 24: 17–43.

Seiffarth, O. 2011. 'The Development of the European Border Surveillance System (EUROSUR)'. In *A Threat against Europe? Security, Migration and Integration*, edited by P. Burgess and S. Gutwirth. Brussels: IES.

Sennett, R. 2006. *The Culture of the New Capitalism*. The Castle lectures in ethics, politics, and economics. New Haven, CT: Yale University Press.

Sewell, G., and J. Barker 2006. 'Weberian thought and the analysis of work'. In *Social Theory at Work*, edited by M. Korczynski, R. Hodson, and P.K. Edwards. Oxford: Oxford University Press.

Sieveking, K. 2001. 'Security of Residence and Expulsion: The German Experience'. In *Security of Residence and Expulsion: Protection of Aliens in Europe*, edited by E. Guild and P. Minderhoud. The Hague: Kluver Law.

Silverman, D. 1975. 'Accounts of Organizations'. In *Processing People: Cases in Organizational Behaviour*, edited by J. McKinlay. London; New York: Holt, Rinehart and Winston.

Softe, W. 1998. 'Evaluation and Measurement of Government Performance'. In *Government and Accountability*, edited by R. Boyle and G. McNamarra. Dublin: Institute of Public Administration.

Soysal, Y. 1994. *Limits of Citizenship: Migrants and Postnational Membership in Europe*. Chicago, IL: University of Chicago Press.

Statistisches Bundesamt 2007. *Bevölkerung mit Migrationshintergrund – Ergebnisse des Mikrozensus 2007*. Wiesbaden: Statistisches Bundesamt.

Statistisches Bundesamt 2011. *Bevölkerung und Erwerbstätigkeit*. Wiesbaden: Statistisches Bundesamt.

Sykes, O.M., and D. Matza 1957. 'Techniques of neutralization: a theory of delinquency'. *American Sociological Review*: 664–70.

Thompson, D.F. 1980. 'Moral responsibility of public officials: the problem of many hands'. *American Political Science Review* 74 (4): 905–16.

Thym, D., and F. Snyder, eds 2011. *Europe – A Continent Of Immigration? Legal Challenges in the Construction of European Migration Policy 7th International Workshop for Young Scholars (WISH) Défis Juridiques Dans La Construction De La Politique Européenne De Migration 7e Rencontre Internationale Des Jeunes Chercheurs (RIJC)*. Travaux du CERIC 24. Bruxelles: Bruylant.

Töpfer, S. 2002. *Diskriminierung durch Gesetze, Vorschriften und Richtlinien*. Duisburg: University of Duisburg, Dissertation.

TRANSIT MIGRATION Forschungsgruppe 2007. *Turbulente Ränder: Neue Perspektiven auf Migration an den Grenzen Europas*. 2. A. Bielefeld: Transcript.

Triandafyllidou, A. 2003. 'Immigration policy implementation in Italy: organisational culture, identity processes and labour market control'. *Journal of Ethnic and Migration Studies* 29 (2): 257–98.

Triandafyllidou, A., and M. Illies 2010. 'EU Irregular Migration Policies'. In *Irregular Migration in Europe: Myths and Realities*, edited by A. Triandafyllidou. Farnham: Ashgate.

Varsanyi, M. 2010. *Taking Local Control: Immigration Policy Activism in U.S. Cities And States*. Stanford, CA: Stanford University Press.

Weber, M. 1968. *Economy and Society; an Outline of Interpretive Sociology*. New York: Bedminster Press.

West, M.D. 2005. *Law in Everyday Japan: Sex, Sumo, Suicide, and Statutes*. Chicago, IL: University of Chicago Press.

Westphal, V. 2009. 'Visumfreie Einreise von türkischen Staatsangehörigen'. Available online: http://www.aufenthaltstitel.de/fremdinhalte/20090416_Einreisebestimmungen_Tuerkei.pdf.

Westphal, V., and E. Stoppa 2001. *Ausländerrecht für die Polizei: Erläuterungen zum Ausländer- und Asylrecht unter Berücksichtigung des Europarechts und des Schengener ... Bundesgrenzschutz und die Polizei der Länder*. 2. Aufl. Westphal, Volker, u. Edgar Stoppa.

Wicker, H.-R. 2012. 'Das Ausschaffungsregime: Die juristische, institutionelle und soziale Konstruktion von Illegalität in der Schweiz'. In *Migration, Differenz, Recht und Schmerz. Sozialanthropologische Essays zu einer sich verflüchtigenden Moderne, 1990–2010*, edited by Hans-Rudolf Wicker, 115–34. Zürich: Seismo Verlag.

Willen, S.S. 2007. 'Exploring 'illegal' and 'irregular' migrants' lived experiences of law and state power'. *International Migration* 45 (3): 2–7.

Wilsher, D. 2004. 'The administrative detention of non-nationals pursuant to immigration control: international and constitutional law perspectives'. *International and Comparative Law Quarterly* 53 (4): 897–934.

Woodhouse, D. 1997. *In Pursuit of Good Administration: Ministers, Civil Servants, and Judges*. Oxford: Clarendon; Oxford University Press.

Wunderlich, T. 2005. *Die Neuen Deutschen: Subjektive Dimensionen Des Einbürgerungsprozesses*. Stuttgart: Lucius & Lucius.

Zaiotti, R. 2011. *Cultures of Border Control Schengen and the Evolution of European Frontiers*. Chicago, IL: University of Chicago Press.

Zincone, G. 2011. 'Conclusion'. In Migration Policymaking in Europe the Dynamics of Actors and Contexts in Past and Present 2011. IMISCOE research. Amsterdam: Amsterdam University Press.

Index

RESEARCH IN MIGRATION AND ETHNIC RELATIONS SERIES

Full series list

European Immigration
A Sourcebook
Edited by Anna Triandafyllidou and Ruby Gropas

Ethnic Diversity and Social Cohesion
Immigration, Ethnic Fractionalization and Potentials for Civic Action
Merlin Schaeffer

Irregular Migrant Domestic Workers in Europe
Who Cares?
Edited by Anna Triandafyllidou

Migrants and Cities
The Accommodation of Migrant Organizations in Europe
Margit Fauser

The Bosnian Diaspora
Integration in Transnational Communities
Edited by Marko Valenta and Sabrina P. Ramet

Negotiating National Identities
Between Globalization, the Past and 'the Other'
Christian Karner

Security, Insecurity and Migration in Europe
Edited by Gabriella Lazaridis

Media in Motion
Cultural Complexity and Migration in the Nordic Region
Edited by Elisabeth Eide and Kaarina Nikunen

Managing Ethnic Diversity
Meanings and Practices from an International Perspective
Edited by Reza Hasmath

Muslim Diaspora in the West
Negotiating Gender, Home and Belonging
Edited by Haideh Moghissi and Halleh Ghorashi

Inclusion and Exclusion of Young Adult Migrants in Europe
Barriers and Bridges
Edited by Katrine Fangen, Kirsten Fossan and Ferdinand Andreas Mohn

Irregular Migration in Europe
Myths and Realities
Edited by Anna Triandafyllidou

Paradoxes of Cultural Recognition
Edited by Sharam Alghasi, Thomas Hylland Eriksen and Halleh Ghorashi

Labour Migration from Turkey to Western Europe, 1960–1974
A Multidisciplinary Analysis
Ahmet Akgündüz

The African Diaspora in the United States and Europe
The Ghanaian Experience
John A. Arthur

Minority Rights Protection in International Law
The Roma of Europe
Helen O'Nions

Diversity Management and Discrimination
Immigrants and Ethnic Minorities in the EU
John Wrench

Cities and Labour Immigration
Comparing Policy Responses in Amsterdam, Paris, Rome and Tel Aviv
Michael Alexander

Immigrant Women and Feminism in Italy
Wendy Pojmann

Moving Lives
Narratives of Nation and Migration among Europeans in Post-War Britain
Kathy Burrell

Migration, Regional Integration and Human Security
The Formation and Maintenance of Transnational Spaces
Edited by Harald Kleinschmidt

Globalizing Migration Regimes
New Challenges to Transnational Cooperation
Edited by Kristof Tamas and Joakim Palme

Migration and its Enemies
Global Capital, Migrant Labour and the Nation-State
Robin Cohen

East to West Migration
Russian Migrants in Western Europe
Helen Kopnina

International Migration Research
Constructions, Omissions and the Promises of Interdisciplinarity
Edited by Michael Bommes and Ewa Morawska

Transnational Social Spaces
Agents, Networks and Institutions
Edited by Thomas Faist and Eyüp Özveren

Nationalism and Exclusion of Migrants
Cross-National Comparisons
Edited by Mérove Gijsberts, Louk Hagendoorn and Peer Scheepers

Citizenship in European Cities
Immigrants, Local Politics and Integration Policies
Edited by Rinus Penninx, Karen Kraal, Marco Martiniello and Steven Vertovec

International Migration in the New Millennium
Global Movement and Settlement
Edited by Danièle Joly

Governance in Multicultural Societies
Edited by John Rex and Gurharpal Singh

Identity and Integration
Migrants in Western Europe
Edited by Rosemarie Sackmann, Bernhard Peters and Thomas Faist

European Encounters
Migrants, Migration and European Societies Since 1945
Edited by Rainer Ohliger, Karen Schönwälder and Triadafilos Triadafilopoulos

Illegal Immigrants and Developments in Employment in the Labour Markets of the EU
Jan Hjarnø

Globalizing Chinese Migration
Trends in Europe and Asia
Edited by Pál Nyíri and Igor Saveliev

Integration and Resistance
The Relation of Social Organisations, Global Capital, Governments and International Immigration in Spain and Portugal
Ricard Morén-Alegret

Ethnicity and Nationalism in Italian Politics
Inventing the *Padania*: Lega Nord and the Northern Question
Margarita Gómez-Reino Cachafeiro

Poland's Post-War Dynamic of Migration
Krystyna Iglicka

South Africa's Racial Past
The History and Historiography of Racism, Segregation, and Apartheid
Paul Maylam

Patriarchal Structures and Ethnicity in the Italian Community in Britain
Azadeh Medaglia

Arguing and Justifying
Assessing the Convention Refugees' Choice of Moment, Motive and Host Country
Robert F. Barsky

Comparative Perspectives on Racism
Edited by Jessika ter Wal and Maykel Verkuyten

Transitions
Russians, Ethiopians, and Bedouins in Israel's Negev Desert
Edited by Richard Isralowitz and Jonathan Friedlander

European Nations and Nationalism
Theoretical and Historical Perspectives
Edited by Louk Hagendoorn, György Csepeli, Henk Dekker and Russell Farnen

New Chinese Migrants in Europe
The Case of the Chinese Community in Hungary
Pál Nyíri

Education and Racism
A Cross National Inventory of Positive Effects of Education on Ethnic Tolerance
Edited by Louk Hagendoorn and Shervin Nekuee

Long-Distance Nationalism
Diasporas, Homelands and Identities
Zlatko Skrbiš

Multicultural Policies and the State
A Comparison of Two European Societies
Edited by Marco Martiniello

Turks in European Cities
Housing and Urban Segregation
Edited by Sule Özüekren and Ronald Van Kempen

For Product Safety Concerns and Information please contact our EU
representative GPSR@taylorandfrancis.com
Taylor & Francis Verlag GmbH, Kaufingerstraße 24, 80331 München, Germany

www.ingramcontent.com/pod-product-compliance
Ingram Content Group UK Ltd.
Pitfield, Milton Keynes, MK11 3LW, UK
UKHW011017180926
475701UK00004B/795

9781138245785